Debt and Democracy in Latin America

EDITED BY

Barbara Stallings
Robert Kaufman

Westview Press

BOULDER, SAN FRANCISCO, & LONDON

Copyright © 1989 by Westview Press, Inc.

Published in 1989 in the United States of America by Westview Press, Inc., 5500 Central Avenue, Boulder, Colorado 80301, and in the United Kingdom by Westview Press, Inc., 13 Brunswick Centre, London WC1N 1AF, England

Library of Congress Cataloging-in-Publication Data
Debt and democracy in Latin America.
  Includes index.
  1. Debts, External—Latin America. 2. Latin America—
Economic conditions—1982–   . 3. Latin America—
Politics and government—1980–   . I. Stallings,
Barbara. II. Kaufman, Robert R.
HJ8514.5.D445 1989   336.3′435′098   88-28009
ISBN 0-8133-7547-9
ISBN 0-8133-7548-7 (pbk.)

Printed and bound in the United States of America

The paper used in this publication meets the requirements of the American National Standard for Permanence of Paper for Printed Library Materials Z39.48-1984.

10   9   8   7   6   5   4

Contents

Acknowledgments

Many people have helped at various stages in the preparation of this book. We would like to thank the contributors as well as the group of scholars who joined them early on to discuss some of the issues developed in the book. The latter group included René Cortázar, Kevin Middlebrook, Carlos Rico, Thomas Skidmore, and Toru Yanagihara. In addition, we are grateful to Eric Hershberg and Barbara Forrest of the Ibero-American Studies Program of the University of Wisconsin-Madison for their administrative assistance. We are also highly indebted to Jayni Edelstein and Kate Hibbard, who ably undertook the time-consuming tasks of typing and copy-editing the manuscripts.

Financial support was received from the Cyril B. Nave Bequest, the Hewlett Fund, the Anonymous Fund, and the University Lectures Committee (all of the University of Wisconsin-Madison) and from the Latin American Studies Center of the University of Wisconsin-Milwaukee.

Barbara Stallings
Robert Kaufman

Introduction

Barbara Stallings and Robert Kaufman

Future historians trying to characterize Latin America during the 1980s are likely to focus on two main processes. In economic terms, virtually all Latin American countries were struggling with balance-of-payments deficits, high inflation, and stagnating production. These problems resulted from many adverse factors, both domestic and international, but the heavy burden of debt service payments certainly loomed large among them. On the political side, the 1980s saw many Latin American nations moving away from authoritarian regimes and toward democracy—or at least toward greater openness and increased space for oppositional activities.

The link between these two processes is controversial. Did the economic crisis trigger the political change? Will the same crisis destabilize the very democracies it brought about? Will the type of regime influence the selection of policies to deal with the economic problems? Will it affect governments' ability to implement chosen policies? It is not coincidence that these questions are controversial, for they are very difficult to answer. Nevertheless, they are sufficiently important—both for the practical future of Latin America and for political-economic theory—that an attempt must be made. This book does just that. Through a series of general essays and case studies, it investigates the two-way relationship between debt and democracy in the 1980s. That is, we examine the evidence about how regime type influenced the choice of policy to deal with foreign creditors and related economic issues. We also reverse the question and look at how debt problems have affected the transition to, and the consolidation of, democratic political systems.

In most of our chapters, two sets of terms are central to the analysis. One is the distinction between democracy and authoritarianism. For our purposes, a regime can be considered democratic to the extent that incumbent governments must win and retain power through competitive elections, tolerate opposition challenges to their incumbency, and deal with relatively independent interest groups. Authoritarian regimes are those that do not permit competitive elections and restrict the space allowed to either oppositional or interest group activity. We also distinguish between orthodox and heterodox policy packages to deal with the economic problems confronting Latin America. The term orthodox refers to market-oriented approaches (often associated with the International Monetary Fund) that emphasize fiscal and monetary restraint, reduction in the size of the state sector, liberalization of trade restrictions, and collaboration with creditors. Although heterodox approaches do not reject all elements of this package, they generally advocate a more active state role in investment and economic regulation, are more willing to risk confrontation with creditors, and attach a higher priority to issues of distribution and employment.

The book is divided into four sections. The first provides an overview of the issues from economic, political, and historical perspectives. To begin, Rudiger Dornbusch's chapter provides the essential background for a discussion of the debt issue. He explains the origins of the debt crisis, including both external and internal factors. Then he goes on to analyze the current problems, focusing on debtor countries' need to grow, banks' need to maintain their solvency, and creditor governments' difficulties in reconciling the two. The outcome up until now has been a strategy of "muddling through." Finally, Dornbusch presents three alternative solutions to the crisis. One is lowering interest payments by capitalizing interest when payments exceed a certain level. A second is the establishment of a "debt facility" or agency that would buy part of the banks' Third World debt at a discounted value and pass on the benefits to the debtors. Third, Dornbusch explains his own preferred solution, which focuses on a "responsible" unilateral decision by debtor nations to reduce debt service in the context of a program to revive growth. The argument in favor of the third strategy is that both debtor and creditor countries will benefit in the long run.

The chapter by Jeffry Frieden turns to the political aspects and implications of the debt crisis. Focusing his analysis on the five largest debtors—Argentina, Brazil, Chile, Mexico, and Venezuela—Frieden identifies the economic interests of different social groups, both during the period of heavy borrowing in the 1970s and early 1980s and after lending ceased in 1982. One of his crucial distinctions is between groups that can easily move their assets and those whose assets are geographically fixed. These economic characteristics are linked to political activities once a crisis sets in. Frieden suggests that those with fixed assets are most likely to engage in political struggle to protect their property. The question then becomes whether they will try to pressure the government from inside or join the opposition. This choice is said to be determined by a group's political weight, its ties to the government, and the existence of a potent opposition whose goals are compatible with those of the group in question.

As the final part of the overview section, Paul Drake's chapter looks back to the debt crisis of the 1930s to draw some historical comparisons with the current situation. In particular, he asks about the effect of economic crisis on the political system. In both decades, he finds a large number of regime changes. The difference is that the change in the 1930s was from democracy to dictatorship, while the reverse occurred in the 1980s. Drake's conclusion is that the sharp negative impact of a debt crisis tends to undermine *whatever* type of regime is in power at the time. Once that change occurs, however, the economic situation has less of an influence on politics. On an optimistic note, he contradicts conventional wisdom and suggests that democracies may have some resources that dictatorships lack, especially their greater legitimacy, in order to resist the negative effects of crisis.

The second section of the book examines three crucial sets of actors in the current crisis. All three—U.S. creditors, Latin American business, and Latin American labor—play political as well as economic roles in the process. Riordan Roett's chapter begins this section with a study of various actors in the United States and their interactions with Latin American governments. He traces out U.S. actions, and European and Japanese lack of action, since the debt crisis began in 1982. He concurs with Dornbusch in describing the approach of the Reagan administration as "muddling through" and portrays recent congressional initiatives as a reaction to the failure of the Reagan strategy. He also contrasts the position of the Latin American presidents to that of the U.S. executive branch. Differing with Drake, Roett strongly endorses the Latin American position that the debt crisis is a major threat to democracy.

A second important set of actors consists of local businesspeople in Latin America. In a chapter that reinforces the major elements of Jeffry Frieden's model, Sylvia Maxfield discusses the economic and political characteristics of business. Concentrating on the three largest debtors—Argentina, Brazil, and Mexico— Maxfield notes that the debt-led growth of the 1970s and early 1980s was especially favorable to the financial sector and large business firms in general. Even these groups, however, felt excluded from economic policy making by the authoritarian regimes in power. When economic problems arose because of the debt crisis, they thus supported the democratic opposition, hoping to increase their own power. Nevertheless, the continuing economic problems have deterred private sector investment, and Maxfield concludes that without such investment, the prognosis for democracy is not auspicious.

In a complementary analysis, which also focuses on Argentina, Brazil, and Mexico, Ian Roxborough discusses the politics of labor during the 1980s. Organized labor, he finds, has not been able to defend itself against wage declines and increased unemployment. Divisions within the labor movement have exacerbated the problem. In the meantime, the three governments have had no consistent policy. The possibility of negotiating a "social pact" among labor, business, and the government has been on the agenda in all three countries, but has not been successfully implemented anywhere. Failing that option, governments have "muddled through," varyingly trying to win support from the labor movement, to divide it, and/or to repress it. Overall, labor has fared poorly, a clear loser despite its organizational potential.

Following these six general essays, the third part of the book features a series of case studies on Mexico, Brazil, Peru, Costa Rica, and Chile. The first country study is Robert Kaufman's analysis of Mexico. Mexico has a peculiar political system. Some label it "quasi-democratic;" others call it "quasi-authoritarian." The delicate balance between the dominant party's labor and business constituencies had been based on a high-growth economy that, in turn, relied heavily on foreign capital. The 1982 crisis threatened that balance, and the de la Madrid government had to make more difficult choices than his predecessors. In the process, opposition parties of left and right have been strengthened, but the implications for democracy remain to be seen.

Brazil shares many economic characteristics with Mexico, but it has a quite different political history. Eul-Soo Pang's chapter describes the political maneuvering among the various political parties as Brazil's military began the process of withdrawal from government. The new democracy was saddled with two sets of problems: an economic crisis that left few resources to meet pent-up demands, and a political crisis after Tancredo Neves' death that left the government searching for legitimacy. Unlike Mexico, Brazil followed a heterodox economic approach, both in regard to macroeconomic policy and debt negotiations. Now that both have failed, a more orthodox period may result, but Pang points to the lack of unity and direction as a powerful deterrent to resolving the political-economic crisis.

The other new democracy among the five cases is Peru, which is discussed by Carol Wise. Under the presidency of Alan García, Peru has taken the most radical stand on the debt issue and proposed a more thorough-going heterodox economic policy package than Brazil. The economic package has failed almost completely now. In part, this was due to the exhaustion of foreign exchange reserves, but Wise points to other reasons as well. One is the underdevelopment of the Peruvian state apparatus, both in terms of institutions and personnel. Another was the infighting and otherwise inefficient management by the political and economic teams around García. A third was the suspicion of groups not associated with the government but whose support was needed—especially business but also labor, other political parties, and the military.

A more established democracy, Costa Rica, is the subject of Joan Nelson's chapter. Although one of the smallest of the countries in Latin America, Costa Rica has a fairly modern economy and an advanced social infrastructure as well as a 40-year functioning democracy. Nelson reports surprising success on the part of the Monge government in dealing with the short-term economic crisis in 1982-83, but less success in pushing forward with structural changes to perpetuate the short-term achievements. She finds that democracy had both positive and negative effects on dealing with the crisis situation (e.g., the slowness with which consensus building had to proceed, but the public support once it occurred). Turning the question around, she asks if the crisis damaged the democratic political system. The answer is no, in part because of the way the situation was handled. Especially important were the provisions to distribute the cost of stabilization more evenly than in some other countries.

Finally, Barbara Stallings examines the experience of the Pinochet government in Chile. Chile suffered the worst economic crisis in Latin America in 1982, and the following year political protests were on the verge of dislodging Pinochet. The government managed to weather the storm, however, and its orthodox economic policies have produced success in terms of growth and inflation, but they have also led to increased inequality and hardship. Stallings suggests that these conflicting economic trends will be crucial factors in determining the outcome of the plebiscite scheduled for late 1988, which will decide whether the military will rule for another eight years. Political variables will also play an important role in this new phase of the ongoing struggle for democracy in Chile.

The last section of the book is the concluding chapter by Kaufman and Stallings. It brings together the themes discussed in the preceding chapters in a comparative analysis that draws not only on the five cases presented in the book but also several others. It asks three main questions. The first is whether political regime character-istics have had much effect on choice of economic policy during the crisis period of the 1980s. Unlike some previous literature—which focused on earlier, more affluent periods—this analysis finds that regime was an important variable in the 1980s. Nevertheless, it must be used in combination with other variables such as state capacity, role of domestic groups, and international factors. Second, the essay looks at the impact of political regime on economic outcomes. Here again there is some evidence of a link. For example, authoritarian regimes have better perform-ance on outcomes like inflation and budget deficits, while transitional democracies do especially poorly. Conversely, authoritarian regimes tend to have a contraction of real wages, while real wages go up rapidly just after democracies return. Not all evidence, however, fits so neatly. Finally, the essay considers the effect of economic crisis on the survival potential for the new democracies. While admitting that the economic problems facing these governments are daunting, the authors basically agree with Drake that many factors other than economics will help determine the fate of the new democracies, and some may provide them with greater strength than their authoritarian predecessors.

PART I

A Political-Economic Overview
of the Debt Crisis

1

The Latin American Debt Problem: Anatomy and Solutions

Rudiger Dornbusch

The Latin American debt crisis now is six years old and growing. When Mexican debts trade at 50 cents on the dollar, and those of Peru at less than a dime, the debt crisis is obviously unresolved. Far from improving their creditworthiness, the debtors are falling behind. Debt ratios are far above the 1982 level, and debtor countries' economies are showing the strains of debt service in extremely high inflation, a deep drop in income, and an unsustainable cutback of investment. The debtors cannot afford to pay, nor can they afford to walk out on the system.

On the side of creditors, reserves are built up to provide a cushion against potential losses. In the meantime, creditor banks are unanimous in their reluctance to continue lending in a situation where the debts are obviously deteriorating. Increasingly, the World Bank is filling the gap left by the debtor countries' inability to pay and the banks' unwillingness to lend. Former Treasury Secretary Baker's "muddling through" remains the Reagan administration's strategy, a treadmill of pretense and make believe in which both debtors and creditors are falling behind. There is a major public interest in changing the course and breaking the deadlock.

This chapter briefly reviews the origins of the debt crisis, then identifies the present dilemmas and recommends interest recycling as a policy that involves fair burden sharing and provides the best chance for all parties to come out ahead in what is presently a negative sum game.

Origins of the Debt Crisis

Debt crises are common in a broader historical perspective.[1] The last worldwide crisis was that of the 1930s when all of Latin America, with very few exceptions (most notably Venezuela and Argentina), went into moratorium for many years. Even as the 1930s defaults got fully underway, Winkler wrote:

The fiscal history of Latin America ... is replete with instances of government defaults. Borrowing and default follow each other with perfect regularity. When payment is resumed, the past is easily forgotten and a new borrowing orgy ensues. This process started at the beginning of the past century and has continued down to the present day. It has taught us nothing.[2]

The cleanup of debtor-creditor relations occurred in the 1950s. Borrowing resumed in the 1960s when first Mexico and then all of Latin America made new forays into the world capital market.

Sporadic debt difficulties occurred throughout the 1970s, but the system-wide problems only emerged in 1982 when Mexico, and soon most of Latin America, had to reschedule its external debt. Three factors account for the generalized debt problem: poor management in the debtor countries, the world macroeconomy that took a singularly bad turn, and initial overlending.

In the late 1970s exchange rates in most Latin American countries were massively overvalued. This was a popular policy because it helped limit or bring down inflation without recession. But the cure was very shortlived, since the resulting loss of competitiveness soon led to large trade deficits and capital flight. The extent of overvaluation is apparent from some data for the period 1977 to 1981. Argentina experienced a real appreciation of 85 percent, Brazil 36 percent, Chile 57 percent and Mexico 30 percent. The resulting trade imbalance was financed by borrowing in world capital markets. Moreover, when capital flight became important, especially in Argentina and Mexico, external loans financed this exodus of private capital. It was a curious spectacle when a central bank borrowed in New York to obtain the dollars that it sold to private citizens who in turn deposited them in Miami.

There is considerable uncertainty about the precise extent of capital flight. One recent study, published by the Institute of International Economics,[3] gives estimates for various countries over the period 1976-82. It shows Argentina with capital flight of $22.4 billion, Brazil $5.8 billion, Mexico $25.3 billion, and Venezuela $20.7 billion. To put these data on capital flight in perspective, it is important to judge them relative to the stock of debts outstanding. In the case of Argentina, for example, the 1982 stock of external debt was $44 billion. Thus capital flight accounted for no less than half of the accumulated debt.

The second element in the debt crisis was the sharp deterioration of the world economy. Under the impact of tightening U.S. monetary policy, with other industrial countries following suit, world interest rates skyrocketed, economic activity declined and real commodity prices plummeted. Table 1.1 shows the relevant data.

Each element in world macroeconomic development was unfavorable for debtors. Higher interest rates implied increased debt service burdens, while lower commodity prices and reduced activity in center countries implied a sharp drop in export earnings. Thus, between increased debt service and reduced export earnings, a large foreign exchange gap resulted. Table 1.2 shows the deterioration in debt and debt service ratios between 1979 and 1982.

Table 1.1

Aggregate World Macroeconomic Indicators, 1970-87

	Real Commodity Prices (1980=100)[a]	Libor[b] (%)	Inflation[c] (%)	Growth Rates[d] (%)
1970-79	115	8.0	11.4	3.4
1980	100	14.4	13.0	0.0
1981	96	16.5	-4.1	-7.0
1982	89	13.1	-3.5	-3.3
1983-87	84	8.5	4.0	3.2

[a]Measured in terms of manufactured export prices of industrial countries
[b]London Interbank Offered Rate, base interest rate for most Latin American loans
[c]Rate of increase of industrial countries' unit export values
[d]Industrial production
Source: IMF and Economic Commission for Latin America.

Table 1.2

Debt and Debt Service Ratios,[a] 1979-82

	1979	1980	1981	1982
Debt[b]	165	152	186	241
Interest and Amortization[b]	27.9	25.4	32.9	40.3
Interest[b]	11.1	13.1	18.6	24.2

[a]Countries with recent debt service problems
[b]As percent of exports of goods and services
Source: IMF.

Without the banks' eagerness to lend, the debt crisis would obviously not have occurred in the first place. In hindsight, why did banks not use more caution? That question is asked in the aftermath of each wave of default, and the answer has not yet been found. The most plausible explanation is that of Guttentag and Herring, who argue that banks have "disaster myopia"—they underestimate the true probability of infrequent events.[4] The combination of overindebtedness and a sharp world deterioration is one such case. The combination makes for pervasive defaults, but it is a rare event.

The banks' role in the debt crisis went beyond the initial overlending. An essential element was the halt on all lending once the debt service difficulties of lenders became apparent. Each bank's attempt to pull out of further lending, seeking recovery of principal at the expense of other creditors, had all the appearances of a bank run. Suddenly, debtors could no longer roll over their interest payments and borrow to finance current account imbalances; they had to adjust. The main feature of the debt crisis was precisely that abrupt halt to all lending. Debtors frozen out of the world capital market learned first hand the old banking truth: "It is not speed that kills, it is the sudden stop."

Current Problems in the Debt Crisis

Debtor adjustment programs were expected to show, in time, an improvement in creditworthiness sufficient to warrant a return to voluntary lending.[5] That remains the official position, but the process is not on schedule, and few believe that the solution lies in the direction of more of the same. A return to voluntary lending is a very remote possibility if one observes the large discounts in the secondary market for LDC debts and banks' attempts to relinquish anything remotely connected to Latin America.

In fact, there is concern that conditions may deteriorate. Over the past five years the non-interest current account of Latin American debtors turned toward a large surplus, and as a result they managed to pay a significant share of their interest liabilities. At the same time, however, investment declined sharply. A cut in investment may be a reasonable response to the crisis for a brief period, but when it lasts year after year it can only lead to severe trouble. Policy makers in debtor countries are concerned that they will ultimately bear the costs for prolonging what they consider a totally unreasonable decapitalization of their economies. Surprisingly no populist government has yet come to power to dramatize this issue, but it is clear that in Brazil, Mexico, and Argentina, the issue is buried only a foot deep.

On the creditor side there is also a deterioration underway. Large banks that are organizing the lending cartel are increasingly disenchanted with Federal Reserve pressure to keep up lending. They would like to see a more substantial takeover by the taxpayers, either overtly or under the cover of expanded loans and guarantees from international agencies. The problem is aggravated by the increasing unwillingness of small banks to participate in new rounds of "involuntary" lending. Their withdrawal puts pressure on loan discounts and thus highlights the fact that loans are traded significantly below par. Dissension between European and New York banks is another factor weakening cohesion.

A final dimension of the crisis is the trade issue. This aspect has been emphasized by Senator Bradley in his proposal for limited, selective and targeted negotiation of debt relief in exchange for conditioned adjustment programs and trade concessions in the debtor countries. Debtor countries today run trade surpluses to earn dollars for debt service. They have achieved these surpluses by substantially depreciating their currencies to gain competitiveness, restricting imports, and expanding exports. At the same time, this large swing in their trade is perceived as a threat to a liberal world trade regime.

Four facts summarize the lack of success of the adjustment efforts so far. First, creditworthiness has been deteriorating. The ratio of debt to exports for problem debtors has risen since 1982 from 269 percent to 350 percent, and the ratio of debt to gross domestic product (GDP) of these countries increased from 44 percent to 54

Table 1.3

Macroeconomic Developments in Countries with Debt Service Difficulties, 1969-87

	1969-78	1979-82	1983-86	1986-87
Per Capita GDP Growth (%)	3.1	0	-0.2	1.4
Inflation(%)	21.9	40.7	75.9	71.0
Investment (% of GDP)	n.a.	24.9	19.0	19.4
External Debt (% of GDP)	n.a.	36.6	48.9	52.6
Resource Transfer Abroad (% of GDP)	n.a.	-1.0	3.4	2.6

Source: IMF.

percent. Five years of adjustment thus have made debtor countries look worse rather than better, at least with respect to their debt burdens. Second, the large swing in trade surpluses that finance much of the interest payments has as a counterpart a decline in investment. Comparing the period 1982-86 with the preceding five-year average, there is an increase in Latin America's non-interest surplus equal to five percent of GDP and an exactly equal decline in investment. When interest is paid by not investing, a serious imbalance builds up. (See Table 1.3.) Third, there is no indication of a return to voluntary lending. Loan discounts are very deep for most debtors, and the case of Colombia shows that even clean debtors cannot gain access when they face a shortage of foreign exchange. Fourth, moratoria are now widespread and discounts in the secondary market, averaging more than 50 percent, indicate that debt has come to be considered both a political and an economic problem. Table 1.4 reviews the debt, growth, and creditworthiness of the main problem debtors.

In fall 1985, Treasury Secretary James Baker proposed a broad-ranging, ambitious plan to cope with the debt crisis. At the center of the plan was the recognition that the debt problem would not go away rapidly and that debts should be serviced and ultimately paid. The strategy to assure that this would in fact happen involved five elements: (1) continued involvement by commercial banks to contribute "new money" as required in the rescheduling of debt; (2) sharply increased participation and lending by multilateral institutions, especially the World Bank; (3) focus on debtor country adjustment not only by belt tightening of the 1982-84 variety, but also a positive focus on free enterprise and supply side economics; (4) a world macroeconomic environment that supplements adjustment of debtors by sustained growth; and (5) a world trade environment of continued and enlarged market access for everyone.

The Baker Plan had few concrete implications other than increased lending by multilateral agencies. It primarily represented a philosophy and an approach to the debt problem. At that general level there is, of course, little disagreement. But without any specificity, there was also very little that could be endorsed. The

Table 1.4
Debt Burden of Highly Indebted Countries

Country	Debt ($ billion)					Per Capita Consumption
	Total	All Banks	U.S. Banks	9 U.S. Largest	Debt per Capita ($)	Growth: 1980-87 (annual average)
Argentina	49.4	42.4	8.5	5.9	1592	-1.2
Bolivia	4.6	1.2	0.1	0.04	407	-5.2
Brazil	114.5	84.2	21.9	15.1	70	1.1
Chile	20.5	17.1	6.4	4.2	1666	-2.2
Colombia	15.1	7.5	2.0	1.5	517	0.2
Costa Rica	4.5	2.3	0.4	0.2	354	-1.4
Ecuador	9.0	6.3	n.a.	n.a.	892	-2.2
Ivory Coast	9.1	5.5	0.4	0.3	892	-4.3
Jamaica	3.8	6.6	0.2	0.2	1583	-1.4
Mexico	105.0	90.5	24.0	13.8	1313	-2.7
Morocco	27.0	5.5	0.8	0.7	1205	0.8
Nigeria	27.0	14.9	0.9	0.7	274	-6.5
Peru	16.7	8.9	1.2	0.7	827	-0.2
Philippines	29.0	17.6	5.0	3.6	527	-1.0
Uruguay	3.8	3.0	0.9	0.7	1267	-2.4
Venezuela	33.9	33.7	16.4	6.2	1904	-4.6
Yugoslavia	21.8	15.2	2.0	1.3	936	-0.5

Source: World Bank, *World Debt Tables 1987-88*; Salomon Brothers Inc.; and Federal Financial Institutions
Examination Council, *Country Exposure Lending Survey* (June 1987).

expectation that the private market could solve the debt problem by a reversal of
capital flight, debt-equity swaps, and foreign direct investment exaggerated the
likelihood and magnitude of these phenomena. The expectation that privatization
and increased efficiency in government could make a significant short-term contribution to a debt overhang problem was bound to be disappointed.

There is a need for a change in strategy. Financial expert Henry Kaufman has
emphasized that this is not merely in the interest of debtors, but in fact is of global
importance:

> The rapid buildup in bank lending to developing countries in the 1970s gave world
> economic activity a temporary boost. However, the current adherence to the creditor/
> debtor commercial arrangements is a powerful limiting force to world economic
> expansion. The restrictiveness of this debt cannot be denied. If the debt blockage is not
> eased, economic growth globally will continue at only a slow pace, risking a major
> worldwide business setback.[6]

There are four basic problems to be solved. One is how to reverse the real
resource transfer and restore the flow of development capital to the debtor countries.
Non-interest surpluses which today service debt need to be turned back into deficits.
This will provide a net resource import to supplement domestic savings in financing

growth. As long as existing debts are judged to be poor, commercial banks will be reluctant to put up new money, even to finance the interest bill. And they most definitely will not lend over and above the interest bill to finance a net resource transfer. The problem goes further because the existing debt has a prior claim on the debtor countries' resources. It therefore stands in the way of new resources from potential lenders or investors not involved thus far (e.g., insurance companies). The existing debt also places a burden on debtor countries' policies, limiting the profitability of direct investment in these depressed or slow-growth economies. Finally, the political backlash in response to the debt collection process may well come one day. At that point, there would be no assurance of a fine distinction between uncooperative banks keeping alive long-dead debts and new investors. In summary, until the problem of old debts is resolved one way or another, fresh capital resources will be very timid.

The second problem is that debtor countries receive no benefit from the implicit or explicit write-offs on commercial bank balance sheets. Even though the market judges that the debts of problem debtors are only worth 46 cents on the dollar on average, reflecting the possibility that some of these debts will not be paid, debtors are still held to the full face value. When a small bank takes a loss, for example, by selling off a claim on Bolivia at 9 cents on the dollar, the buyer acquires a claim with uncertain payoff that he will seek to enforce to the full value. The debtor country still owes a dollar and thus bears the full burden of trying to service that debt. The burden, even if nothing is paid in fact, becomes an uncertainty that adversely affects the macroeconomic environment. Thus not only are there no net resource transfers, but even countries that are not paying suffer from the lack of resolution over their ultimate debt service liability. This uncertainty in itself may be costly for both creditors and debtors, raising the possibility of write-offs that help all parties.

The third set of problems involves the commercial banks, their ability to take the accounting losses involved in any debt consolidation, and the ease or difficulty posed by the regulatory environment. The issues that arise here stem from the divergent interests of large and small banks, and the differences between U.S. banks and those abroad. The starkest difficulty is that at least one major money center bank could not survive reducing the book value of its loans to market value. Difficulties also arise from the fact that the U.S. regulatory environment remains consciously ambiguous on the consequences of consolidation. There is little doubt that *ex post* the costs to banks will be minimized, but *ex ante* consolidation is discouraged by regulatory requirements that make it very expensive for banks. Indeed, even competitive reserve provisions have been frowned upon by the regulatory authorities. This may represent a strategy to suppress any excessive eagerness on the part of creditors to give in to consolidation. Of course, it thereby also stands in the way of reasonable settlements for some claims, which as a result may deteriorate.

The fourth problem concerns the difficulty creditor countries have in reconciling the conflicting interests of commercial banks, foreign policy, and manufacturing. Maintaining the stability and profitability of the banking system is rightly singled out as an important national objective, but it may compete with other objectives. The U.S. interest in stable democratic governments on its borders is one; the interest in the health of U.S. manufacturing sector, which pays some of the costs of debtor country adjustment, is another.

Some Possible Solutions to the Debt Crisis

Solutions to the debt problem must address two questions. The first is who pays for the debt relief—the debtor, the bank stockholder, Japan, or the taxpayer? The second question is who takes the initiative—creditor governments, debtors and creditors jointly, or debtors unilaterally?

There is also ambiguity overt the role the taxpayer will play. The possibility that the taxpayer could enter, directly or via a sharply increased funding of the World Bank or a new institution, makes talk of concessions premature. Countries should borrow rather than adjust and banks should lend at the highest interest rates possible. It is difficult to see how to establish a precommitment that would define the limits on the role of the taxpayer and thus facilitate voluntary deals between banks and debtors. But along with more clarity on the regulatory treatment, there is a need to define more clearly what the taxpayer is willing to do.

In the discussion that follows, three general types of solutions are described: interest capitalization, a public "debt facility" to purchase part of the debt, and unilateral action by key debtor countries combined with a plan for reconstruction. As will be seen, the author strongly recommends the third approach.

Interest Capitalization

Debtor countries and some European bankers (especially the Swiss) have advocated interest capitalization as an immediate step to halt the outward transfer of real resources. The system is designed to minimize the possibility of confrontation in the context of a liquidity crisis and thus eliminate any plausible excuse for default. This mechanism, however, runs directly counter to the concerns of U.S. banks who reject capitalization and insist on the full *current* payment of interest.

In the interest capitalization proposal, automatic capitalization might have as a counterpart objective indicators that trigger enhanced debt service. These would involve, for example, the price of oil for an oil exporter. If oil prices came to exceed a particular level, increased revenues would be used to bring debt service up to the full level and perhaps to provide amortization of principal.

The attraction of the plan for European banks is that they have already set aside provisions amounting to a large part of their claims. Hence *any* receipts are good news. Many of the major U.S. banks, by contrast, are excessively concerned with quarterly receipts and thus severely aggravate the debt problem by forcing debtor countries into much more dramatic adjustments. The attraction of the plan is that it improves debts by relaxing the timing of interest rate receipts. In doing so it removes the risk that a debtor, strained by excessive insistence on current service, might default. At the same time, however, the scheme also means that creditors forego some of the leverage that they now exercise through requiring specific economic policy changes as part of reschedulings. There might be a middle ground between the quarterly emphasis of U.S. banks and the infinite horizon of a Swiss banker.

The capitalization proposal is very different from a scheme where there is an automatic cap on interest payments, say at 6 percent, with the excess automatically forgiven. The capitalization scheme implies that the portion that is capitalized retains an option value, should matters improve. The alternative scheme makes an automatic and unconditional gift to debtors, even if their conditions should subsequently improve. Needless to say, the Swiss proposal is more attractive to the banks since it affords them with an opportunity to make larger concessions today because they have as a counterpart the potential of a payback down the road.

It might be argued that the present rescheduling practice is not very different from capitalization. After all, when countries cannot pay, creditor banks grant loans as "new money" to pay the interest they are owed. But the Swiss proposal goes much further. It not only removes the difficulty and confrontation of rescheduling and the problems of organizing the creditors' cartel; it also locks all creditors into refinancing in a way that is now impossible. Most importantly, it gives macroeconomic planning a much longer horizon because it removes the threat that a country unable to come up with a rescheduling agreement would be forced to choose between a dramatic depression or an equally dramatic default. The resulting uncertainty is, of course, a major mortgage on investment and growth. The Swiss proposal is a front-end commitment that if things are bad the debt is forgiven, and if they turn out well it is payable in full.

A Debt Facility

The stock of old, bad debt stands in the way of a resumption of lending. Since Princeton economist Peter Kenen first advanced the proposal in 1983, there has been an interest in the idea of moving debt, which is now trapped in the hands of banks, into some public agency or "facility." In the process, both an improvement in bank balance sheets and a reduction in debt burdens for the debtors would be achieved. The idea of a debt facility has received reinforcement from the large and increasing discounts in the secondary market, as shown in Table 1.5. The discounts suggest that an agency could buy up debt and pass on partial relief to debtors, if only the right institutional vehicle could be created.

There is an obvious opening for the taxpayer to step in. A public body would be created with the task of bringing about renewed resource flows to debtor countries. The concrete proposal is to create an agency which takes over debts from banks (at a discount and in exchange for government-guaranteed bonds) and renegotiates them with debtor countries. Debtor countries would receive the benefit of the discount, and the time stream of payments would be structured to match reconstruc-

Table 1.5
Prices in the Secondary Market for Bank Loans
(Bid price, percent of face value)

	7/85	7/86	7/87	3/88
Argentina	60	63	47	28
Brazil	75	73	57	46
Mexico	80	56	54	48
Peru	45	18	11	5
Philippines	n.a.	n.a.	73	50
Venezuela	81	75	69	54

Source: Shearson, Lehman Brothers and Salomon Brothers Inc.

tion programs. Contingency clauses might be used to link payments to the state of objective economic indicators, such as GDP growth or the prices of key commodities in a debtor country's trade. If the facility enjoyed a government guarantee, significant debt relief would become a real possibility.

One important difficulty with the facility scheme is that the discount in the market reflects not only inability but also unwillingness to pay. It is essential therefore, as emphasized by Weinert, that implementation be conditioned on adjustment programs and, indeed, serve as incentive for such programs.[7] In this manner, countries whose debts trade at the largest discounts—such as Bolivia and Peru—would get the maximum debt relief. In this swap arrangement the sponsor of the facility assumes the default risk, the debtor obtains the full benefit of the implicit bank write-off in the form of interest relief, and the bank restores its balance sheet by acquiring low yield, safe claims in place of precarious ones. The taxpayer does have exposure now because of the remaining default risk.

There is no free lunch in this scheme since the taxpayer's assumption of the default risk is the *sine qua non* for the debtor to capture the full benefit of the discount. It is true that passing debt relief on to debtors in the form of lower interest rates or reduced principal reduces their debt burden, but the debt reduction may not be enough to eliminate default risk or the risk of sustained payments difficulties.

Among the important issues in designing such a facility is the choice between a multilateral approach, using, for example, the World Bank, and a U.S. option. There are good arguments for a facility that is operated only by the United States, with beneficiaries targeted by their importance from a U.S. foreign policy perspective. Access to the facility would be restricted to U.S. banks. This would exclude European banks that have already fully reserved their loans from being the main beneficiaries, while their governments might be the most reluctant contributors. A U.S. facility would also highlight the foreign policy interests of the United States— in Central America and the Philippines, for example—and thus would stand a much better chance of congressional approval.

Since the facility can only be effective if the government provides guarantees, there is an obvious question of how much liability taxpayers are willing to assume. It would be a good idea to target an initial plan on countries other than the major debtors—Brazil, Mexico, Venezuela and Argentina. A given budget for guarantees—say $20 billion—could make a major difference for many small debtors like Bolivia, Ecuador or Costa Rica, while it would make only a minor dent in the problems of Brazil or Mexico. The facility might set itself two major objectives. First, for very poor, small debtors, all commercial bank debt should be restructured, even if that meant buying up debts from foreign banks. Second, there should be a maximum possibility for small U.S. banks to exit; regulatory facilitation should make this especially easy.

What could be expected from such a fund and how much would it cost? Debts to U.S. banks of the Philippines and Latin America (excepting the four major debtors) amount to $18 billion at face value. They represent about one third of those countries' total debt. At the secondary market valuation, these bank debts amount to approximately $13 billion. Thus for a $13 billion government guarantee, a $7 billion or 12 percent debt reduction for problem debtors could be secured by the facility taking over the entire stock of U.S. bank debt for the entire group of countries. (This $7 billion represents the difference between the hypothesized $20 billion budgeted for debt purchase and the $13 billion valuation in the secondary market.)

These numbers seem very disappointing: the budget commitment in terms of guarantees is large and the debt relief seems almost negligible. Nevertheless, it can be seen another way. Bolivia's external bank debt is $1.2 billion and trades at only 11 cents on the dollar. For a guarantee of less than $200 million, there could be an altogether dramatic reduction in external debt pressure for Bolivia (assuming, of course, that the discount remained low). The reality of a fund lies somewhere between those two extremes. If the access rules were well structured, a relatively small guarantee commitment could have an astounding impact on the external outlook for a host of small countries and small banks that are now caught by a lack of solutions. There is another reason why the facility would be more important than the 12 percent debt reduction suggests: bank debt carries far higher interest rates than official debt. Thus the 12 percent reduction in total debt, given that all of this reduction comes from high interest bank debt, would lower overall interest obligations by perhaps as much as 20 percent.

The government budget of creditor countries would have to absorb the contingent liability involved in underwriting the bonds issued by the facility but serviced by the income from LDC debts. If default should occur, the government would have to assume debt service. Such a guarantee used to be given quite freely by the U.S. government, but is now harder to extract from Congress. The scheme, if it were operated by the U.S. government, would therefore have to pass through the full rigor of congressional budget action. There are, of course, other possibilities. One obvious direction is to use World Bank capital as a means of guaranteeing debt. Other possibilities focus on industrial countries with strong currencies and external surpluses. Many observers have also looked to Japan as a candidate for assuming the guarantees.

We have discussed here how a facility could use the secondary market as a way of intermediating between banks that want to get out and countries that cannot pay. In addition, there is the possibility of a more aggressive role. Concerned with the solvency and productivity of the facility, the facility's management could potentially act in rescheduling agreements to assure that the value of the assets it carried were not impaired by extortionary settlements or unreasonable adjustment programs. One might even imagine, in a particular situation, that the facility makes available long-term reconstruction loans to particular countries. In exchange for participating in the financing, it secures from the banks extraordinary reductions in spreads or maturities. Of course, to perform this function aggressively would require a facility manager to be of sufficient stature and independence to be beyond the immediate reach of the U.S. Treasury.

The bottom line on such a facility remains the participation of taxpayers' capital. This may be accomplished away from public sight, by World Bank borrowing, or through pressure on Japan to do something. Unless the taxpayer in some incarnation takes over the default risk, however, the debtors cannot get the full advantage of the discounts at which the debts are now traded.

Unilateral Action

The obstacle to organized debt relief comes from taxpayers' unwillingness to underwrite debtor country growth. Even if the case is compelling, politicians do not want to confront the banks. U.S. banks are reluctant to consider write-offs as long as there is no outright crisis of default, and even then they would prefer to wait for someone else to pick up the tab. No one can blame the banks for that. In the meantime, the debt problem proceeds with frequent reschedulings, general uncertainty, and a pervasive deterioration of economic and social conditions in the debtor countries. The problem posed itself quite concretely in Brazil, as the country first announced a moratorium and then abandoned that policy.

The most reasonable course would be for Brazil unilaterally to announce the amount of interest automatically capitalized, the form in which creditors could manage the capitalized portion, and the applicable rates. But there are two reasons that it is likely to continue to shy away from such a unilateral course. One is the threat of sanctions. The other is the possibility that the international financial system is in fact already moving in the direction of change, offering once again the mirage of a significantly different debt process in the near future.

It would be difficult for a debtor to find evidence of officially-sponsored changes in debt strategy. Internationally, debt has made only a minor appearance at summit meetings. The summits merely reiterate the belief of the heads of state that solutions to the debt problem must follow a case-by-case approach and that adjustment of debtor countries and a favorable international climate are essential elements of a successful debt strategy. Hence, on an international level, debt is simply a non-issue.

The scope for sanctions to be imposed on debtor countries is poorly understood. The realistic view must be that when the chips are down, there is very little that can be done to a country like Brazil. Overwhelming U.S. political and economic interests dictate that a *responsible* unilateral action would be accepted and quietly welcomed. We discuss below what responsible action might mean. A further issue is whether a debtor country that adopts a unilateral action by that very fact excludes the possibility of returning to the world capital market in the future. In one sense the answer is quite obvious: all of Latin America adopted unilateral action, ranging from moratoria to outright defaults, in the 1930s. None paid more than 50 cents on the dollar and yet all returned to voluntary lending. In fact Latin American countries, as we saw before, have defaulted not once but many times. Thus there is little reason to accept a categorical assertion that there is no credit again after unilateral action, but it is equally important to recognize that the imminent return to voluntary lending is a myth.

A solution to the debt problem is unlikely to emerge until a major debtor, calmly and responsibly, defines *unilaterally* the terms of debt consolidation it imposes on the creditors. It is essential for success, and for avoiding sanctions, that the action be sufficiently limited to be acceptable. It must take place in the context of a realistic restructuring of domestic economic policies. There must also be some serious prospect that the unilateral restructuring of debt service would significantly improve the quality of the consolidated debt. Moreover, the restructuring should definitely carry a provision that would entitle creditors to participate in any significant improvement of the country's economic position and ability to pay.

What might such a unilateral proposal look like? The first objective is to simplify the debt rescheduling process, and the second is to reduce the immediate debt service burden. A program of reconstruction is built on two principles: a temporary suspension of resource transfers abroad and major policy reform. The Baker Plan failed because it made debt collection and immediate resource transfers too central and, as a result, had no bargaining chip for policy reform. Immediate write-downs are not much better, however, since they conclude prematurely that countries cannot pay before giving them the support needed for reconstruction.

To accomplish these two tasks, a debtor country, such as Brazil, could announce two plans between which creditors could choose. Plan A would provide an exit bond: debt service in dollars, but at the price of a reduction in principal and interest. Plan B would maintain the principal in dollars, but require that any interest be invested in Brazil for a specified minimum period of time. Those banks opting for Plan A would enter an auction where they could bid to exchange their current claim for a thirty-year dollar bond carrying the U.S. treasury bill rate. The debtor government would explicitly agree to give these bonds seniority over any other claims. Banks electing Plan B would not suffer any reduction in principal, and their interest claim would be calculated at Libor plus 1 percent. But rather than receiving payments in dollars, interest payments would be made in cruzados at the official exchange rate. Creditors could maintain these cruzados in the central bank with an exchange rate guarantee and interest accumulating at a modest rate. Alternatively they could lend cruzados in Brazil to private businesses, hold government bonds or sell their claims to other parties, including banks or foreign investors. The ability to invest would be restricted only to preclude remission under the guise of repatriation of principal or dividends on previous foreign direct investment. A further provision of Plan B would be that if economic conditions turned out favorably, the government would allocate foreign exchange to debt service in dollars.

The suspension of resource transfers abroad clearly does not mean that creditors are left stranded. Debtor countries must make a commitment to free budget resources to actually pay the creditors; it is not a question of simply inflating away the interest payments. Debtors must also overcome nationalism to create a climate that turns local currency payments into profitable, inflation-proof investments. The implementation of the debt plan would be accompanied by a new economic program that would remove the extreme uncertainty that has been detrimental to the economic climate. Investment would ultimately resume, and the quality of debts and captive deposits would improve over time.

The argument for such a unilateral policy is different, but even stronger, for countries like Argentina that are in especially bad economic conditions. Even if a facility managed to write down half the Argentine debt, the country's situation would be largely unchanged; Argentina has never paid more than half the interest. Whether one wrote off the other half or created fictional new loans would make little difference. The half that matters is that which that Argentina is paying now, but cannot afford to pay since the country is on the verge of economic collapse. A facility would leave that problem entirely untouched unless the write-off amounted to 90 percent, something no one has been willing to suggest for a major debtor. With economic reconstruction, at least part and perhaps all the debt could be paid some day. Argentina is potentially prosperous, but trying to squeeze out dollars too fast has virtually destroyed its economy.

The advantage of accepting this unilateral plan over write-downs comes to this: Why should banks write down debts to 50 cents on the dollar (or more) if there is another strategy that may ultimately give them a good name and their money back? The discounts, for many (although not all) countries, reflect a short-run inability— or even unwillingness—to pay, not a basic insolvency. The challenge is to bring countries like Mexico or Brazil to the point where debt service can be achieved without economic distress. That is mostly a question of reconstruction and time. Rather than writing off their loans, we should help debtor countries implement hardnosed adjustment programs that support growth and hence make it possible to resume debt service.

Growth and financial stability in Mexico, Brazil or the Philippines would help create a business climate where investment would be profitable. With any luck, ten years later all the debt could be paid routinely out of the reflow of flight capital and voluntary foreign investment. Even if it is not a sure thing, it is a more promising way to get one's money back than subjecting debtor countries to depression and hyperinflation. Mexico has undergone many of the necessary reforms to make such a scheme plausible. It would be a good time to put one in place before renewed growth cuts the current account surplus and brings up the next rescheduling confrontation.

How should the governments of creditor countries react to such a unilateral measure? Provided the action is limited and accompanied by positive steps to enhance the prospects for sustained growth and an ultimate ability to service the debt in dollars, we should welcome the action. We should applaud and encourage measures that get the debtor countries, the banks and the world economy out of the current impasse.

In the summer of 1982, Mexican Finance Minister Silva Herzog went to Washington to report that his country could not service its debts. In the midst of confusion and a flurry of rescue activity, he received one clear message: above all, don't do anything unilateral. Now, five years later, we have come full circle: someone, please, do something unilateral.

According to debtor country rhetoric, debt service has stopped growth and investment in their economies. Creditors keep telling us about the wonderful investment opportunities (for others) in developing countries; the unilateral proposal takes up the challenge. Debtors get the resources to support reconstruction, but they cannot dissipate them by poor fiscal policies or premature growth of consumption. Creditors are put on hold, but their claims are enhanced by a sharply improved business climate and growth performance in debtor countries. Surely our public interest, whether from the point of view of trade or foreign policy, is better served by debtor country reconstruction than by the Baker treadmill.

Notes

1. See Max Winkler, *Foreign Bonds* (Philadelphia: Roland Swain Co., 1933); Willy Feuerlein and Elizabeth Hannan, *Dollars in Latin America* (New York: Council on Foreign Relations, 1940); James Gantenbein, *Financial Questions in United States Foreign Policy* (New York: Columbia University Press, 1939); U.S. Senate Committee on Finance, "Sale of Foreign Bonds or Securities in the United States," January 1932; and Eliana Cardoso and Rudiger Dornbusch, "Private Capital for Economic Development," in *Handbook of Development Economics,* ed. Hollis Chenery and T. N. Srinivasan (Amsterdam: North-Holland, forthcoming).

2. Winkler, *Foreign Bonds.*

3. Robert Cumby and Richard Levich, "On the Definition and Magnitude of Recent Capital Flight," in *Capital Flight and Third World Debt,* ed. Donald Lessard and John Williamson (Washington, DC: Institute for International Economics, 1987).

4. Jack Guttentag and Richard Herring, *Disaster Myopia in International Banking,* International Finance Section, no. 164 (Princeton: Princeton University, 1986).

5. Voluntary lending is the "normal" type of transaction, responding to market forces.

Since the debt crisis began, voluntary transactions have been replaced by "involuntary" loans which were organized by bank committees (with help from the IMF and Federal Reserve) as part of the debt rescheduling process. (See Roett chapter in this volume.)

6. Henry Kaufman, "The Risks in the World Economic Order," public lecture, New York University, February 24, 1987.

7. Richard Weinert, "Swapping Third World Debt," *Foreign Policy* (Winter 1986-87).

Suggestions for Further Reading

Cline, William. *International Debt and Stability of the World Economy.* Washington, DC: Institute for International Economics, 1983.

Dornbusch, Rudiger. "Our LDC Debts." In *The U.S. in the World Economy,* ed. Martin Feldstein. Chicago: University of Chicago Press, 1988.

Kahler, Miles, ed. *The Politics of International Debt.* Ithaca: Cornell University Press, 1985.

Kaletsky, Anatoly. *The Costs of Default.* New York: 20th Century Fund, 1985.

Kuczynski, Pedro-Pablo. "Latin American Debt." *Foreign Affairs,* Winter 1982-83.

_____. "Latin American Debt: Act Two." *Foreign Affairs,* Fall 1983.

Smith, Gordon W., and John Cuddington, eds. *International Debt and the Developing Countries.* Washington, DC: World Bank, 1985.

2

Winners and Losers in the Latin America Debt Crisis: The Political Implications

Jeffry A. Frieden

Latin American debt has been politicized since the financial crisis began in 1982. It is easy to understand why international debt has become an international political issue, for the renegotiation of cross-border loans inevitably involves governments. Continued bargaining over the terms of debt service among debtor states, creditors, and creditor states confirms expectations that this international political interaction will reflect the wide variety of material interests and institutional forces at play.[1]

Foreign debt has also become an extremely important political issue *within* Latin American countries. It has been central to Latin American domestic politics since 1982, affecting such significant processes as democratization, oppositional protests, and repression in a variety of countries. Indeed, domestic political strife over the external debt has often spilled over into the international bargaining process, as countries have found their international negotiating stance constrained by domestic pressures.

Recent experience demonstrates the weakness of existing approaches to Latin American political economy. The modernization tradition, which argued for a positive relationship between economic development and political democracy, was largely discredited by the wave of authoritarian coups that swept Latin America in the late 1960s and early 1970s. The most common alternative, the "bureaucratic authoritarian" approach that suggested a causal link between economic crises and political authoritarianism in countries at middle levels of economic development, has been undermined by the wave of democratization that, in the midst of serious economic distress, swept the region in the early 1980s.[2]

This essay suggests an alternative based on the broader political economy literature. The approach explores how socio-economic actors, in pursuit of their material interests, interact with existing institutions. The result is not a constant assertion that economic growth leads toward or away from democracy, but rather a mode of analysis that allows us to understand the relationships among economic interests, political behavior, and social outcomes.

The essay summarizes the domestic political impact of the debt crisis in the five largest Latin American debtor nations: Argentina, Brazil, Chile, Mexico, and

Venezuela. It emphasizes how the domestic distributional effects of the financial crisis have been reflected in the domestic political arenas of the major Latin American debtors. A simple analytical framework focusing on the impact of the crisis on different social groups, the distinction between liquid and fixed asset-holders, and the availability of a sympathetic government or attractive oppositional coalition partners is used to explain the responses of different economic agents to financial distress. The evidence mustered is not exhaustive or systematic, but meant to illustrate the analytical points being made. First is a general survey of the distributional effects of international financial relations. The next two sections of the essay discuss these distributional effects during the borrowing process and the financial crisis respectively. The final section explores the political implications of these distributional effects during the debt crisis.

International Finance and Domestic Interests

Foreign debt is often a source of domestic political conflict, for it can raise important distributional issues. An inflow of capital as debts are contracted, or an outflow of capital as debts are repaid, affects different economic agents variably. Some do especially well during an expansion in borrowing, while others do especially poorly during a contraction in new borrowing or reversal of financial flows. The possibility of an unequal distribution of gains and losses in borrowing booms and financial crises makes foreign debt potentially controversial within borrowing countries.

Beyond market forces, government policy can also affect who wins and who loses in borrowing and financial crises. During financial expansions the government may channel foreign loans to favored firms, while during times of crisis it may use taxpayers' money to bail out the indebted enterprises. External finance may be used to allow industrialists to purchase cheap capital goods from abroad, while a financial cut-off may be dealt with by repressing industrial wages to increase exports. In such instances, the relative distribution of costs and benefits in both boom and bust is amenable to government policy, and is thus the focus of political conflict. To clarify the issues involved, we first consider the economic impact of a capital inflow (or outflow) in the absence of government policy, and then consider how government policy can affect this economic impact.

We begin our analysis at the point where financial resources start to flow into the country, which affects three important economic variables: the availability of capital, foreign currency, and government finance. This is of course only part of the story—the pattern of borrowing presumably responds to the prior structure of domestic socio-economic and political interests—but it is ambitious enough for our purposes.[3] We take as given the structure of economic interests, political institutions, and government policy when borrowing begins.

Inasmuch as foreign finance increases the supply of capital available for domestic investment, it lowers domestic interest rates. A capital inflow thus makes borrowing cheaper and saving less attractive. When the capital inflow is channelled through domestic financial intermediaries, as occurs frequently, it benefits the national financial sector as well. Of course, here as elsewhere the capital inflow has a number of crosscutting effects. Borrowers eventually have to service their debts, and savers who are also consumers may benefit in the long run if the capital inflow leads to higher levels of productivity and thus lower prices. Nonetheless, the principal short-term result is straightforward: borrowers benefit from the increased supply and lowered price of capital.

As external borrowing increases the domestic supply of foreign currency, it cheapens foreign exchange relative to the domestic currency. Without getting into thorny analytical debates about currency "overvaluation," we can safely say that in most instances the borrowing country's currency is stronger than it would otherwise be; domestic prices rise relative to world prices.[4] This benefits those who purchase imports and harms exporters, although the ultimate result depends on the structure of protection. In the usual Latin American context, in which there are many barriers to the import of finished goods, cheap foreign exchange generally helps protected domestic producers who use imported capital goods or inputs.

When foreign capital is used to cover the public sector deficit, it has distributional effects analogous to those of more general government spending. Some benefit by the public programs made possible by external public borrowing; others benefit by the short-term reduction in taxation that public borrowing allows. When, as is common, public borrowing is done by parastatal firms, the position of three groups is improved: employees of the firms whose debt allows increased wages or payrolls, suppliers of the firms that use debt to increase orders, and customers of the firms where debt leads to increased output and lower prices for the firms' products.

Of course, the differentiated effects of a capital inflow are reversed in the case of a capital outflow or a cessation of new lending. When a country with previous access to foreign capital is cut off, the supply of capital is reduced and domestic interest rates rise. Foreign exchange dries up and the currency depreciates, while the public spending-revenue gap must be closed without recourse to foreign funds. The society also has to mobilize domestic resources and foreign exchange to maintain service payments on the external debt. National savings, exports, and government revenue have to increase, or investment, imports, and government spending must decrease, or some combination of these. As foreign finance disappears and domestic interest rates rise, borrowers lose and savers gain. As foreign exchange becomes scarce and the currency depreciates, consumers of imported goods suffer and exporters benefit. As it becomes harder to finance the public deficit, spending is cut and employees, suppliers, and consumers of the public sector suffer the consequences.

Government policy can affect the distribution of foreign finance and thus the costs and benefits of a country's international financial position. When loans flow in, the government can channel capital and foreign exchange to favored sectors of the economy, thus concentrating the availability of cheaper capital or imports on a few government-backed borrowers. It is precisely this ability of government policy to affect the impact of international financial flows on different groups in society that makes these flows politically controversial. On the basis of these general observations, we can move on to discuss the Latin American experience, both while finance was readily available and once the financial crisis hit.

Politics and Economics in the Borrowing Process

The economic effects of Latin American borrowing were the result of both market factors and government policies; they thus varied from country to country. We can nonetheless identify general patterns among the economic actors who were especially assisted by foreign borrowing; that is, those on whom the positive effects of the capital inflow were concentrated. It should be kept in mind that our analysis uses the borrowing period as a somewhat artificial starting point, especially since many of the effects discussed here were the result of government policies already in place when borrowing began.

In virtually all borrowing countries, the financial and commercial sectors grew very rapidly. The banking system was a major conduit for funds in all countries, and its role as intermediary between foreign lenders and domestic borrowers was extremely lucrative. By the same token, the greater availability of foreign exchange increased foreign trade, thus helping the commercial sector.[5]

Other consequences of external borrowing depended on the specifics of national government policy. In Brazil, Mexico, and Venezuela, the significant portions of foreign borrowing that went to finance parastatal investment improved the position of the parastatals themselves, as well as that of the suppliers and customers of the parastatals. This included construction firms and capital goods producers which received lucrative orders to supply the huge parastatal petrochemical, hydroelectric, mining, and steel projects. It also included the consumers of industrial inputs produced and sold at subsidized prices by these new parastatal investment projects. At the same time, domestic industry was accorded significant protection from foreign competition, even as it was generally able to purchase relatively inexpensive foreign capital goods. In all three countries, therefore, the public industrial corporations and the private firms tied to them grew very substantially.

In the Southern Cone, neo-liberal policies meant that external finance went largely to the financial and commercial sectors. Despite the general availability of cheap imported capital equipment and inputs, trade liberalization made the countries' mostly uncompetitive industrial firms particularly unattractive to external lenders. Meanwhile, concurrent booms in consumer goods, financial, and real estate markets made firms in these sectors especially attractive. Chile is the most striking case: the public sector did almost no borrowing, and most of the country's external debt was accumulated by diversified conglomerates based in financial, commercial, and real estate activities. In Argentina the pattern was similar, although some military-controlled public corporations were major borrowers there.

Foreign borrowing led to little domestic political conflict in Latin America before the financial crisis. This is easy to understand, since an inflow of foreign resources has far more visibly positive effects than negative ones.[6] Whatever unfavorable impact a capital inflow may have had on savers and exporters was generally overshadowed by the general prosperity it brought. The borrowing phase of recent Latin American financial experience was in fact one of relative well-being, as debt went to finance an expansion of consumption or investment or both.

Although debt-financed consumption or investment booms were generally uncontroversial, two criticisms of Latin American borrowing were voiced in some quarters even before 1982. One explicitly political objection came from opponents of the many authoritarian regimes then in power, who viewed foreign borrowing as a contribution to strengthening the *status quo*. The most obvious examples of this first criticism were in the Southern Cone, where policies of financial liberalization and resultant borrowing sprees were closely tied to the anti-labor bent of the military dictatorships and their supporters. The left and much of the labor movement in Chile and Argentina were just as hostile to foreign borrowing as they were to the regimes' neo-liberal policies.

The second pre-1982 criticism of external debt was explicitly economic, focusing on the role of foreign borrowing in validating or reinforcing undesirable domestic resource transfers. The most egregious target of such critics was the linked financial and currency speculation that went on in most countries, especially after 1979. As international interest rates rose in 1981 and 1982 and domestic interest rates followed suit, financial investors reaped very large profits. At the same time, as currencies became increasingly overvalued, the availability of a "one-way bet" against the national currency led financial investors in many countries to buy dollars and transfer their portfolios to Miami, London, or New York. Moreover, the major currency overvaluations of the early 1980s were generally possible because national monetary authorities could borrow heavily abroad and resell borrowed dollars at home at bargain basement prices.

Despite some complaints about the distributional effects of foreign borrowing—especially in the Southern Cone—the prevailing affluence among the upper and middle classes, and of parts of the working classes, muted most of the discontent that existed. The external debt did not become a major domestic political issue until the financial crisis began in 1982.

Distributional Effects of the Debt Crisis

The sudden disappearance of external sources of finance in 1982, exacerbated by the need to make service payments on large accumulations of external debt, had important macroeconomic consequences for countries that relied on foreign loans to finance investment and/or to cover their trade and budget deficits. Access to foreign capital dried up, which drove interest rates substantially higher everywhere. The reduced supply of foreign exchange led to rapid currency depreciation and a major compression of imports. The public sector's inability to finance its deficit abroad forced it to borrow more at home, driving interest rates up still further. It also forced the public sector to reduce its expenditures (other than debt service) and increase its revenues.

The debt crisis was disastrous for virtually everyone in Latin America. In one sense, of course, the crisis hit the poor hardest, since they had the least reserves to cushion the impact of the worst depression in modern Latin American history. While this is an important fact to keep in mind, it is far too undifferentiated to be of much explanatory power in understanding the political fallout of the crisis. Poverty is endemic in Latin America, the poor are always in conditions of relative deprivation, and most of the region's political systems have long succeeded in systematically excluding the poor from effective political activity.

Leaving aside the undifferentiated mass of the impoverished, the effects of the debt crisis fell unevenly on other economic agents. Those who bore the exchange risk for major foreign debts were probably the hardest hit. In some countries this was the domestic financial system itself, but in most cases local banks had passed the exchange risk on to local borrowers, and the massive crisis-driven devaluations bankrupted virtually all such ultimate borrowers. In one fell swoop many of Latin America's leading private firms were made insolvent, with dollar liabilities often many times larger than their assets.

The identity of those hit hardest by crisis-induced devaluations depended on the major borrowers in the financial expansion. In Brazil, where the devaluation was only moderate and most of the borrowing had been done by the public sector, the impact on the private sector was less severe than in Chile, where the devaluation was massive and the vast majority of the borrowing had been done by private firms. Mexico and Venezuela both had important private-sector borrowers that were bankrupted by the crisis, but the public sector still accounted for most external debt. In Argentina the mix was about half and half. In these last three countries, the devaluations were substantial, and the impact was felt throughout both the private and public sectors.

Another important group of economic actors who shared the brunt of the crisis in many countries was the network of firms tied to the public sector. The crisis forced a major curtailment of public investments expanded by borrowing, which hit hard at the parastatals' former suppliers. This was very much the case in Brazil, Mexico, and Venezuela. By the same token, where debt-financed parastatals had offered subsidized inputs to private industry, the crisis forced them to raise prices to maintain debt service. The resultant increase in utility rates, energy prices, transportation costs, and the cost of basic industrial inputs again hurt important industrial sectors in Brazil, Mexico, and Venezuela. Both of these outcomes—reduced parastatal orders and reduced public-sector subsidies to industry—were far less significant in Argentina and unimportant in Chile, which had fewer orders and subsidies to begin with.

Other beneficiaries of government spending were also affected by the crisis in public finance brought on by external debt difficulties. This was especially important in Mexico and Venezuela, both of which had relatively well-developed social programs for politically important popular-sector groups. The urban working class in both nations was an important source of political support for the ruling parties—the Partido Revolucionario Institucional (PRI) in Mexico, and Acción Democrática in Venezuela between 1974 and 1979—and had received some social programs during the financial expansion. These programs were drastically curtailed during the crisis. And, of course, public employees were major victims of the government budget cutting that inevitably followed the crisis.

Besides the ever-present and disenfranchised poor, then, the crisis was also disastrous for certain economically and politically influential sectors and groups. At the risk of over simplifying, the modern industrial sector was hit hardest in Brazil, Mexico, and Venezuela. This included especially the capital goods and basic industries that relied heavily on government orders and subsidies; it of course included both owners and workers. In Argentina and Chile the financial sectors were very hard hit. The end of the debt-financed consumption boom pulled the rug out from under middle classes that had experienced unprecedented prosperity in the late 1970s. The economic catastrophe that began in 1982 drove economic actors into the political arena to fight for protection or support. The result was a bewildering array of domestic political battles over economic policy in all Latin American nations.

Latin American Politics in the Debt Crisis

To explain the structure of domestic political activity in the debt crisis, we begin with an analysis of the different effects on various economic sectors. We then take into account the implications that different underlying economic positions, and the availability of viable political coalition partners and institutional settings, have for political activity. The goal of the exercise is to combine our rudimentary map of the economic effects of the crisis with a simple analytical framework that helps explain the patterns of political behavior observed in Latin America since 1982. The focus is on political behavior in the relatively short run—the immediate aftermath of the crisis. Political trends over the long term may differ from the initial response to the crisis.

We use the familiar notions of "exit" and "voice" introduced into the political economy literature by Albert Hirschman.[7] This allows for a distinction between actors who respond to adversity by leaving their surroundings for greener pastures (exit), and those who respond by attempting to improve the pasture they are in (voice). For our purposes the analysis is dichotomous and can be regarded as a series of decisions. First, actors decide whether to respond to the crisis by taking their assets elsewhere (exit) or by struggling for economic assistance in the political arena (voice). Second, those who opt for political activity decide whether to exert pressure as loyal supporters of the government (voice) or as defectors to the opposition (exit).

The first step is to examine how the position of various economic actors gave them different incentives to divert resources from economic endeavors to political activity. Throughout Latin America, investors whose assets were very mobile could easily exit from the local economy and thus had less incentive to exert political pressure on the government. Other groups whose assets were relatively immobile had no choice but to engage in political activity to protect their interests.

There is a continuum in the political behavior of economic actors from complete reliance on the market to total dependence on government favors. The endpoints are unrealistic—few firms devote none or all of their resources to political pressure— but there is substantial variation. Whether social actors exit the system or give voice to their demands is a function of the economic position of the actors themselves— the economic feasibility of each option—and of the domestic political environment—the expected results of protest. Leaving aside for now the likelihood of the success of political pressure, there are clear reasons why different sorts of investors with different kinds of assets will respond differently to identical economic events.[8]

Some economic actors can easily move their assets among sectors and jurisdictions, and thus respond rapidly to changes in economic conditions without loss of revenue. Those whose savings are in very liquid domestic financial instruments can easily respond to national economic difficulties and uncertainty by shifting their savings to Miami, where both the currency and the underlying economic and political environment are presumably more stable. Financial institutions can similarly shift their short-term assets from Mexico City to London. Investors with easily-marketable assets, such as gold, can readily liquidate their holdings.

Other investors, however, have assets tied to activities that cannot easily be liquidated without a significant capital loss. Capitalists may have production facilities with which they are very familiar, informal contracts from which they alone can benefit, expertise that can only be used in certain lines of production, or other sector- or site-specific assets that bind them to the local economy. Managers or employees may have skill, language, or personal ties that make it very difficult to move. Investors with assets that cannot easily be sold at the price they are worth to the investors, and who would have to take a major loss to liquidate their holdings, are relatively immobile economically.

The former investors, whom we shall call liquid assetholders, are far more likely to take their investments elsewhere in times of crisis than the latter investors, whom we shall call fixed assetholders. In response to serious domestic economic difficulties, which lower local rates of return or introduce unacceptable risk into local economic activities, liquid assetholders will tend to change their portfolios or even to flee the jurisdiction, while fixed assetholders will tend to stand and fight to protect the value of their assets.

In all of Latin America, important economic groups with liquid assets responded to the debt crisis with a combination of hedging and capital flight. Some got into extremely short-term deposits (often overnight accounts) indexed to the inflation rate or the dollar, or otherwise relatively protected against domestic instability. Others bought consumer durables, dollars, or gold, which could easily be sold at

Table 2.1

Estimates of Latin American Capital Flight and Total Debt, 1976-84

Country	A Capital Flight, 1976-1984 ($ billion)	B Gross External Debt, end-1984 ($ billion)	A/B
Argentina	$16	$46	35
Brazil	9	104	9
Chile	-2[a]	20	0
Mexico	27	97	28
Venezuela	30	34	88

[a]Indicates unregistered capital inflows

Source: Donald R. Lessard and John Williamson, eds., *Capital Flight and Third World Debt* (Washington, DC; Institute for International Economics, 1987), 88, 155 and 206. It should be noted that estimates for capital flight vary widely; figures presented here should be regarded only as indicative.

predictable prices in case of further trouble. Still others took their assets elsewhere, to establish dollar accounts or buy condominiums in Miami, San Diego, New York, London, or Geneva.

The precise mix of such asset movements was largely a response to national economic conditions as well as geographical and historical factors. Table 2.1 presents estimates of capital flight in the five major Latin American borrowers. In Brazil there was only a moderate currency overvaluation, a long tradition of capital controls, and general confidence in the country's long-term prospects. Liquid assetholders there generally got into real estate, index-linked Treasury securities, or physical dollars they kept inside the country. In Chile, the principal economic actors had substantial liquid assets, and reshuffled them in response to the crisis. Few engaged in capital flight, despite the massive peso overvaluation. The reasons for this are not entirely clear. Investors may simply have believed the dictatorship's continual insistence that there would be no devaluation, or astronomical domestic interest rates may have offset devaluation expectations.

Recourse to capital flight was most common in Mexico, Venezuela, and Argentina. In Mexico and Venezuela, with long traditions of easy movement to and from the United States and few or no capital controls, many investors already had U.S. bank accounts. The principal response of liquid assetholders in these countries was to buy dollars and take them overseas. To some extent, relatively inexperienced or trusting Mexican middle-class savers established legal dollar accounts inside Mexico; they were rewarded for their inexperience and faith by having their accounts frozen and converted to pesos at an artificially low rate once the crisis struck. Argentina's chronic economic and political instability since World War II had made many investors wary of fixed assets, so flight into overseas dollar accounts was widespread in Argentina.

While liquid assetholders responded primarily by protecting their assets—shifting their investments into new instruments or taking them abroad or both—they also engaged in some political action. Their primary concern was to ensure the continued liquidity, availability, and profitability of their assets. Thus they lobbied against exchange controls, for freer financial markets, and for government support for failing financial institutions. Although such demands for economic liberalization were limited in the initial phases of the crisis, since investors with such interests were relatively protected against the worst effects of the financial turmoil, pressures from market-oriented liquid assetholders have mounted over time.

In all countries liquid assetholders, many of whom now hold internationally-diversified portfolios, have come to support more orthodox macroeconomic measures, financial and commercial liberalization, and a more cooperative stance toward international financial institutions. The most visible such movement has been the increased support for the right-wing Partido Acción Nacional (PAN) by a portion of the Mexican business community, especially those in the North and/or those tied to trade and finance. Whether through Mexico's PAN, Venezuela's Grupo Roraima, or through other means, liquid assetholders have exerted some political pressure on the government. Nevertheless, because they concentrated most of their resources on economic diversification rather than political activity during the first stages of the crisis, their initial political successes were quite limited.

All of this explains why the foremost political pressures on Latin American governments in the aftermath of the financial crisis came from sectors that could not easily shift their economic activities and so were forced to fight for state support. The most prominent such group was made up of industrial capital and labor. Everywhere in Latin America the industrial sector was the strongest opponent of debt crisis-induced domestic austerity measures.

Our first step was to explain why some social groups engaged in intense political activity as the financial crisis hit. Our second step is to explain why this activity took different forms. Within the political arena, we are primarily interested in explaining a group's choice between exerting political pressure on the government and engaging in oppositional activity. The sort of political activity chosen depends on the likelihood that such activity will matter, which is largely a function of the institutional and political environment faced by social actors. Firms, sectors, and groups are most likely to make demands on governments perceived to be responsive. By the same token, they are most likely to support an opposition that has both the willingness to endorse their demands and some prospect of taking power.

The sort of political action engaged in by a social group thus depends on its assessment of the likelihood of success of the various options. This in turn is a function of the strength of the group, its ability to ally with other groups, its existing ties to the government, and the strength and availability of an oppositional alternative. We can highlight this process by focusing on how and why industrial capitalists, the most important group of fixed assetholders in industrializing societies, chose to exert pressure on the government or defect to the opposition.

The ability of industrialists to obtain the policies they sought without defection from the government was largely due to the economic importance of domestic industry, the degree to which industrial labor and management were able to unite in support of common demands, and the existence of close ties between industrialists and the government. A turn toward oppositional activity depended both on an inability to meet these conditions and on the availability of an acceptable opposition partner with reasonable chances of eventual success.

The general openness of the government to various social demands and the availability of an attractive opposition were indeed important factors in the political behavior of the Latin American private sector after 1982. In Chile, ties between domestic industrialists and the military regime were weak. Leaders of industry had little say in or sympathy for the government's neo-liberal economic policies after 1973. Indeed, industry had been substantially weakened by neo-liberal policies, as manufacturing value added dropped from 25 percent of gross domestic product (GDP) in 1970 to 19 percent in 1982.[9] In addition, labor-management relations were extremely hostile, so that industrial capital and labor could not unite to pressure the government. Industrial pressure on the Chilean government was weak, and the industrial sector had almost no success in obtaining government support. The government was willing to assume some responsibility for the financial catastrophe, but mostly in support of the heavily-indebted conglomerates whose position affected the country's overall international creditworthiness. After some initial vacillation, however, the dictatorship was generally indifferent to the pleas of the domestic industrial sector.

Despite their inability to influence government policy, Chilean industrialists engaged in little political protest. This was primarily because the existing opposition to the military did not enjoy the confidence of the private sector. The left, of course, was a traditional enemy, but even the Christian Democrats and the right were discredited in the eyes of the business community by their pre-1970 behavior. The moderate Chilean opposition complained bitterly that the private sector was cowardly, and at the same time attempted to tie itself to business discontent by assuring investors that the opposition would respect property rights and otherwise encourage private enterprise. Few businessmen were convinced. Another factor was the apparent willingness of the regime to use brute force to repress most opposition; there seemed little likelihood of anyone dislodging Pinochet. The opposition's ambiguous economic preferences and poor prospect of taking power meant that the business sector, discontented as it might be, remained politically passive. The exception that proved the rule, of course, was the brief participation of business groups in the opposition demonstrations in 1983-84. The government's success in co-opting business was a key factor in the failure of the protest movement.

In Argentina, industrialists had more options. Although Argentine deindustrialization was almost as significant as in Chile—manufacturing value added went from 27 to 23 percent of GDP between 1970 and 1982—the sector maintained ties with some military factions. At the same time, Argentine labor-capital relations, although not fully cooperative, were better than in Chile, and most of the opposition was less suspect. The industrial sector thus used a combination of pressure on the dictatorship and defection to the opposition. The 1981 Viola presidency reversed the anti-industrial course of previous economic policy and bailed out many private firms, raising the hopes of the industrialists. When Viola was eased out by hard-line officers, however, industrialists lost faith in the military. After the Falklands/ Malvinas disaster discredited the hard-liners still further, it seemed a safer bet to dissent from the military, and much of the industrial sector openly opposed the country's military-run neo-liberal policies. The industrial sector in fact received support during both the 1981 Viola presidency and after Raúl Alfonsín's accession to power.

In Brazil, Mexico, and Venezuela industrial production led the pre-1982 economic expansion, and the industrial sector was both economically and politically influential. The three countries differed primarily in government responsiveness to industrial demands.

In Mexico and Venezuela the industrialists were economically crucial, and labor-management relations were such that unified sectoral demands could be made. In both countries, the industrial sector worked through the existing political structures of the ruling party, and it received substantial support. Government assistance given in response to industrial pressure ranged from subsidized loans to trade protection. Perhaps the most important aid to industry took the form of schemes allowing industrial firms with overseas liabilities to service their foreign debts at a preferential exchange rate rather than at the vastly more expensive market rate, thus effectively transferring most of private industry's debt burden to the government. After the initial shock of the crisis, Mexican policy did gradually move toward liberalization, but by then much of the industrial sector had been cushioned against some of the most severe effects of the financial distress, whether by access to loans at subsidized interest rates or to artificially inexpensive foreign currency for debt service payments.

In Brazil there was a both a history of government sympathy for the industrial sector and a vibrant opposition. Brazilian industry had grown extremely rapidly during the borrowing period, and both labor and management in modern industry were well-organized. Brazilian industrialists thus reacted to the crisis in two ways. First, they protested vehemently to the military government about the policies being undertaken. When their protests went more or less unheeded, the industrialists defected to the opposition, either leaving the official party for the new Liberal Front or joining the leading opposition party, the Partido Movimento Democrático Brasileiro (PMDB). Eventually the military and its civilian supporters were replaced by a broad anti-austerity PMDB-Liberal Front movement of the modern industrial sector, the urban middle class, and parts of the working class.[10]

All of these cases are far more complex than this rudimentary summary allows. The structure of labor-management relations, private sector ties with the military, the traditional party system, and a host of other considerations need to be investigated in much more detail and factored into an accurate account of the crisis. Our purpose has been only to sketch the implications and demonstrate the potential usefulness of an approach that directs attention to the economic position of social actors and, given this economic position, to the choices they made within their economic and political environment.

Conclusion

This chapter has presented a framework for analyzing the political effects of the Latin American debt crisis. International financial relations have differential consequences, and their political implications follow from their distributional effects. These distributional effects are filtered through two prisms. The first is economic, and determines the probable response of economic agents to economic difficulty, especially the likelihood that they will have recourse to the political arena. The second is political, and determines the form of the political response, especially the likelihood that a group's political activities will occur within the existing government's support apparatus, rather than taking the form of oppositional protest.

The first step in understanding the politics of the debt crisis, then, is accurately to characterize the economic interests of the various social forces at work. We have argued that there is a crucial difference between liquid and fixed assetholders, since the former can easily leave the domestic economic environment, while the latter are tied to it and thus driven to the political arena in times of distress. As the debt crisis hit, the response of the two broad groupings of investors was substantially different: one engaged primarily in asset diversification (such as real estate speculation or capital flight), while the other moved primarily into political action.

The second step is to specify the political environment faced by various social forces. We have explored the circumstances in which a group's political activity takes the form of "loyal" pressure on the government, and those in which the group resorts to political opposition. This set of choices is determined by the group's economic importance, its ability to unite with other forces, its ties to the government, and the availability of an opposition attractive to the group in question.

The discussion in this chapter is preliminary and suggestive, rather than detailed and definitive. It does, however, indicate the possibility of going beyond *ad hoc* description and abstract theorizing to analyze the sources of domestic political conflict in Latin America. The essay demonstrates the utility of the approach put forward and holds out the prospect that further investigation and analysis will help us explain Latin American political behavior, both in the debt crisis and more generally.

Notes

Thanks, for useful comments and suggestions, to David Dollar, Barbara Geddes, Kevin James, Robert Kaufman, David Lake, Sylvia Maxfield, Ron Rogowski, and Michael Wallerstein.

1. For some representative examples of the burgeoning literature on this international bargaining, see Charles Lipson, "Bankers' Dilemmas: Private Cooperation in Rescheduling Sovereign Debts," *World Politics* 38, no. 1 (October 1985); Jeffrey Sachs, "Theoretical Issues in International Borrowing," *Princeton Studies in International Finance*, no. 54 (Princeton: International Finance Section, 1984); and Vincent Crawford, "International Lending, Long-Term Credit Relationships, and Dynamic Contract Theory," *Princeton Studies in International Finance*, no. 59 (Princeton: International Finance Section, 1987).

2. On the approaches and their deficiencies, see, for example, J. Samuel Valenzuela and Arturo Valenzuela, "Modernization and Dependency: Alternative Paradigms on the Study of Latin American Underdevelopment," *Comparative Politics* 10, no. 4 (July 1978) and *The New Authoritarianism in Latin America*, ed. David Collier (Princeton: Princeton University Press, 1979).

3. For a more ambitious attempt to explain both the origins and the effects of national borrowing experiences, see my "Classes, Sectors, and Foreign Debt in Latin America," *Comparative Politics* (forthcoming). More detailed references can be found there; surveys include Andrés Bianchi et al., *External Debt in Latin America* (Boulder: Lynne Rienner, 1985); Carlos Díaz-Alejandro, "Latin American Debt," *Brookings Papers on Economic Activity* 2 (1984); Inter-American Development Bank, *External Debt and Economic Development in Latin America* (Washington: IADB, 1984); *Latin American Political Economy: Financial Crisis and Political Change*, ed. Jonathan Hartlyn and Samuel Morley (Boulder, CO: Westview Press, 1986); and Joseph Ramos, *Neoconservative Economics in the Southern Cone of Latin America, 1973-1983* (Baltimore: Johns Hopkins University Press, 1986).

4. In the simplest sense, "overvaluation" results when an inflow of resources leads to an increase in the demand for non-traded goods, whose prices thus move upward. Inasmuch as traded goods prices are constrained by international competition and the exchange rate is set by the traded goods sector, the exchange rate will tend to drift toward "overvaluation" as it rises more slowly than domestic inflation. See, for example, Arnold Harberger, "Economic Adjustment and the Real Exchange Rate," in *Economic Adjustment and Exchange Rates in Developing Countries*, ed. Sebastian Edwards and Liaquat Ahamed (Chicago: University of Chicago Press, 1987). The well-known and controversial literature on the "Dutch disease" discusses a special case of this phenomenon.

5. In a more nuanced vein, the benefits accruing to the financial and commercial sectors, and to the non-traded goods sectors more generally, depended on the degree to which financial resources flowed to these sectors or "leaked" into them in large amounts. To the extent that government policy limited borrowing to producers of traded goods and forced borrowers to use borrowed funds directly for imports, there was little overvaluation and thus little switching of domestic expenditures from domestically-produced traded goods to foreign and non-traded goods. Where government policy allowed significant amounts of borrowed funds to be used for non-traded goods purchases, the resultant overvaluation exacerbated the first-order effect by cutting into the domestic demand for domestically-produced traded goods.

6. This implies, of course, that agents were not accurately forecasting the future costs of

current borrowing. Given the catastrophic and relatively sudden nature of the crisis, this is hardly a controversial assertion. For an argument that even "prudent planners" would have been swamped by the events of 1982-1983, see Carlos Díaz-Alejandro, "Some Aspects of the 1982-1983 Brazilian Payments Crisis," *Brookings Papers on Economic Activity* 2 (1983).

7. Albert O. Hirschman, *Exit, Voice, and Loyalty* (Cambridge: Harvard University Press, 1970).

8. In what follows we focus almost exclusively on real capital; the argument could easily be extended to include human capital, and thus the specific skills of workers. The political implications of the inclusion of human capital are clear and significant. It should also be noted that the following discussion assumes that investors' portfolios are not completely diversified. This is a reasonable assumption, especially in Latin America, where capital markets are extremely underdeveloped and almost all firms are family-owned.

9. Manufacturing value added as a percentage of GDP calculated from Inter-American Development Bank, *Economic and Social Progress in Latin America: 1986 Report* (Washington, DC: IADB, 1986).

10. For more details on the Brazilian case, see Jeffry Frieden, "The Brazilian Borrowing Experience," *Latin American Research Review* 22, no. 2 (1987).

Suggestions for Further Reading

Bianchi, Andrés et al. *External Debt in Latin America*. Boulder: Lynne Rienner, 1985.

Díaz-Alejandro, Carlos. "Some Aspects of the 1982-1983 Brazilian Payments Crisis." *Brookings Papers on Economic Activity* 2, 1983.

Frieden, Jeffry A. "Classes, Sectors, and Foreign Debt in Latin America." *Comparative Politics* (forthcoming).

Hartlyn, Jonathan, and Samuel Morley, eds. *Latin American Political Economy: Financial Crisis and Political Change*. Boulder, CO: Westview Press, 1986.

Inter-American Development Bank. *External Debt and Economic Development in Latin America*. Washington, DC: IADB, 1984.

Sachs, Jeffrey D. "External Debt and Macroeconomic Performance in Latin America and East Asia." *Brookings Papers on Economic Activity* 2, 1985.

Thorp, Rosemary, and Laurence Whitehead, eds. *Latin American Debt and the Adjustment Crisis*. London: Macmillan, 1987.

3

Debt and Democracy
in Latin America, 1920s–1980s

Paul W. Drake

In the mid-1980s, Latin America presented a seemingly glaring contradiction. The region enjoyed one of the best moments ever for liberal democracy amidst one of its worst economic crises in history. That paradox challenged longstanding social science assumptions. Explicitly or implicitly, scholars have frequently argued that the pacts and compromises underlying democratic stability normally benefit from reasonable levels of prosperity.

Consequently, experts warned that the nagging debt crisis was undermining fragile civilian governments.[1] Doomsayers pointed to the previous crash in the 1930s, when the Great Depression triggered military *coups d'état* throughout the hemisphere. To compare those two crises, it becomes necessary to examine the historical record of the interaction between debt and democracy.

In broad terms, scholars must ask what is the long-term relationship—causal or casual—between external finance and regime type in Latin America. Most social science attempts to establish macrolevel cross-national correlations between such economic and political variables have failed. For example, statistical exercises linking economic growth with democracy or authoritarianism have borne little fruit.[2] Over many years and many countries, is there any pattern indicating that positive or negative net resource transfers particularly encourage dictatorships or democracies in Latin America? Is it correct to assume that capital inflows disproportionately favor dictators while capital outflows disproportionately damage democrats? Appearances to the contrary, there may be no verifiable or predictable influence of debt on democracy.

Nevertheless, at first glance there does seem to be some connection between changes in financial flows and changes in political systems. The two great debt crises of the 1930s and the 1980s clearly coincided with massive shifts between democracies and dictatorships. As can be seen in Table 3.1, the depression of the 1930s was associated with an initial switch from fourteen democracies and six dictatorships to ten democracies and ten dictatorships. By the middle of that decade, Bolivia, Ecuador, Nicaragua, Paraguay, and Peru had also moved firmly into the dictatorial column, leaving five democracies and fifteen dictatorships. In a mirror

Table 3.1
Debt and Democracy in Latin America, 1920s-1930s

Country	Approximate External Public Long-Term Debt in 1929 ($ million)	Formal System of Government, 1928-30		Downfall of Indebted Govt. (! = coup)	Formal System of Government, 1932-34	
		Democracy	Dictatorship		Democracy	Dictatorship
Argentina	$1,202	X		1930!		X
Bolivia	55	X		1930!	X	
Brazil	1,059	X		1930!		X
Chile	499		X	1931!	X	
Colombia	88	X		1930	X	
Costa Rica	18	X		1932	X	
Cuba	85		X	1933!		X
Dominican Republic	19	X		1930!		X
Ecuador	20		X	1931	X	
El Salvador	19	X		1931!		X
Guatemala	14	X		1930!		X
Haiti	13		X	1930		X
Honduras	27	X		1932		X
Mexico	826	X		1934	X	
Nicaragua	3	X		1932	X?	
Panama	18	X		1931!	X	
Paraguay	4	X		1932	X	
Peru	113		X	1930!	X	
Uruguay	138	X		1934		X
Venezuela	4		X	1935		X
		14	6		10	10

Note on Debt: Numerous sources give slightly different figures, but the data here represent reasonable approximations of magnitudes. These numbers come from the United Nations, Department of Economic and Social Affairs, External Financing in Latin America (New York: United Nations, 1965), 27.

Note on Democracy: My definition of "democracy" is, of necessity, very loose and relative; it mainly includes constitutionally elected, civilian governments, however elitist and contrived. "Dictatorship" refers to blatantly more authoritarian regimes. Those democracies with a question mark were particularly dubious and short-lived.

image, Table 3.2 shows how the depression of the 1980s ushered in a reversal from seven democracies and thirteen dictatorships to seventeen democracies and three dictatorships.

Admittedly, there is a potential methodological problem with these tables. It is intrinsically difficult to classify and quantify crudely-defined and roughly-measured regime types. The categorizations here reflect a reasonable consensus gleaned from numerous scholarly secondary sources. Among contemporaries, most of these governments enjoyed the reputations recorded in these columns. The term "democratic" is used in a very narrow reference to the prevailing procedures of political competition; it implies nothing about mass participation in the inputs and outputs of government.

Moreover, the classification scheme is relative in two senses. First, for any one time period, those governments labeled democratic might not meet some absolute criteria, but they were more freely-elected, representative, constitutional, and civilian based than those labeled dictatorial, which were more imposed, authoritarian, arbitrary, and military-dominated. By the same token, movement from one column to another indicates that a government became significantly more democratic or despotic than its predecessor. Obviously, there are some close calls and mixed breeds, such as civilian governments that were installed by force or army generals elected president under dubious circumstances. Some "paper" democracies are so limited as to be barely distinguishable from rather "liberal" dictatorships. Mexico's authoritarian, elected, civilian government is always an anomaly; it is placed in the more-or-less democratic camp here, by contrast with the harsher military autocracies. In both eras, the most ambiguous cases resided in Central America and the Caribbean, where both democracies and dictatorships were often under the tutelage of the armed forces and the United States.

Although some individual choices in the tables remain contentious, the general scope and trajectory of political movement seems, nonetheless, undeniable. Virtually all Latin Americanists would agree that there was a general swing toward dictatorship in the 1930s and toward formal democracy in the 1980s. Barring astonishing coincidences among countries, there should be some logic to these cyclical transformations.

This chapter will first examine the implications for political systems of financial inflows in the 1920s and outflows in the 1930s. Then it will sketch some comparisons with the political economy of the debt influx and efflux of the 1970s and 1980s. Finally, a few tentative conclusions are offered on historical relationships between foreign loans and regime types.

The Politics of Debt Infusion in the 1920s

To analyze the political impact of external financing, it is necessary to distinguish between the consequences of positive and negative net resource transfers from abroad. During the infusions of the 1920s and the 1970s, U.S. financiers were often

Table 3.2
Debt and Democracy in Latin America, 1970s-1980s

Country	Formal System of Government, 1978-1981		Turnover of Indebted Government	Formal System of Government, 1983-1986	
	Democracy	Dictatorship		Democracy	Dictatorship
Argentina		X	1983	X	
Bolivia		X	1982	X	
Brazil		X	1985	X	
Chile		X			X
Colombia	X		1982	X	
Costa Rica	X		1982	X	
Cuba		X			X
Dominican Rep.	X		1982	X	
Ecuador	X		1984	X	
El Salvador		X	1984	X	
Guatemala		X	1985	X	
Haiti		X	1986	X?	
Honduras		X	1982	X?	
Mexico	X		1982	X?	
Nicaragua		X	1984	X?	
Panama		X	1984	X	
Paraguay		X			X
Peru	X		1985	X	
Uruguay		X	1984	X	
Venezuela	X		1983	X	
	7	13		17	3

Note on Democracy: My definition of "democracy" follows that of the U.S. Department of State, Bureau of Public Affairs, "Democracy in Latin America and the Caribbean," *Current Policy*, no. 605 (August 1984), emphasizing elected, representative, constitutional, civilian governments, more or less conforming to Western, liberal models. Even in dubious cases, I have accepted their classifications, except in Nicaragua.

accused of bankrolling tyrants in Latin America. Did those investors prefer dictators and did their funding especially help dictators? Was there any natural bond between foreign loans and authoritarianism? Specifically, did external lending particularly encourage (1) powerful outside actors to resort to authoritarian interference in Latin American politics; (2) the creation or consolidation of authoritarian regimes; or (3) dictators or democrats adopting or intensifying authoritarian governing practices? Or, to the contrary, did loans from abroad reinforce more democratic regimes and governing methods? To begin to answer those questions, it is necessary to look at the politics of debt during the "Dance of the Millions" in the 1920s, the greatest influx of private Yankee dollars prior to the 1970s. We will examine the policies of the key players in both the United States and Latin America toward debt and democracy.

From World War I to the Great Depression, the United States extended its economic hegemony from the Caribbean and Central America into South America. U.S. citizens displaced the British everywhere except on the east coast. In its trade with the United States, Latin America's exports doubled and imports tripled. Total U.S. investments in the region also tripled. Over one fourth of that total was in indirect investments, which accounted for approximately three fourths of the increase in the 1920s. Most of that new money went into South America and to national governments.[3]

U.S. investment bankers competed with each other and with Europeans to arrange those loans. At the start of the 1930s, Francis White, the U.S. Assistant Secretary of State for Latin American Affairs, concluded, "In the carnival days from 1922 to 1929, when money was easy, many American bankers forsook the dignified, aloof attitude traditional of bankers and became, in reality, high pressure salesmen of money, carrying on a cutthroat competition against their fellow bankers, and once they obtained the business, endeavored to urge larger loans on the borrowing countries." Those bankers sometimes pressed imprudent loans because they were not risking their own money. In contrast with the direct financiers of the 1970s, they mainly served as intermediaries who sold Latin American government bonds to individual U.S. investors in the New York market. Normally, the bankers' profits came from commissions in the original contract, not from eventual servicing of the debt. Consequently, many of these investment houses cared little about the character of the borrowing regime. They eagerly generated financing for democrats or dictators.[4]

Nevertheless, some U.S. bankers did meddle in Latin American politics. They hoped to forge long-term relationships with both the debtors in Latin America and the creditors in the United States. Therefore, they attempted to assure the credit-worthiness of the borrowers. These bankers went to great lengths to investigate, solidify, and even control Latin American finances. Their concerns and demands favored authoritarian regimes, or at least undemocratic governing behavior.

Naturally, bankers preferred to arrange such deals behind closed doors. They found it easier to work out contracts quietly with the executive branch, away from the spotlight of legislative bodies or the press. Confidential negotiations proved especially desirable on sensitive matters such as pledging future fiscal revenues to loan repayments. Such guarantees appeared quite reasonable to U.S. bankers, attractive to U.S. bond purchasers, and necessary to Latin American borrowers. Once revealed, however, these commitments could outrage nationalistic politicians from opposition parties.

To safeguard investments, U.S. bankers preferred technocratic management of fiscal and financial institutions, especially by U.S. experts. In order to husband resources for debt servicing, they wanted to shield economic agencies—such as the national budget office, the customs department, and the central bank—from interference by politicians, who had other spending priorities for local projects and clienteles. In other words, foreign investors sought to insulate economic decision making from democratic pressures. In order to exert the budgetary and banking control expected by foreign lenders, even formally democratic governments in Latin America became increasingly authoritarian in behavior.

In one extreme case, the Bolivian government in 1922 accepted a Permanent Fiscal Commission dominated by U.S. bankers in return for a $33 million loan. The Commission was empowered to supervise all taxes, customs duties, government expenditures and banks. Once those terms became public, critics assailed the arrangement as "an alienation of Bolivia's economic sovereignty, which imposes upon our institutions and upon the popular will the absolute discretion of a group of foreign bankers whose actions do not and can not have any other guide than profit...Such regulations try to impose on this part of America the imperialist sentiment of some bankers."[5]

In the 1920s, the U.S. government did not play a large role in either international debt or democracy. It encouraged foreign lending to generate purchases of exports and return payments on interest and principal. At the same time, it hoped the borrowers would become more receptive to U.S. influence. U.S. policymakers also believed that loans would fuel prosperity overseas and thus reduce the likelihood of disorder or, worse, revolution. By the 1920s, particularly in South America, they hoped to achieve their objectives by eschewing either military intervention or coercive diplomatic lobbying on behalf of U.S. businesses. Instead, they relied on the "open door" and the "diplomacy of the dollar."[6]

The "open door" assumed that equal opportunity and reciprocity in a nation's economic policies were sufficient conditions for U.S. entrepreneurs to prevail over weaker European and local Latin American competitors. The "diplomacy of the dollar" envisioned U.S. foreign investments automatically enhancing U.S. international interests. To facilitate that process, the U.S. government would encourage laissez-faire practices abroad, generally promoting the overseas expansion of U.S. traders, companies, investors and banks. Only minimal assistance ("good offices") was provided to most U.S. firms, except in rare instances affecting national security. The State Department realized that in most cases further interference was not only unnecessary but also counterproductive. It wanted to quell fears that the flag would follow the dollar. Avoiding entanglements with individual U.S. enterprises also kept the State Department out of inter-firm conflicts and above disputes between them and Latin American governments. Although abridged at times, official policy stated that U.S. investors in Latin America took their own risks, with no guarantee of protection from their government.[7]

Applying that principle to foreign loans proved particularly delicate. Beginning in 1922, investment bankers were required to notify the State Department of contracts for foreign bonds to be sold to the public. This procedure did not imply government approval. The State Department normally refused to judge the business merits of the loans or to back them in any way. It merely told the bankers whether or not it had any objections on foreign policy grounds, which it rarely did. In the few instances that a loan was not approved, private bankers almost always suspended financial negotiations. For example, in 1925 a loan to Brazil was blocked because it would have subsidized a coffee monopoly. In another case, a Central American loan that might have conflicted with treaty provisions was rejected.[8]

In most cases, the State Department did not employ overtly political criteria in evaluating these loans. It could afford to be neutral because in the 1920s virtually no governments adamantly hostile to the United States existed. One criterion that might have had a significant political impact in Latin America was the disapproval of loans for armaments. That proviso was never invoked, however, even though one Bolivian issue went partly for that purpose. Whereas the U.S. government often closely supervised lenders and borrowers in the strategic Caribbean region, it seldom interfered with South American transactions. As the 1920s progressed, it rendered fewer and fewer judgments on Latin American deals. When the Great Depression capsized the international financial system, the major complaint from U.S. bondholders and politicians was that the U.S. government had played too small a role in policing foreign investments.[9]

Despite its relative passivity in the 1920s, the U.S. government still exerted some authoritarian pressures in pursuit of its economic objectives abroad. In parts of the Caribbean and Central America, the United States retained economic privileges through the use of troops and treaties. It viewed landing the marines farther south as too expensive, politically as well as economically. For example, during the Great Depression, one New York banker asked the head of the State Department's Latin American division about using military force to protect U.S. properties in Chile. The government official replied

> . . . that the properties in Chile were inland, the copper properties at least being high up in the Andes, and that a battleship could not climb mountains . . . I pointed out that we had never done anything of this sort before and had not landed troops in any country south of the canal. I told him it was my personal opinion that if we did so we could not accomplish what he wanted and our action would be such that there would be no benefits in Chile itself, and still less in the rest of South America. I said I thought it would be the end of our trade in South America for some time.[10]

Nevertheless, many Latin Americans feared that the potential for violence lurked behind the quest for economic concessions. The specter of that violence made a few South Americans, fearing that bullets might follow the bonds, resist U.S. economic penetration. Many more, however, welcomed U.S. investments, partly in hopes that voluntary receptivity would avert armed intimidation.

Other coercive levers used by the U.S. government included withholding recognition, blocking arms shipments, and promoting friendly political factions. For example, in Chile in 1912, a short-lived Socialist Republic threatened to nationalize all foreign deposits in the Central Bank. The U.S. State Department dissuaded the Chileans by holding up recognition of the government, delaying oil shipments, and warning that U.S. banks would not pay out drafts and would deny international trade credits.[11] The most common device was formal and informal diplomatic lobbying. More explicitly economic measures involved encouraging or discouraging U.S. investments in a particular country and directly or indirectly supervising its finances.

At the start of the 1920s, the recognition policy, inherited from Woodrow Wilson, was not officially connected to economic issues. Instead, it denied diplomatic recognition to unconstitutional governments. Such a denial automatically discouraged U.S. investors. Thus, in theory, the United States was intervening on behalf of democrats rather than dictators or bankers. In practice, the doctrine of constitutionalism proved very difficult to apply to poorly-defined and unstable regimes. In some cases, a dictatorship might plausibly claim to be just as "constitutional" as a democracy. Consequently, Latin Americans resented the policy as a subterfuge for discriminating among friendly and unfriendly governments, for example in Mexico and Nicaragua. In order to reduce resentment against U.S. interventionism, President Herbert Hoover scrapped the nonrecognition policy in 1930 and returned to the traditional practice of accepting *de facto* as well as *de jure* governments.[12]

In the 1920s, most direct U.S. political interference in Latin America occurred through financial supervision. Economic institutions, policies, and behavior designed to assure debt repayment were imposed to reduce uncertainties for U.S. lenders. This also increased the host country's creditworthiness in the eyes of U.S. investors. Therefore, Latin American as well as U.S. elites often welcomed such external proctoring and certification.

Neither U.S. government nor banking officials wanted to bear direct responsibility for this assertion of authority over another country's public decision making. After World War II, they relied on international devices, especially the International Monetary Fund, to enforce conformity to the rules of the game of western capitalism. Prior to the era of multilateral agencies, the instruments of financial supervision evolved from public to private operations.

That privatization of financial monitoring went through four stages. To a significant extent, the procedures became increasingly democratic. First, at the turn of the century, the U.S. government directly and officially dispatched economists along with soldiers to recast and administer financial institutions in the colonies of Puerto Rico and the Philippines. In this first modality, there was virtually no pretense about policy decisions being made voluntarily, democratically, or independently by the debtor country. A second public device subsequently channeled U.S. economic administrators throughout the client states of the Caribbean and Central America under the provisions of the treaties signed with occupied countries, such as the Dominican Republic, Haiti, and Nicaragua. From 1911 to 1923, a third semi-official practice emerged. Rather than treaties, private contracts between Latin American governments and U.S. investment bankers stipulated that loans would be safeguarded by placing that country's fiscal affairs under the control of a U.S. adviser. In many cases, that official was approved, though not appointed, by the State Department. Such private individuals, outside of government but intrinsically helping to advance U.S. objectives, were called "chosen instruments." They played a role in contractual arrangements between lenders and borrowers in Guatemala, Honduras, El Salvador, Bolivia and Peru.[13]

From the early 1920s onward, the U.S. State Department further shielded itself from charges of interventionism by favoring a fourth mechanism: independent economic missions hired voluntarily by governments seeking loans. In most cases, the State Department's only involvement consisted of helping the country find advisers and quietly nudging all parties from behind the scenes. The archetype of these private emissaries in the 1920s was Edwin W. Kemmerer, Professor of Economics at Princeton University and known around the globe as the "Money Doctor." A sort of one-man IMF, Kemmerer thoroughly revamped the monetary, banking, and fiscal systems of Guatemala, Colombia, Chile, Ecuador, Bolivia, and Peru, not to mention South Africa, Poland, China, and Turkey.[14]

In almost every case these economic missions by Kemmerer and other such experts stabilized exchange rates and controlled domestic credit by establishing the gold standard, a central bank, and strict banking regulations. They also made government finances more orderly, efficient and reliable by recommending new laws for budgeting, accounting, collecting taxes, and servicing debts. For example, these advisers shifted budgetary authority from the legislative to the executive branch and imposed strict auditing under an independent national comptroller. Frequently, they placed U.S. specialists in charge of those new institutions.

Kemmerer and his fellow economic missionaries advised democratic as well as dictatorial governments. At the time of his South American assignments, the Money Doctor was brought in by two "democracies" (Colombia and Bolivia) and three "dictatorships" (Chile, Ecuador and Peru). Such foreign advisers saw their primary purpose as the neutral transfer of technology from the universal science of economics. They were not committed to the advancement of narrow corporate or political interests. Nevertheless, they found it easiest to get their prescriptions accepted by authoritarian regimes, and so came to prefer working with dictators or dictatorial methods. For example, in Ecuador in 1927, Kemmerer urged the U.S. Embassy to recognize the dictatorship there despite its lack of constitutionality. He preferred that regime to a democracy because it could impose his laws by decree without prior debate, implement their provisions "with a strong hand," and staff the new institutions with U. S. citizens, despite nationalistic opposition.[15]

Whether dictatorial or democratic, host governments had little choice but to implement the bulk of Kemmerer's recommendations. It was hard for Latin Americans to reject or even modify expert advice after having invited a foreign mission with great fanfare, exposed their financial flaws to it, and staked their external credit rating and domestic political credibility on its success. Because of their ability to elicit external loans, foreigners possessed leverage to restructure Latin American economies more than recipient governments could have done on their own. Not unlike the "Chicago Boys" of the 1970s, Kemmerer's anointment elevated certain ideas, institutions, and individuals as sacred and above normal public debate and political struggle. Whatever their motivations, making policies in consultation with foreign advisors rather than with national interests was inherently undemocratic. Government by experts was inevitably less open than government by elected representatives.

Dictatorships used such economic missions and the need for sweeping economic restructuring to justify staying in office. They shared with foreign advisers a belief in government by technocrats, rather than by allegedly petty, partisan politicians. Their own citizens, they argued, lacked sufficient wisdom or objectivity to pass judgment on the virtues of imported economic models. Beyond their transfer of knowledge, these missions served as mechanisms of legitimation; employing such renowned outside experts improved the prestige of these governments at home and abroad. Governments used their reports to blame previous administrations for mismanagement and to recast local economic institutions. Above all, they took advantage of the experts' seal of good housekeeping to attract new loans from New York.

Especially for authoritarian regimes, external financing made it easier to survive with only a slim base of domestic support. One anti-imperialist charged in the 1930s that Kemmerer "helped dictators put their abused revenue sources in order, so they could squeeze out more funds to pay more debts, buy more munitions, and pay their police forces to keep the people down and avoid revolution. He was hailed in Wall Street and he was hailed by the dictators of a continent and a half as a wonder worker. . . . Now, even the dictators are wiser, especially as the udders of American loans have gone dry."[16]

Whatever the regime type, they used these financial supervisors and the accompanying loans to expand their country's extractive and distributive capabilities. Contracting foreign debts was mainly a power capability of the central government, which became more subservient to external authorities but more autonomous from internal elites. The central administration became larger and better managed. Foreign financing alleviated the need to tax domestic elites and enhanced the ability to satisfy the military, the bureaucracy, and new urban groups. Most foreign dollars went into public works, which pleased industrialists with infrastructure and middle-

and working-class elements with jobs. Swelling national budgets underwrote reforms and participation, reducing the need to repress demands. External loans helped paternalistic, clientelistic political systems—whether installed through the ballot box or the barracks—keep afloat.

Thus U.S. economic advisers and investors contributed to both authoritarian and democratic systems and practices, but the general state of the economy and the constellation of domestic forces mainly determined the type of regime and its behavior. At least in Mexico and South America, political outcomes were primarily decided by the ability of local elites to take advantage of outside as well as inside resources to achieve their own objectives. Latin Americans themselves made the key decisions about the local political and economic beneficiaries of debt accumulation. Regardless of the preferences and operating methods of external agents, the types of political regimes neither determined nor were determined by the flow of foreign capital.

In the 1920s, most of those loans ended up in the hands of elected, constitutional governments, as Table 3.1 shows. Foreign financing in the 1920s did encourage external authoritarian interventions and internal authoritarian governments and operations, but not much. In contrast with the 1970s, debt infusion did not primarily sustain dictatorships, mainly because blatantly authoritarian regimes happened to be in the minority. In individual cases, external financing may have been more essential for dictators than democrats, as a substitute for internal support. In the aggregate, however, portfolio investments were more abundant for democrats.

The Politics of Debt Hemorrhage in the 1930s

Just as debt accumulation aided all types of regimes, so net outflows to service debt wreaked havoc on both democracies and dictatorships. As Table 3.1 indicates, the debt crisis of the 1930s provoked a violent switch from democratic to authoritarian regimes. The primary reason for regimes changing direction was that so many constitutional governments had held office on the eve of the Crash. What were the politics of default?

When the Great Depression struck, overextended Latin American governments had become heavily reliant on loans through foreign bankers. In hopes of new credit, they initially tried to ride out the crisis by acquiescing to U.S. government and business demands. From 1929 to 1931, U.S. advisers recommended balancing the budget, slashing domestic expenditures, sustaining the gold standard, meeting foreign obligations, and awaiting the revival of the world economy. But neither U.S. government officials nor bankers came forward with any significant emergency relief, whether for democrats or dictators. To the contrary, the U.S. Congress aggravated the situation by passing the highly protectionist Hawley-Smoot tariff of 1930.

From 1925-29 to 1930-34, Latin America's exports declined 48 percent and imports 56 percent. Foreign credits disappeared, while government revenues, central bank reserves, and the money supply shrank commensurately. Latin American leaders found it extremely difficult to reduce their bloated expenditures as fast as revenues were plummeting. If a strapped administration cut public works, bureaucracy and the military, social and political stability were endangered. If it pruned foreign debt payments, any hope of being rescued by external creditors was destroyed. Nevertheless, as in the 1980s, Latin American governments made herculean efforts to impose austerity, adjust to the catastrophe, and maintain the international financial system. Mounting protests from their own dominant elites, however, soon drove them to default.[17]

Since governments that had contracted those debts were reluctant to declare bankruptcy, the first defaults transpired in the wake of existing regimes being overthrown. Bolivia set off that chain reaction in January of 1931, followed by Peru in March and Chile in July. After England abandoned the gold standard in September of 1931, the contagion swept the hemisphere during 1932-34. International sanctions against isolated defectors became ineffective. Since the debts were sprinkled among thousands of bondholders, there was no powerful external creditor, government, or multilateral institution with whom to negotiate or from whom to receive relief. No pressure of assistance from abroad could offset domestic demands. Therefore, Latin American governments rushed to impose import restrictions and exchange controls. They jettisoned free trade and the gold standard, regulated remittances abroad, and suspended foreign debt payments. Expanding the role of the state, they promoted economic recovery under more insulation from external shocks.

By 1934, Latin America had defaulted on 85 percent of its dollar bonds. Only Argentina (under heavy British influence) and Haiti and the Dominican Republic (under direct U.S. control) continued servicing their external debts. No Latin American government, however, repudiated its foreign obligations. Default was a response to a crisis of resources, rather than to any overwhelming wave of economic nationalism, ideological hostility, or alternative theory of development. From the mid-1930s to the early 1950s, most of those debts were renegotiated and settled at greatly reduced amounts with associations of bondholders in New York and London.[18]

How do the timing and sequence of these events in the 1930s compare with the 1980s? From the onset of the crisis in 1929, it took approximately three years for most of the countries to default by 1931-32. By contrast, the debt disaster beginning in 1982 has lasted six years without an epidemic of defaults. Another contrast (perhaps merely a fortuitous one) was the opposite direction of regime changes. In both cases, the turnover time for most existing governments was three years: 1929-32 and 1982-85. Also similar was the economic recuperation period of four to six years, if we accept that at least mild recovery commenced in most countries during, respectively, 1933-35 and 1986-88. Thereafter, greater political stability ensued, at least in the 1930s.

In sum, the result of the first great debt crisis of the twentieth century was severe depression, nearly universal default, and widespread takeover by military dictatorships. Those governments forced regime changes, brought social disorder under control, and rammed through new economic policies. In the long run, however, that debt cycle of boom and bust had some democratizing consequences.

The influx of dollars in the 1920s had helped underwrite the rise of new urban industrial, middle- and working-class groups. Their demands for participation, social welfare, and economic nationalism propelled the rise of reform movements dedicated to the expansion of more democratic central governments. When the Great Crash exacerbated those demands, it also discredited the previous elitist model of development, so heavily reliant on foreign trade, capital and control. Dictators temporarily held those new social forces in check. Nevertheless, reformist coalitions continued to grow, later becoming the foundation for populist movements and governments. From the late 1940s to the 1960s, on the whole, authoritarianism receded. Meanwhile, many civilian governments promoted import-substituting industrialization, social reforms for urban groups, and expanded electoral participation.

During those latter decades, foreign investment bankers stayed away from Latin America. Instead, external financing came mainly from the U.S. government or multilateral agencies. Foreign technocrats poured into Latin America to give advice and write reports rationalizing and justifying outside funding. Although those public monies were frequently dispensed by creditors with political criteria, they were seldom allocated preferentially to democracies. Even during the decade of the Alliance for Progress, most development assistance from the United States went to dictatorships. There was no clear pattern of connection between foreign lending and regime type.[19]

Then financial conditions in the 1970s came to resemble more closely those of the 1920s. Private bank loans to Latin American governments ballooned. To acquire finance capital, some countries had to obtain a passing grade from the International Monetary Fund, which required such austerity measures as reductions in budgets, wages, and exchange value of the currency. Sometimes similar policies were adopted on the recommendation of private U.S. economists, most notably from the University of Chicago. In many cases, the resulting flood of loans benefited authoritarian governments. Soon, more open economies, more loans, and more belt tightening became necessary to continue servicing the mushrooming debts. As a result, the Latin American borrowers became extremely vulnerable to the international recession in the early 1980s.[20]

Just as the 1970s in Latin America echoed the 1920s, so the 1980s evoked comparisons with the 1930s. From 1982 to 1985, the hemisphere suffered the worst depression since the Great Crash. Once again, an economic catastrophe helped topple many governments, this time mainly military regimes. It ushered in an unprecedented wave of democratization.

In contrast with the 1930s, most countries in the 1980s continued to at least minimally service their staggering foreign debts. They did so even though those debt obligations loomed much larger—absolutely and relatively—than during the previous Great Depression. They continued to pay even though their struggling democracies desperately needed relief and even though anti-austerity domestic groups were far better articulated, organized and mobilized than in the 1930s. Regime changes in Latin America fostered surprisingly few innovations in economic policy in the 1980s. Most governments labored mightily to squeeze their budgets and meet a portion of their foreign obligations.

In contrast with the 1930s, why did the 1980s fail to witness rampant defaults? One key explanation was that in the 1980s, debts were owed mainly to huge banking consortia rather than scattered individual investors. These bankers could pressure, negotiate, and extend emergency credits. They could argue that full-fledged default threatened the entire international financial system and western capitalism itself, which Latin American elites were loathe to abandon. The bankers bargained as unified creditors versus divided debtors. In each iteration of the negotiating game, they kept each Latin American government hoping it would receive more lenient terms and more generous loans than its neighbors. Moreover, multilateral agencies existed to help ease the debt burden. Despite the vaunted Baker Plan, however, the U.S. government did little more to help than it had in the 1930s. Once again it took the position that this was essentially a private problem between U.S. lenders and Latin American borrowers. Although dire predictions of widespread defaults did not come to pass, it remains possible that the day of reckoning has merely been postponed. Equally dire predictions that the debt burden would crush shaky democracies were not fulfilled either, at least through 1987.[21]

In other words, two oft-repeated prognostications about debt and democracy had not yet been borne out by 1987: that democratization would unleash popular demands rendering debt servicing impossible and/or that debt servicing would destabilize the democracies. Why did these democracies not default? Why did these democracies not fall? If we have given a partial answer to that former question, now we must address the latter.

Conclusion: Debt and Democracy, 1930s and 1980s

For a final comparison of the crises of the 1930s and the 1980s, it is necessary to look back at the two tables on debt and democracy. There it can be seen that the two debt crises were associated with enormous regime changes, at least in terms of correlations. Obviously, it was very hard for governments with economies and treasuries so vulnerable to world market fluctuations to weather such financial storms. As long as the current debt crisis lingers on, these tables are ominous forecasts for the ability of existing democracies to survive. Many observers feared that after the first wall of the debt hurricane smashed the dictators, the second wall would dash the democrats. Consequently, most experts from 1982 on called logically and compassionately for debt relief for elected civilian governments.[22]

Table 3.3
Latin American Political Regimes Surviving Debt Crises, 1930s and 1980s

Country	Democracies		Dictatorships	
	1930s	1980s	1930s	1980s
Bolivia	X			
Chile				X
Colombia	X	X		
Costa Rica	X	X		
Cuba			X	X
Dominican Republic		X		
Ecuador		X		
Haiti			X	
Mexico	X	X		
Nicaragua	X			
Panama	X			
Paraguay	X			X
Peru		X		
Venezuela		X	X	
Totals	7	7	3	3

Beyond highly laudable ethical considerations, such a policy recommendation implied two corollary arguments. One was that these democracies would be much more viable with additional resources to pursue economic growth and social justice. That seems irrefutable. The second implication was that dictatorships would be better able to cope with sustained debt servitude. The presumption was that authoritarian regimes were better equipped to make and keep private deals with foreign bankers, to enforce the technocratic rules of the game. Dictators have freer rein to slash the budget, to allocate the costs (mainly to the masses), and to suppress discontent from the downtrodden or even the elites. Perhaps, however, dictators are actually more vulnerable than democrats to debt crises.[23]

Two arguments suggest that democracies may be more resourceful and resilient than dictatorships, at least in the 1980s. First, while scores of scholars and commentators predicted that continued debt outflows were likely to bring down these flimsy regimes, up to 1988 none had actually reverted to authoritarianism (with the possible exception of Panama). Peruvian President Alan García warned that the choice was "debt or democracy," but the reality was "debt *and* democracy." That does not mean that none of the democracies will collapse, or that they would not be sturdier without the debt drainage. It does suggest that the truly surprising story into the late 1980s was the survivability of these rickety political systems under extremely inauspicious economic circumstances.

Second, Table 3.3 indicates that democracies may be more durable than dictatorships. Its tabulations show not only which regimes changed but also which did not. During the two debt crises, by these admittedly crude measures, fourteen democracies (seven out of fourteen in the 1930s and seven out of seven in the 1980s) survived—at least momentarily—but only six dictatorships (three out of six in the 1930s and three out of thirteen in the 1980s). For the two periods combined, democracies displayed a 67 percent survival rate, dictatorships only 32 percent. One could also tabulate just the ten South American cases, where regime types were somewhat more sharply defined. There, the early 1930s witnessed the endurance of three out of six democracies but only one out of four dictatorships. Similarly, the mid-1980s saw the durability of four out of four democracies but only two out of six dictatorships.

Throughout the hemisphere, however, the evidence from the 1930s is at best ambiguous. Soon after the time period in the table, Bolivia, Ecuador, Nicaragua, Paraguay and Peru switched from at least quasi-democratic to openly authoritarian governments. Nevertheless, the 1930s do not suggest that dictators had any greater staying power than democracies, while the 1980s suggest they had much less. Over the span of both crises, particularly noteworthy continuities occurred in Colombia, Costa Rica, Mexico and Venezuela—some of the most stable political systems in Latin America. If these indicators of systematic stability are correct, then military dictatorships may be more susceptible than democracies to destruction by debt peonage. Following are some speculative ideas as to why that might be.

The Achilles heel of dictatorships is their narrow base of legitimacy and support. Their legitimacy often rests largely on their purported ability to provide economic efficiency and social order. Depression and debt disaster severely undermine those capabilities. At the same time, their slender base of support leaves little room for shifting coalitions or policies. The crisis compresses that base further to a hard core among the elites and armed forces. Those groups may resist reduction of their privileges or budgets by governments wanting to continue debt service. Dissent, even among elites, over who will bear the costs of austerity can become difficult to manage under an authoritarian as well as a democratic system. Although military governments may seize power to "clean up the mess," they can also return to the barracks to "leave the mess." It is easier for soldiers than for democratic civilians to exit the presidential palace of their own accord. Nevertheless, dictators may persist if they continue rewarding enough owners of the means of production and deploying security forces against the opposition.

More significant may be the advantages of democracies. One virtue is that they have other sources of legitimacy. They can claim to be elected, representative, popular, and fair. They can convey a more equitable image of the distribution of sacrifices. In the absence of "economic goods," democracies can distribute "political goods," such as freedom of speech and assembly, which also provide safety valves for discontent. Presumably, they can call upon the ideological sympathy of democratic creditor countries, though the results of such appeals have been minimal to date.

Democracies also possess a broader base of support than most dictatorships.

Even the opponents of many democratic governments have a stake in the system. Since democracies can mobilize numerous bases of support, they may even be able to use the need for general austerity to justify reducing the size of the armed forces. Conceivably, they might also have more bargaining power with foreign creditors. Democrats can refer to irrepressible domestic pressures against full debt payments, though there is scant evidence that democracies actually receive any better financial treatment than dictatorships. Above all, a democracy's broader base of support makes it less dependent on foreign lenders to stay in power.[24]

Equally important, democratic systems boast more varied and flexible means of absorbing, deflecting and diffusing the economic crisis. Rather than all pressures falling on the dictator, they can be dispersed through legislative bodies, political parties, and the press. It is easier for countries to change leaders or administrations than to change regimes. The public can register its discontent with a democracy's economic performance by simply blaming and voting out the previous government.[25]

Indeed, the main challenge to democratic leaders in Latin America today may not be to effect a quick solution to the debt crisis, which would be virtually impossible. Rather, it is to convince people that democracy is valuable in and of itself, regardless of short-term economic outcomes. Democrats are trying to forge a consensus that economic dissatisfaction should be expressed through regular changes of governments rather than irregular changes of regimes. Elected leaders are trying to persuade citizens that authoritarian systems have proven themselves even less capable of solving economic crises. Argentine President Raúl Alfonsín and his counterparts argue that any alternative to democracy would only be worse. To the extent possible, such uncoupling of economic and political issues may be the key to democratic consolidation.[26]

Perhaps the most important reason that current democracies may persist is the timing and sequence of economic crisis and regime change. Whereas the 1930s depression happened to devastate democracies, the 1980s version happened to undermine dictatorships. It is that initial, sudden drop in resources, production and incomes that is most disruptive to governments. The subsequent slow, grueling process of adjustment and recuperation is much less destabilizing. After the original shock and plunge, expectations have been lowered. Persistent poverty seldom spawns upheaval.

Following the first wave of the debt crisis, political inertia may be on the side of the subsequent regimes. It took Latin America over two decades to fully recover from the Great Depression. Nevertheless, most post-crisis governments—of whatever type—in the 1930s proved remarkably durable: Lázaro Cárdenas in Mexico, Getúlio Vargas in Brazil, Arturo Alessandri in Chile, Rafael Trujillo in the Dominican Republic, the Liberal Party in Colombia, and others. In the 1930s, defaults did not free up funds for democratization but did buoy governments that defaulted. In the absence of another economic downturn of the magnitude of 1981-83, the current post-crash political systems may also have more stamina than one might expect. The newly-elected democratic governments can blame the debt debacle on their predecessors, and the military may be reluctant to reassume responsibility for governing over the continuing painful adjustment.

None of the above arguments deny that the smoldering debt crisis jeopardizes democracy in the 1980s, just as it did in the 1930s. In Latin America, the politics of scarcity leave little room for maneuver; severe poverty and inequality spawn conflicts difficult to solve with compromise. In all likelihood, relief from the debt burden will be needed to fund the economic growth and social reforms essential for the long-run maintenance of democracies.

Amidst the continuing crisis, this essay merely sounds a small note of guarded optimism. Neither the strengths of dictatorships nor the weaknesses of democracies should be overestimated. Obviously, both types of regimes benefit from debt inflows and suffer from outflows. In comparative terms, the historical evidence suggests that debt infusion may be even more crucial to unpopular dictators than to broad-based democrats, but that debt hemorrhage may be even more damaging to the former. By denying dictators loans or relief from their strict payment, financial powers can probably shorten their tenure. By providing democrats with economic assistance, world leaders might well be betting on the future of Latin America. But what if the debt crisis deepens or the more hopeful arguments presented here prove wrong? Then observers of Latin America may have to shift their concerns from debt and democracy to default and dictatorship.

Notes

1. Riordan Roett, "Democracy and Debt in South America: A Continent's Dilemma," *Foreign Affairs* (Winter 1984).

2. For example, see Clarence Zuvekas, Jr., "Political Democracy and Economic Growth in Latin America, 1980-1985," *LASA Forum* (Fall 1986).

3. Barbara Stallings, *Banker to the Third World: U.S. Portfolio Investment in Latin America, 1900-1986* (Berkeley: University of California Press, 1987); Joseph S. Tulchin, *The Aftermath of War: World War I and United States Policy toward Latin America* (New York: New York University Press, 1971); Cleona Lewis, *America's Stake in International Investments* (Washington, DC: The Brookings Institution, 1938); Max Winkler, *Investment of United States Capital in Latin America* (Boston: World Peace Foundation, 1928).

4. Memorandum, February 6, 1931, "Latin America-General," Box 3, Francis White Papers, United States Department of State; John T. Madden, Marcus Nadler and Harry C. Sauvain, *America's Experience as a Creditor Nation* (New York: Prentice Hall, 1937).

5. Margaret Alexander Marsh, *The Bankers in Bolivia* (New York: Vanguard Press, 1928); Edmundo Vázquez, *Nociones de finanzas generales y hacienda pública de Bolivia* (La Paz: 1939), 328-329.

6. Emily S. Rosenberg, *Spreading the American Dream: American Economic and Cultural Expansion, 1890-1945* (New York: Hill and Wang, 1982); Joan Hoff Wilson, *American Business and Foreign Policy, 1920-1933* (Lexington, KY: University of Kentucky Press, 1971); Robert N. Seidel, "Progressive Pan Americanism: Development and United

States Policy toward South America, 1906-1931" (Ph.D. dissertation, Cornell University, 1973).

7. William Appleman Williams, *The Tragedy of American Diplomacy*, rev. ed. (New York: Dell Publishing Co., 1962); Herbert Feis, *The Diplomacy of the Dollar: First Era, 1919-1932* (Baltimore: Johns Hopkins Press, 1950).

8. Tulchin, *Aftermath of War*, 104-243; Charles Evans Hughes, *Our Relations to the Nations of the Western Hemisphere* (Princeton: Princeton University Press, 1928), especially 54-72.

9. Madden, Nadler and Sauvain, *America's Experience*, 240-247.

10. Conversation with Mr. W.W. Lancaster of National City Bank, March 7, 1932, "Colombia," Box 1, Francis White Papers.

11. Paul W. Drake, *Socialism and Populism in Chile, 1932-1952* (Urbana: University of Illinois Press, 1978), 71-83.

12. Federico G. Gil, *Latin American-United States Relations* (New York: Harcourt Brace Jovanovich, 1971), especially 87-116; Alexander DeConde, *Herbert Hoover's Latin American Policy* (Stanford: Stanford University Press, 1951).

13. Emily S. Rosenberg, "American Foreign Financial Advising in Latin America before the Great Depression: Form and Structure" (St. Paul, MN, 1985, typescript); Richard Hemmig Meyer, *Bankers' Diplomacy: Monetary Stabilization in the Twenties* (New York: Columbia University Press, 1970); Charles Lipson, *Standing Guard: Protecting Foreign Capital in the Nineteenth and Twentieth Centuries* (Berkeley: University of California Press, 1985).

14. Paul W. Drake, *The Money Doctor in the Andes* (Durham, NC: Duke University Press, forthcoming 1989).

15. United States Department of State Archives, from Quito, February 11, 1927, 822.51A/41.

16. Carleton Beals, *The Coming Struggle for Latin America* (Philadelphia: J.B. Lippincott, 1938), 198-199; John J. Johnson, "Foreign Factors in Dictatorship in Latin America," in *Dictatorship in Spanish America*, ed. Hugh M. Hamill, Jr. (New York: Knopf, 1965).

17. Rosemary Thorp, ed., *Latin America in the 1930s: The Role of the Periphery in the World Crisis* (London and New York: St. Martin's Press, 1984); United Nations, Department of Economic and Social Affairs, *External Financing in Latin America* (New York: United Nations, 1965), 23-30.

18. United Nations, Department of Economic and Social Affairs, *Foreign Capital in Latin America* (New York: United Nations, 1955), 7-11.

19. Jerome Levinson and Juan de Onis, eds., *The Alliance that Lost Its Way: A Critical Report on the Alliance For Progress* (Chicago: Quadrangle Books, 1970).

20. Barbara Stallings, "Peru and the U.S. Banks: Privatization of Financial Relations," and Roberto Frenkel and Guillermo O'Donnell, "The 'Stabilization Programs' of the International Monetary Fund and Their Internal Impacts," both in Fagen; Milton Friedman, *Milton Friedman en Chile: bases para un desarrollo económico* (Santiago: Fundación de Estudios Económicos BHC, 1975).

21. Carlos F. Díaz-Alejandro, "Latin America in the 1930s," and Charles P. Kindleberger, "The 1929 World Depression in Latin America—From the Outside," both in Thorp. Among scores of publications on the debt crisis of the 1980s, three particularly useful books include Richard E. Feinberg and Valeriana Kallab, eds., *Adjustment Crisis in the Third World* (New

Brunswick: Transaction Books, 1984); Miguel S. Wionczek, ed., with Luciano Tomassini, *Politics and Economics of External Debt Crisis: The Latin American Experience* (Boulder, CO: Westview Press, 1985); and Miles Kahler, ed., *The Politics of International Debt* (Ithaca: Cornell University Press, 1986).

22. Roett, "Democracy and Debt in South America."

23. Robert R. Kaufman, "Democratic and Authoritarian Responses to the Debt Issue: Argentina, Brazil, Mexico," in Kahler, *Politics of International Debt*; James M. Malloy, "The Politics of Transition in Latin America," in *Authoritarians and Democrats: Regime Transition in Latin America*, ed. James M. Malloy and Mitchell A. Seligson (Pittsburgh: University of Pittsburgh Press, 1987).

24. Ellen Comisso, "State Structures and Political Processes Outside the CMEA: A Comparison," in *Power, Purpose and Collective Choice: Economic Strategy in Socialist States*, ed. Ellen Comisso and Laura D'Andrea Tyson (Ithaca: Cornell University Press, 1986).

25. Peter H. Smith, "Restructuring Political Regimes (University of California-San Diego, 1987, typescript).

26. In addition to the paper by Smith, key publications on the wave of democratization in the 1980s include Mitchell A. Seligson, "Democratization in Latin America: The Current Cycle," in Malloy and Seligson, *Authoritarians and Democrats*; Paul W. Drake and Eduardo Silva, eds., *Elections and Democratization in Latin America, 1980-1985* (San Diego: Center for Iberian and Latin American Studies, Center for U.S.-Mexican Studies, Institute of the Americas, University of California-San Diego, 1986); and, above all, Guillermo O'Donnell, Philippe C. Schmitter and Laurence Whitehead, eds., *Transitions from Authoritarian Rule*, 4 vols. (Baltimore: Johns Hopkins University Press, 1986).

Suggestions for Further Reading

Drake, Paul. *The Money Doctor in the Andes*. Durham, NC: Duke University Press, forthcoming 1989.

Fishlow, Albert. "Lessons from the Past: Capital Markets during the 19th Century and the Interwar Period." *International Organization* 39, no. 3 (Summer 1985).

Maddison, Angus. *Two Crises: Latin America and Asia, 1929-38 and 1979-83*. OECD, 1985.

Stallings, Barbara. *Banker to the Third World: U.S. Portfolio Investment in Latin America, 1900-1986*. Berkeley: University of California Press, 1987.

Thorp, Rosemary, ed. *Latin America in the 1930s*. New York: St. Martins Press, 1984.

Tulchin, Joseph. *The Aftermath of War: World War I and United States Policy toward Latin America*. New York: New York University Press, 1971.

PART II

Key Actors in the
Debt-Democracy Dilemma

4

How the 'Haves' Manage the 'Have-Nots': Latin America and the Debt Crisis

Riordan Roett

A remarkable aspect of the debt crisis that began in 1982 has been the unwilling-ness of the West European and Japanese governments to assume any significant responsibility for its resolution. The implicit decision to leave the process of crisis management entirely in the hands of the United States has had serious implications, both in terms of the debt crisis itself and for U.S.-Latin American relations.

As we enter the seventh year of the crisis, the essential elements remain the same, although two important differences merit discussion. First, a new actor has entered the arena in the United States: the U.S. Congress. In the absence of executive branch leadership, the Congress has increasingly begun to explore and define alternatives. The main impetus is not debt relief for Latin America—although that may be the result of some congressional initiatives—but the necessities of the U.S. economy and political system. Late in 1987, a second difference also emerged: the private commercial banking community agreed to disagree. A number of regional and smaller banks began to increase their reserve levels, and individual money center banking institutions devised innovative forms of debt relief with the blessing of the U.S. government.

These two differences are significant. The election of a Democratic president in 1988 would increase the likelihood of a political solution for the debt crisis. All of the debt-relief proposals that Congress has discussed have been proposed by members of the Democratic Party. Over time, congressional Democrats have argued that "muddling through" is insufficient. If the White House and the Congress are in Democratic hands in January 1989, it is highly probable that one of the Democratic policy alternatives for debt will be adopted.

The second issue is also relevant. The increasing disarray among commercial banking institutions signals that a change in strategy may be required to maintain both the credibility and the asset quality of the major banks. Leading banking institutions such as Citicorp have created massive reserves against the possibility of default on Latin American debt. Others banks have sold outright their Latin American loans. Many have refused to participate further in new lending to Latin

American debtor countries. When combined with the weak loan portfolios in the U.S. energy and agricultural sectors, the Latin American debt exposure provides major U.S. banking institutions with a continuing source of concern about their health and continued success.

This chapter will explore how the industrial world views the debt crisis, the strategy the industrial countries have employed to keep the major debtors working within the system, and the relevance of democratization in Latin America to bank and multilateral institutional decision making.

Background on the Debt Crisis

The origins of the Latin American debt crisis have been fully discussed elsewhere.[1] The immediate consequences of the breakdown of the financial system in 1982 have also been analyzed by a number of writers.[2] The crisis mentality of 1982-1984 slowly abated, and by early 1985 it was widely believed in the industrial countries that the worst was over. That year brought a number of surprises, however, among them the precipitate drop in oil prices driving Mexico into a new round of negotiations, the election of Alan García in Peru who announced a *de facto* moratorium, and the hardening of Brazil's position on debt with the transition to a civilian regime in March. Data published by the United Nations Economic Commission for Latin America and by the Inter-American Development Bank highlighted the tremendous social toll the debt has taken. Of equal concern was the massive export of Latin American capital to service the debt.

Throughout this period the only interlocutors of the indebted countries had been the private commercial banks. The industrial countries' governments had refused to recognize the debt as a foreign policy issue. Indeed, in 1984, at the height of the first phase of the crisis, seven Latin American presidents sent a letter to the industrial countries' leaders, then preparing for the annual economic summit to be held in London. In the communication the presidents called for a "constructive dialogue among creditor and borrowing countries."[3] It was impossible to imagine that their financial problems could be resolved only by "contacting banks or through the isolated participation of international financial organizations."[4]

The final communique of the London Summit brusquely rejected the call for negotiations. The industrial countries offered "help," but only if the Latin American governments reduced their spending and worked to put their houses in order. The growing frustration of the Latin American political leaders led to the organization of the Cartagena Consensus group in June 1984. Speaking at the opening of the meeting, then-President Belisario Betancur of Colombia stated: "Latin America's foreign debt service has become so burdensome that it threatens the very stability of the international monetary system and the survival of the democratic process in various countries."[5]

Follow-up meetings of the Cartagena Consensus produced few results. During the autumn 1984 meetings of the World Bank and the International Monetary Fund

(IMF), it was agreed to hold a 1985 conference on the debt, but the results of that subsequent encounter were meaningless in providing debt relief for Latin America.

Growing evidence that the debt crisis had not abated led to the announcement of the Baker Plan at the 1985 annual meetings of the World Bank and the IMF in Seoul, South Korea. The initiative identified three key players in the next phase of the debt crisis: indebted countries, who were required to adjust; international financial institutions; and private commercial banks. Very pointedly, the Baker Plan did not assign a role to the governments of the industrial countries.[6]

Throughout 1986, there was much talk but little action on the Baker Plan. The highly politicized Mexican debt negotiations of late 1986 were touted as a sign of the plan's success, but most observers viewed the Mexico agreement as the burial of the initiative. Mexico's deal with its creditors had taken an inordinately long time to put together. The private banks were reluctant to participate, and they resented pressure from Washington to do so. Clearly, Mexico represented a special case, given the 2,000-mile common border and the related agenda of bilateral foreign policy issues. While a solution was needed for Mexico, the application of the Baker Plan there did not mean that it would necessarily be relevant in other Latin American crisis situations.

The apparent failure of the Baker Plan has led the U.S. government to support the concept of a "menu" of responses by private commercial banks, ranging from new funding to debt-equity conversions, swaps, exit bonds, and other financial alternatives. This approach has not produced a very enthusiastic or optimistic response from either the debtors or the creditors.

The strategy devised by the industrial countries to deal with the debt crisis has been either one of "quarantining" the most dangerous debtor or of "muddling through." The former refers to the process during the 1982-88 period of isolating the Latin American debtor that appeared closest to default or radical action. A special arrangement would be made and the errant player would return to the game. The "muddling through" approach has been just that—bits and pieces of a response to systemic trauma. By September 1987, even the conservative *Financial Times* of London questioned how far that approach would take the international financial system:

> The question is whether muddling through is still the best strategy or whether the governments of the developed countries should themselves provide resources to solve the problem. Muddling through is always easy, but is it enough? It is difficult to believe that the running sore of developing country debt will be healed without a willingness of major developed countries to contribute to the treatment.[7]

At the end of 1987, eight Latin American heads of state gathered at a summit meeting in Acapulco, Mexico, the first of what was planned to be an annual event. In the final document of the meeting, the presidents declared:

> Recovery of sustained economic growth, improvement in our peoples' standard of living and strengthening of democratic processes in the area require a just and

permanent solution to the external debt problem, in addition to unpostponable measures to reduce the burden of servicing the debt.[8]

The Industrial Countries and the Debt

A number of factors led other industrial governments to support the Reagan administration's approach to the debt crisis. First, there appears to have been a tacit understanding that the industrial countries would assume responsibility for those areas within their spheres of influence and/or those countries that were formerly colonies. That led to a natural division, with the Western European banks dealing principally with Eastern Europe and Africa.[9] Japan, to the degree that it participated, impliciitly accepted a role in Asia. That left Latin America for the United States.

The geographical division of labor, however, does not explain the approach taken by the industrial countries. The second factor is ideology. When the debt crisis erupted, the Reagan Revolution was in full swing. Following his inauguration in January 1981, the President and his team initiated a series of fiscal and monetary policies designed to restore the health of the U.S. economy. In so doing, they created a world recession. Two other key players—Prime Minister Margaret Thatcher of Great Britain and Chancellor Helmut Kohl of West Germany—enthusiastically endorsed these policies. Both European leaders shared Reagan's conservative, market-oriented approach to economics, and both were undertaking their own domestic versions of Reagan's American Revolution. A businesslike approach to Third World debt, in which creditors and debtors worked out their problems, was considered appropriate. And it was key that all three would remain in office throughout the debt crisis. As late as the 1986 Summit in Tokyo, the Economic Declaration laconically repeated past policy:

> ...developing countries, particularly debtor countries, can fit themselves to play a fuller part in the world economy by adopting effective structural adjustment policies, coupled with measures to mobilize domestic savings, to encourage the repatriation of capital, to improve the environment for foreign investment and to promote more open trading policies.

> We reaffirm the continued importance of the case-by-case approach to international debt problems. We welcome the progress made in developing the cooperative debt strategy, in particular building on the United States initiative. The role of the international financial institutions, including the multilateral development banks, will continue to be central, and we welcome moves for closer cooperation among these institutions, and particularly between the IMF and the World Bank. Sound adjustment programs will also need resumed commercial bank lending, flexibility in rescheduling debt and appropriate access to export credits.[10]

A third factor, related to the economies of the industrial countries, was the relative inability of the European countries to respond to Latin America's needs.

High protectionist barriers already existed to guard domestic industry, and they would not be sacrificed for Latin American exports. Domestic pressures from labor unions concerned about rising unemployment worked against relaxation of such measures. Moreover, trade concessions were granted through the successive Lomé Conventions to Caribbean and African states, representing Europe's "contribution." The implication was that the U.S. economy would have to take up the slack within the industrial world to absorb Latin America's exports.

The summit process also reflected an important fourth factor. To the degree that the debt issue was not viewed as political by the leaders of the industrial countries, it was left in the hands of their finance ministers. Donald Regan, who served as U.S. Treasury Secretary during the first Reagan administration (1981-1985), played a crucial role in relegating the debt crisis to minor status.[11]

Regan's philosophy, akin to the President's, emphasized the play of market forces. His Wall Street background and his handling of the Reagan Revolution made him incapable of understanding the political implications of the debt. Moreover, when he moved to the White House as the President's chief of staff after the first administration, he continued to exercise strong influence over Reagan's thinking. James Baker, former chief of staff, took Regan's position at Treasury. He brought in a new team, and started constructing the Baker Plan over Regan's opposition. Only Baker's close ties to the President and his control of the Treasury bureaucracy, as well as the tactical alliance he constructed with Federal Reserve Chairman Paul Volcker, allowed the Treasury Secretary to take hold of the Third World debt issue in 1985. It was well known in Washington that Volcker and Regan were barely on speaking terms. Baker quickly changed the nature of that relationship and the two became a critically important team, forging the Baker Plan in response to the rapidly changing global environment in 1985-1986.

A fifth factor that led to the "apolitical" approach to debt by the leaders of the industrial world was the particular historical moment at which the crisis erupted. The debt crisis exploded in Latin America in mid-1982, when a series of governments were making a complicated transition from military rule to democratic regimes.[12] For years the industrial countries had been used to dealing with military rulers in Argentina, Brazil, Uruguay, and Peru. The significance of the transitions was lost to a large degree among the "big three"—Reagan, Thatcher, and Kohl. To them, Third World stability was more important than democratic transitions. Their tendency to see democratic transitions as potentially destabilizing was natural, if inaccurate. Nor did Alfonsín, Neves and Sarney, Sanguinetti, or García have strong personal ties with leaders in the industrial nations. Thus, the relatively unknown political leaders of the new democracies could not effectively influence the calculations of the industrial world.

Moreover, Reagan's foreign policy focus in the Western Hemisphere had become Central America. Save for Secretary of State Alexander Haig's ill-fated effort to mediate the 1982 Malvinas conflict, neither Haig nor his successor, George Shultz, demonstrated any interest in South America. Both viewed the creation of the

Cartagena Consensus with suspicion and distrusted the Support Group for Contadora, which had formed in July 1985. To the degree that the continent had an impact on the thinking of Washington policy makers, these initiatives were viewed as vaguely confrontational.

The new Latin American political leaders' lack of political experience was a sixth factor that conditioned the response of the leaders of the industrial nations. Unknown and untested, the new leaders were at best marginal players in world affairs. The economic crisis at home gave them even less space to maneuver internationally. Washington suspected that they would identify with leaders such as Belisario Betancur of Colombia, whose populism and penchant for disagreeing with the United States were well known. That fear was confirmed with the election of APRA (Alianza Popular Revolucionaria Americana) candidate Alan García in Peru. García announced at his July 1985 inauguration that henceforth Peru would allocate no more than ten percent of its foreign exchange earnings to debt service. Nevertheless, lack of experience does not fully explain the plight of the new leaders. The debt crisis clearly made the Latin American leaders feel impotent. From their actions, if not their words, the leaders communicated their feelings of futility and marginalization. Although their public documents and speeches rang with fervor, their diplomatic and political actions seemed hollow. Their aggregate irrelevance reflected the superior-inferior relationship that has traditionally characterized links between North and South, particularly between the United States and its neighbors in the hemisphere.

In that case, why didn't the Latin American leaders take a more radical stance? They judged that remaining within the international financial system was preferable to being excluded, as Alan García discovered after 1985. Moreover, the longer-range implications of default or a moratorium were not clear, although they were sure to be negative. Not until February 1987 would a major Latin American country—Brazil—confront the system with a *de facto* moratorium. By early 1988, Brazil had another new finance minister who began to lift the moratorium. Blessed by the U.S. Treasury and Federal Reserve, a new understanding with the private commercial banks allowed Brazil to repay overdue interest and to finance needed interest payments in 1988.   On the regional level, the Acapulco Summit of November 1987 was generally ignored in Washington as well as in the major capitals of the industrial countries. The crisis continued in 1988, but radical new departures by Latin America seemed unlikely in the short run.

The Domestic Political Context of the Debt

While the industrial governments continued to ignore the plight of Third World debtors, discourse began to shift in the United States.[13] By 1985, the debt situation had been somewhat defused because the Latin American states were making massive efforts to adjust and to export.[14] Given the structural barriers in Western Europe and the political barriers in Asia, the U.S. market absorbed the lion's share of the hemisphere's exports. Those exports, of course, earned the foreign exchange required to service the outstanding debt. Beginning in 1985, politicians complained that exports from Latin America were flooding the U.S. market and taking jobs away from U.S. workers.[15] A complementary argument held that serious efforts to adjust their internal economies had caused the Latin American countries to massively cut back on imports. Given the trade flows, U.S. exporters had lost large shares of the Latin American market. That meant laying off workers and postponing new investments.

By early 1988, the trade statistics were dramatic. While exports to most other world areas were rising, shipments of goods to Latin America had fallen sharply, from $42.1 billion in 1981 to $31.1 billion in 1986. From 1981 to 1986, imports of the region's four largest debtor countries (Brazil, Mexico, Argentina, and Venezuela) fell by nearly 50 percent.

U.S. senators and representatives began to feel local constituency pressure as the debt crisis continued, and Congress became the new forum for discussing this aspect of the debt. Labor unions as well as manufacturers were being hurt. Immediately following the 1982 crisis, the congressional position had been to simply "bash the banks." Heated exchanges took place between congressional committees and the administration, in which committee members warned that they would not "bail out the banks."[16] In other words, bad loans were bad loans, and the U.S. taxpayer was not going to be asked to pick up the cost of those loans if the debtors could not repay them. Financial relief would have to come out of bank earnings or reserves.

By 1985-86 a more sophisticated Congress had stopped discussing the debt crisis in terms of who was to blame for the huge debt overhang and began to focus on medium and long-term implications. The absence of executive branch leadership spurred Congress to action. A staff study prepared for the Joint Economic Committee of the Congress in May 1986 stated flatly that U.S. policy toward Latin American debtor nations had seriously hurt U.S. farmers and manufacturers without accomplishing much to resolve the crisis itself. According to the report, "nearly 50 percent of the trade surplus that Latin America needed to pay interest was generated by reducing its purchases of United States products."[17]

The debt crisis has not only caused a shrinkage in Latin American and other Third World markets, it has also exacerbated a rush of goods to the United States and intensified competition between U.S. exporters for markets outside of Latin America. In 1981, the United States took one third of exports from developing countries; by 1986, the figure had risen to 60 percent. Debtor countries struggled fiercely to expand their exports. Suddenly, U.S. producers were being shut out of their home market because of cheaper Latin American products.

Slowly, members of Congress realized that they had to respond to the trade/debt question regardless of whether the executive branch understood the issue. Congress also began to understand that poor growth performance, structural protectionism, and high unemployment in Western Europe limited the extent to which the United States' industrial allies could share the burden.[18] Japan was the exception. And it was precisely at this point that Japan-U.S. trade relations deteriorated. Japan's unwillingness to open its markets and assume more responsibility for world growth makes the U.S. trade deficit worse. It is also a significant factor in Latin America's continued dependence on the U.S. market.

The Congressional Initiatives

In June 1986, Senator Bill Bradley (D-New Jersey) launched a highly controversial proposal for dealing with the debt crisis.[19] Since the Baker Plan was based on new private commercial bank lending, Bradley charged it would only pile new debt on old, thus increasing the precarious exposure of the banking system. Bradley proposed a three-year program of interest rate cuts and debt relief by the commercial banks. His plan would reduce the interest rates developing countries paid by up to three percentage points, while also writing off a maximum of three percent of the loan principal. The governments of industrial countries would simultaneously lend as much as $3 billion per year. This debt relief was to be granted only if the borrowers spurred economic growth and stemmed capital flight. Other steps included reducing subsidies and ending restrictions on investment and trade. Sure to attract attention, Bradley challenged the president of the United States to call an annual trade relief summit: "The purpose of the summit would be to secure agreement among the major creditors of Latin American and other indebted developing countries to provide yearly trade relief packages to eligible debtors."[20]

Other members of Congress quickly jumped on the bandwagon. In December 1986, Senator Paul Sarbanes (D-Maryland) and Representative David Obey (D-Wisconsin) proposed the creation of a new facility run by the World Bank and the IMF. The special facility would serve as a secondary market buyer for developing country debt. Banks holding loans could sell to this facility at a "realistic" discount. Then the facility would renegotiate terms with the developing country. Representatives Bruce Morrison (D-Connecticut) and Sander Levin (D-Michigan) proposed the Debt Deconcentration and Growth Promotion Act. The Act would instruct the Reagan administration to create a new entity affiliated with the World Bank. The Act would instruct the Reagan administration to work with U.S. allies who have also lent money to Third World nations in order to create a new entity affiliated with the World Bank. The new entity would buy troubled loans at a discount and negotiate with the debtor country to repackage the loans for marketability throughout the world capital markets. (See the Dornbusch chapter in this volume for further discussion of how such a facility would operate.) Representative John LaFalce (D-New York) proposed that U.S. regulatory authorities provide maximum flexibility to commercial banks in negotiating any principal and/or interest reduction on Third World loans. He also called for the establishment of a new International Debt Management Facility which would offer to purchase sovereign debt from the banks at a discount.

These and other proposals address a number of key issues. First among them is the health of the U.S. private banking system. Bashing the banks is out; Congress is seeking ways to guarantee the integrity of the system, critical to the health of the global financial system. Second, all the proposals are predicated on the need for economic growth, rather than further adjustment, in Latin America. Third, all of the proposals recognize the close linkage between trade and debt. And, fourth, all of the proposals see the debt issue as both an economic and political problem.[21]

Other members of the Congress are proposing protectionist legislation that would be damaging to the Third World, particularly Latin America. As the trade deficit worsened from 1987 to 1988, measures were introduced in the Congress to retaliate against those Third World countries having large trade surpluses with the United States. The most controversial was an amendment to the 1987 Trade Bill introduced by Representative Richard Gephardt (D-Missouri). It set numerical targets for reducing the trade surpluses of key U.S. trading partners. While the Gephardt amendment did not survive, it signified the high level of congressional frustration regarding both the U.S. exporters' lack of competitiveness and the Third World countries' success in penetrating the U.S. market.

The various debt relief, trade expansion, and trade protectionism measures under consideration demonstrate that the debate over debt and trade has moved from the executive branch to the Congress. The shift is due to Democratic Party control of Congress in recent years, and to the loss of markets in Latin America that has been prejudicial to U.S. exporters. As jobs are lost in the United States and factories close, export-industry workers and manufacturers have become an increasingly important lobby group.

But growing congressional interest is also due to the failure of the Baker Plan and the realization that the United States and its industrial allies have failed to come to grips with issues that have grown more serious since the onset of the crisis in 1982. No longer is the debt crisis seen as a "we" versus "they" question. Congress has come to understand that the debt crisis threatens both the North and the South in very real ways.[22] What is underway is a redefinition of the problem and the search for new solutions.

The Commercial Banks React

In 1987 and 1988, the private commercial banks began to react against their traditional strategy. Although hostile to the concept of debt relief and still willing to "muddle through," they became increasingly concerned about the negative impact of their Third World debt portfolio on earnings as well as on bank assets. Citicorp chairman John Reed set the mood for rethinking the debt in May 1987 when he dramatically set aside $3 billion in reserves to cover bad loans in the Third World. Reluctantly, other money center banks followed. The move was supported by the Treasury and Federal Reserve as a prudent measure.

By late 1987, another crucial step was taken when important regional banking institutions decided to actually write off loans that they judged would never be repaid. The Bank of Boston took the lead in December 1987 with a $200 million write-off. The move implied that the bank had given up hope of repayment on that portion of its portfolio and went far beyond merely adding to loan loss reserves. Other banks followed in 1988, but none of the money center banks were involved. With the write-off decision gaining favor, two groups have emerged among U.S. banks: a small group of money center banks with comparatively thin reserves against large loans to developing countries, and regional institutions with relatively small exposure to developing countries. These banks are willing to establish big reserves against such loans or to completely write off some loans as uncollectible.

While unable to afford such drastic action, the money center banks have been exploring other alternatives. In late 1987, Morgan Guaranty Trust proposed the exchange of debt for long-term bonds. The scheme was backed by the U.S. Treasury, which sold zero-coupon bonds to Mexico to use as collateral for its own new bonds. The banks bid for the Mexican bonds at a discount, thus losing capital with respect to their existing loans but gaining assets that were arguably safer. Although the new program did not receive universal support from the banking community, many viewed it as an innovative initiative to seek relief from the constant crisis management that has characterized the financial community since 1982.

Perspectives for the Future

West European governments are content to leave the next phase of the debt crisis in the hands of the United States. European banks are less exposed, and European accounting and regulatory procedures facilitate writing down some of the exposure. In addition, the European banks have built up larger loan-loss reserves against Third World debt. The Japanese have taken a separate path. Twenty-eight commercial banks have established a company that will assume part of their loans outstanding to Latin America. Primarily aimed at helping the Japanese financial institutions remain healthy, the company will issue preferred stock, which the participating banks will purchase. Proceeds from the stock sales will be used to buy Latin American loans from the banks at a discount. Then the company will either pool the loans and try to resell them to investors, or hold them to maturity.[23]

Given the protective measures taken by the West Europeans and the Japanese, the time has come for the United States to change policies. The U.S. Congress apparently has decided to disregard the Reagan administration's criticism of the various plans under discussion. From the point of view of the Europeans and the Japanese, the U.S. banking system still needs to be strengthened and protected from the impact of Third World debt. Simultaneously, the United States is beginning to link its trade problems with the Third World debt. The linkage has created friction with the Japanese that will continue as long as the U.S. trade deficit grows. It may lead to friction with the Europeans as well, as U.S. attention turns to the protective walls around European markets and Europe's unwillingness to absorb additional exports from Latin America.

The reluctance of the European and Japanese governments to accept greater responsibility for the Latin American debt has forced the issue to become a principal focus of U.S.-Latin American relations. Indeed, debt and trade matters dominate the agenda. The U.S. rejection of all pleas to deal with the debt on a government-to-government basis has introduced a new set of frictions in the relationship. The Reagan administration's apparent endorsement of adjustment and austerity and its rejection of growth has further weakened an already tenuous relationship between the United States and its neighbors in the Western Hemisphere.

The Acapulco summit of Latin American presidents made its position very clear in its final communique: "We call on the Heads of State of the industrialized countries to join in political dialogue that will make it possible to surmount the obstacles to development, to the restructuring of the world economy, and to decision making related to peace and security."[24] But the call for a political dialogue will undoubtedly go unheeded. The rhetoric of the Latin American heads of state is strong, but they have not yet devised the strategy needed to link words with action in their dealings with the industrial countries.

In the aftermath of Argentina's war with Great Britain in 1982 and the U.S. endorsement of the British position, the debt crisis again placed the Reagan administration in what appeared to be an anti-Latin American posture. The growing protectionist trend in the United States, which will have a devastating impact on Latin America's capacity to export, will further exacerbate the tendency. The cumulative effect of the last few years has further alienated the United States from trends developing in the region. These include a heightened awareness of the need for regional integration, symbolized by the Argentine-Brazilian-Uruguayan accords of recent years and the commitment to further collective consultation as witnessed by groups such as those organized to debate the debt (Cartagena) and the crisis in Central America (Contadora). Growing out of the meetings of the Contadora group, the Group of Eight, which first met in Acapulco at the end of 1987, is further evidence of this commitment. All of these efforts have been justified by Latin America's political leaders as efforts to preserve and strengthen democratic institutions in the region. The failure to make the link between the consolidation of democratic regimes in the hemisphere and the overhang of debt has frustrated the political leadership Latin America. It was the prime motivation for Alan García's 1985 moratorium decision, and certainly a key element in President José Sarney's decision to establish a debt moratorium in February 1987.

West European political leaders are concerned about the apparent sense of drift in the relations between the United States and Latin America, but they are unwilling to confront the Reagan administration. Other matters are more pressing—defense, trade, and the dollar are the issues of highest priority. In addition, Prime Minister Thatcher and Chancellor Kohl appear firmly in control of their governments and will remain so for some years to come. Their philosophical bent remains conservative, and they continue to define the debt in narrow financial terms. The answer to Latin America's economic and financial woes remains firmly linked to U.S.

policy—and U.S. policy problems. The twin deficits in the budget and balance of payments, which explain the trade protectionist syndrome, for example, require firm political decisions in Washington. It appears unlikely that the Reagan administration will take the steps needed to begin the appropriate adjustments.

Democracy and the Debt Crisis

An underlying theme in many of the debt crisis proposals put forward in the U.S. Congress has been a growing concern about the survival of democratic regimes in the hemisphere. The background is simple. Many of the debtors—Argentina, Brazil, Chile, Peru, and Uruguay, among others— were ruled by the military during the years in which much of the debt was accumulated. Little of the borrowed money was invested for developmental purposes. Many of the loans turned around as flight capital, while others disappeared in either speculation or outright corruption. The portion of the borrowed funds that was invested domestically made little contribution to alleviating poverty or responding to social needs at home.

With the transitions to democracy that took place in South America in the early 1980s, citizens of those countries released their pent-up desires for government policies that would respond to social needs and priorities. Unfortunately, as the transitions were taking place, the debt crisis erupted. Since 1982-83, democratic governments in Latin America have been waging a losing battle to honor their countries' debt obligations, while attempting to demonstrate that they are effective at responding to domestic social demands. They have not been successful. The need to export, to earn foreign exchange, and to cut back imports to free up foreign exchange, has severely constrained the ability of democratic regimes to increase their legitimacy through effective domestic policies.

It is now widely understood that U.S. security interests in the Western Hemisphere are better met when working with democratic regimes. While they may appear more compliant in the short-term, military governments do not provide any medium or long-term guarantees that their interests are at all compatible with those of the United States. A long list of examples demonstrates that common sense in policy making should favor civilian, democratic institutions. One has merely to review U.S. relations with Pinochet in Chile, Somoza in Nicaragua, or Noriega in Panama to understand that short-term expediency is rarely a justification for prolonging military rule and undercutting transitions to democratic regimes.

While the initial democratic transitions of the early and mid-1980s have survived—there have been no military takeovers of those regimes that restored democracy—the second round of national elections is now approaching in 1988 and 1989. In the intervening years, expectations that the quality of life would improve have been cruelly dashed. Given an option, voters may favor a populist leader who promises a better future. The issue is less whether democratic regimes will be forcibly overthrown than whether Latin America will slowly return to the irresponsible, populist politics of a bygone era. Promises of distribution cannot be met given the current economic crisis. What will follow the failure of populist policies? Will populist regimes so radicalize the policy process that polarization will inevitably result, with the armed forces then becoming a real threat in the 1990s?

The Latin American countries need room to grow. While their commitment to introduce structural reforms has been largely unsuccessful, a good case can be made that democratic governments have been unable to do so because of the scarcity of economic resources. Newly restored regimes cannot service the debt, practice belt tightening policies, and also respond to social pressures. As part of the search for a political solution to the debt, it is necessary to recognize that reform can only succeed if it is supported by adequate resources. It is also true that conditionality—the requirement for certain kinds of changes in policy in the Latin American countries—should be linked to a renewal of resources for development. Since 1982, it has been totally unrealistic to expect conditionality to succeed when the political space to support it has dramatically diminished. A serious approach to seeking new alternatives to the debt crisis would require conditionality, but link it directly to the availability of resources to support meaningful internal changes in the region.

The linkage between debt and democracy has been difficult to establish for the governments of industrial countries. Witness the fact that the Reagan administration has touted its support for democracy in Latin America while ignoring one of the basic forces weakening democratic institutions—the debt crisis. The Group of Eight, meeting in Acapulco, have made the linkage. Individual Latin American presidents have done so as well. Most observers of the region have commented that the environment for democracy to grow and become stronger is constrained by the lack of economic opportunity, which in turn is a direct result of the debt burden under which the entire region has labored since the early 1980s.

Conclusion

The industrial countries have never developed a common policy regarding Latin American debt; each has taken a separate path. But primary responsibility has been clearly delegated to the United States as the principal lender and as the country with a sphere of influence to protect in Latin America. The Reagan administration's failure to address the security interests involved in the debt and trade issues has forced the U.S. Congress to seek alternatives. That implies a merger of the debt and trade issues with U.S. domestic politics. The engine that drives congressional decision making is local constituency pressure and concerns. It would be ironic if the six-year old Latin American debt crisis were now intelligently addressed by the industrial countries because it has become an issue of deep concern in the rust belt region of the United States.

The Latin American debt problem is now understood by many in Congress as an issue with serious consequences for the U.S. domestic economy. Moreover, the Congress is increasingly sensitive to the national security argument—that it is against U.S. interests to allow either further polarization between Latin America and the industrial world or to jeopardize the fledgling democratic regimes in the hemisphere. To survive they must have economic growth, but they cannot service the outstanding debt and grow simultaneously. What is needed is vigorous and courageous political leadership by the United States and its industrial allies. The 1987 Acapulco summit meeting of Latin American presidents put the issue succinctly:

> The economic crisis undermines democracy in the region because it neutralizes the legitimate efforts of our peoples to improve their living standards. In addition, it is contradictory that those who call for democracy also impose, in world economic relations, conditions and adjustments that compromise that very democracy and that they themselves do not apply in correcting their own imbalances.[25]

Notes

1. For an overview see Benjamin J. Cohen, *In Whose Interests? International Banking and American Foreign Policy* (New Haven: Yale University Press, 1986).

2. See Ricardo Ffrench-Davis and Richard E. Feinberg, eds., *Más allá de la crisis de la deuda: bases para un nuevo enfoque* (Santiago: CIEPLAN/Diálogo Interamericano, 1986).

3. Quoted in Riordan Roett, "The Debt Crisis: Economics and Politics," in *U.S. Policy in Latin America: Quarter Century of Crisis and Challenge*, ed. John D. Martz, forthcoming.

4. Ibid.

5. Ibid.

6. See Riordan Roett, "Beyond the Baker Initiative," *SAIS Review* 6, no. 2 (Summer-Fall 1986).

7. "Strategy for LDC Debt," *The Financial Times* (London), September 30, 1987.

8. Acapulco Summit Meeting of Latin American Presidents, "Final Comminque," November 30, 1987, mimeo.

9. For an interesting European perspective, see Manfred Mols, *El marco internacional de América Latina* (Barcelona: Editorial Alfa, 1985).

10. "Text of Economic Declaration Issued at End of Tokyo Summit Conference," *New York Times*, May 7, 1986.

11. While little has been written about Regan's role in the debt crisis, one can sense his position by reading, for example, references to Regan in John H. Makin, *The Global Debt Crisis: America's Growing Involvement* (New York: Basic Books, Inc., 1984).

12. See Riordan Roett, "The Foreign Debt Crisis and the Process of Redemocratization in Latin America," in *A Dance Along the Precipice: The Political and Economic Dimensions of the International Debt Problem*, ed. William N. Eskridge, Jr. (Lexington, MA : Lexington Books, 1985).

13. See Christine A. Bogdanowicz-Bindert, "World Debt: The United States Reconsiders," *Foreign Affairs* 64, no. 2 (Winter 1985-86). Although this article focuses on the changes in the executive branch, it offers a good overview of the rethinking of the debt issue by Baker and his associates.

14. For an excellent overview of the problem, see Ricardo Ffrench-Davis, ed., *Las relaciones financieras externas: su efecto en la economía latinoamericana* (Mexico: Fondo de Cultura Económica, 1983).

15. See Gabriel G. Manrique and Stuart K. Tucker, "Costs to the United States of the Recession in Developing Countries," Working Paper No. 8, Overseas Development Council, Washington, DC, 1984.

16. Makin, *Global Debt Crisis*, 16.

17. "The Impact of the Latin American Debt Crisis on the U.S. Economy," (Staff study prepared for the use of the Joint Economic Committee, Congress of the United States, May 10, 1986, mimeo).

18. See Riordan Roett, "The Brazilian Debt Crisis," Statement before the Subcommittee on International Finance, Trade and Monetary Policy of the Committee on Banking, Finance and Urban Affairs, U.S. House of Representatives, April 23, 1987.

19. Senator Bill Bradley, "A Proposal for Third World Debt Management" (Speech delivered in Zurich, Switzerland, June 29, 1986, mimeo).

20. The congressional initiative was so welcome that it received support from unlikely allies. See Rudiger Dornbusch, "The Bradley Plan: A Way Out of the Latin Debt Mess," *The Washington Post*, August 27, 1986; and Jeane Kirkpatrick, "Bradley Debt Plan Deserves Consideration," *The Philadelphia Inquirer*, July 20, 1986.

21. See Riordan Roett, Statement before the Subcommittee on International Development Institutions and Finance of the Committee on Banking Finance, and Urban Affairs, U.S. House of Representatives, March 18, 1986.

22. See Albert Fishlow, Statement before the Subcommittee on International Finance, Trade and Monetary Policy, Committee on Banking, Finance and Urban Affairs, U.S. House of Representatives, April 23, 1987.

23. For a further discussion of Japanese policy, see Barbara Stallings, "The Reluctant Giant: Japan and the Latin American Debt Crisis," in *Japan and the Third World*, ed. Susan J. Pharr (forthcoming).

24. Acapulco Summit Meeting of Latin American Presidents, "Final Communique," November 30, 1987, mimeo.

25. Ibid.

Suggestions for Further Reading

Amuzegar, Jahangir. "Dealing With Debt." *Foreign Policy*, no. 68 (Fall 1987).

Feinberg, Richard E. "Third World Debt: Toward A More Balanced Adjustment." *Journal of Interamerican Studies and World Affairs* 29, no. 1 (Spring 1987).

Foreign Policy Institute. *The U.S. Approach to the Latin American Debt Crisis*. Washington, DC: The Johns Hopkins School of Advanced International Studies, 1988.

Islam, Shafiqul. "Breaking the International Debt Deadlock." *Critical Issues* 2. New York: Council on Foreign Relations, Inc., 1988.

Kuczynski, Pedro-Pablo. "Latin American Debt." *Foreign Affairs* 66, no. 1 (Fall 1987).

Lever, Harold, and Christopher Hume. *Debt and Danger: The World Financial Crisis*. Boston: The Atlantic Monthly Press, 1986.

Roett, Riordan. "Brazil and the Debt: Is the Cost Too High?" In *The Latin American Debt: Problems and Policies*, ed. Robert Wesson. Stanford: Hoover Institution, forthcoming 1988.

Watkins, Alfred J. *Till Debt Do Us Part*. Lanham, MD: University Press of America, 1986.

5

National Business, Debt-Led Growth and Political Transition in Latin America

Sylvia Maxfield

Debt-led growth, and the austerity programs that followed it, have had important consequences for the distribution of wealth and income between capital and labor. In addition, indebted development has also changed the distribution of wealth and income *within* the business sector. The latter trend has had important political ramifications in the major Latin American countries. On the one hand, the business sector has redefined its relationship to the state. On the other hand, it has been a potential force in changing the nature of the state. Thus, in the 1980s, business groups have joined with other sectors of society to promote a transition from authoritarian regimes to political democracy. Their commitment to democracy, however, remains in doubt.

Focusing primarily on Brazil, Argentina, and Mexico, this essay discusses the effects of the borrowing boom and debt bust on the internal composition of business. Three related trends emerge. First, debt-led growth contributed to the creation of "wealthy businessmen and bankrupt businesses." In other words, the owners of corporations often benefited personally from debt-led growth even when their businesses suffered. Second, in combination with government policy, the foreign borrowing of the 1970s and early 1980s led to a boom for domestic financiers all over Latin America. The boom in short-term financial activity drew resources away from long-term industrial projects, so that financiers fared better than industrialists. Finally, through its impact on domestic financial systems, debt-led growth contributed to industrial concentration. Large-scale industrialists and entrepreneurs in commerce who were linked to financial institutions reaped profits from the boom and were partially bailed out during the crash. Small and medium-sized entrepreneurs were squeezed; many went bankrupt or were bought out by large conglomerates.

The essay also deals with the political repercussions of these economic trends. It describes how Argentine and Brazilian industrialists, disgruntled with government management of the borrowing binge and crisis, began to criticize authoritarianism and support calls for political opening. In a similar manner, it argues that business opposition to the Mexican ruling party, the Partido Revolucionario Institucional (PRI), is one of several trends that may contribute to regime change there. By and large, however, this political behavior appears to be a means to an end. Argentine and Brazilian industrialists could just as easily support a return to authoritarianism if convinced that political opening is not likely to improve their economic situation. Likewise, Mexican entrepreneurs could support increasing authoritarianism if they believed it would bring them more control over economic policy.

Debt-Led Growth and the Fortunes of Domestic Entrepreneurs

Among Latin American countries, there are several important cross-national differences in terms of the impact of foreign borrowing on capitalist development. In both Chile and Argentina, the combination of foreign borrowing with trade and financial liberalization led to a decline in the size of the industrial sector. Brazil was much more successful in harnessing foreign exchange inflows to medium- and long-run trade and industrial development goals. Mexico and Venezuela stand somewhere in between; in both countries debt fueled new industrial investment as well as tremendous capital flight. Despite these differences among Latin American countries, each has been affected by the three regionwide trends mentioned above.

Wealthy Businessmen, Bankrupt Businesses

During the borrowing boom, the trade openings and the relaxation of capital controls in many Latin American countries provided opportunities for capital flight and purchase of luxury consumer imports. With little regulation of foreign borrowing or foreign exchange transactions, individual entrepreneurs could take out loans for business activities and transfer a portion to personal accounts in the United States as a hedge against economic uncertainty. Reduction of trade barriers and exchange rate overvaluation provided incentives to spend loans on imports, both of production goods and luxury consumer items. Since this forced domestic suppliers out of business, industrial enterprises became more dependent on access to foreign exchange for production.

One might expect more capital flight and use of foreign loans for nonessential imports in the countries where private sector borrowing was relatively high, but the picture sketched in Table 5.1 is more complicated than this simple assumption suggests. Capital flight was low in Chile, where a high proportion of borrowing was by private entities, and in Brazil, where most loans were contracted by the state. Although Mexico and Argentina had different patterns of public and private borrowing, both had relatively high capital flight. In all cases, it is true that the portion of loans to the private sector increased towards the end of the borrowing boom, and capital flight rose. Nevertheless, to account for cross-national differences in the use of foreign loans, we also need to look at variation in financial regulation, trade, and exchange rate policies.

Table 5.1

Foreign Borrowing, Capital Flight, and Investment Patterns in Latin America, 1975-85

	Capital Flight ($ billion)		Growth Rate Financial Services/ Manufacturing	Average Annual Real Change in Private Gross Fixed Capital Formation		Foreign Borrowing, Cumulative Disbursements ($ billion)	
	1976-82	1983-85	1970-80	1975-81	1982-84	1975-82 Public	Private
Argentina	-27	1	2.95	-.03	-.45[a]	17	19
Brazil	-3	-7	.79	.16	-.23	45	38
Chile	0	1	3.92	.24	-.21	5	12
Mexico	-36	-17	.60	.20	-.20	52	30
Venezuela	-25	-6	.76	.02	-.21	12	20

[a]1982-83

Sources: Calculated from data provided by the Inter-American Development Bank, Morgan Guaranty Trust Company, International Monetary Fund, and the United Nations.

In Argentina, extreme financial liberalization, an overvalued exchange rate, and elimination of exchange controls encouraged capital flight. While the value of the Argentine currency was relatively high compared with the dollar, Argentines could buy dollars "cheaply"—with relatively few pesos. The mechanism was for the government to use foreign loans to buy pesos, making them relatively scarce and expensive compared to relatively plentiful and inexpensive dollars. Without the foreign loans that made this government intervention in the currency market possible, the peso's value relative to the dollar would have fallen and the cost of capital flight would have been higher.

In Chile, the exchange rate was also overvalued, but there was less capital flight than in Argentina, partly because the Chilean government maintained stricter exchange controls. Given these conditions, Chile's dramatic trade liberalization encouraged foreign imports. Private entrepreneurs used loans to import luxury items for personal consumption. They forced many domestic enterprises out of business by shifting their purchases from domestic to foreign markets. Mexican policy included an overvalued exchange rate, a moderate trade opening, and no restrictions on currency exchange. As a consequence, Mexico suffered both a rise in consumer imports and tremendous capital flight.

Since the late 1970s and early 1980s, correction of the overvalued exchange rates that subsidized capital flight has become part of International Monetary Fund (IMF) austerity packages. As foreign loans dried up, the consequences of spending those loans for personal consumption or short-term financial or commercial operations hit home. Many large and small industrial enterprises faced bankruptcy, particularly as devaluation made their dollar debts harder to pay off. To help local elites and their international creditors, Latin American governments provided subsidized bail-out loans and/or took over private debts. Ironically, the devaluations made individuals who held assets abroad even wealthier in domestic terms. The dollars that they had bought cheaply, with relatively little local currency, were now worth much more in local currency and domestic purchasing power. Thus, while wealthy businesspeople's companies were bailed out by the state, their foreign assets remained untouched.

Financial Boom

A second consequence of foreign borrowing in the 1970s and early 1980s was a boom for Latin American financiers. Domestic deregulation of local financial markets, coupled with growing international liquidity, spurred a tremendous short-term financial binge. In Mexico, high domestic interest rates—relative to international loan rates—created attractive opportunities for short-term financial speculation. Dollar loans converted into pesos were deposited for a short time in Mexican banks and then reconverted into dollars, earning the speculator a considerable profit between 1979 and mid-1982. Anyone who succeeded in obtaining cheap credit was assured large profits, whether through exchange speculation or other short-term use.

The boom in such short-term financial activity clearly came at the expense of long-term lending for industrial development. Between 1978 and 1982 Mexican private banks' nonliquid time deposits with maturities over one year fell more than 75 percent, from 48 percent of total deposits to 12 percent.[1] Long-term credits extended by public-sector banks fell from 36 percent of commercial bank assets in 1970 to 27 percent in 1979. Private financing for industry fell, while financing for services rose. Between 1977 and 1981, the percentage of private financing to manufacturing fell to decade-long lows.[2]

As in Mexico, there was a tremendous boom in Argentine financial markets. Similarly, growth of short-term financial activity responded to a combination of domestic policy and international liquidity. The military regime that overthrew the civilian government of Juan Perón's widow in 1976 instituted a far-reaching financial reform following the "structural monetarist" blueprint. The military government freed interest rates, eliminated barriers to entering the financial market, and removed restrictions on international capital movement. In the context of high liquidity in global financial markets, Argentina's reforms engendered financial sector growth but no increase in national savings or net new capital accumulation. The private financial sector boomed but grew increasingly concentrated. It was the only sector with steadily growing income between 1977 and 1986.[3] At the same time, the number of financial institutions shrank from 725 in 1977 to 449 in 1981.

The Argentine financial boom reflected the rise of a large, short-term financial market with rapid turnover. Between 1976 and 1981 the share of time deposits (mostly short-term) in total commercial bank deposits grew from 40 percent to 79 percent. In 1981, 70 percent of all time deposits were 30 days or less.[4] Nominal interest rates were so high that few activities other than speculation were profitable.

Despite growth in the financial sector, aggregate financing to industry fell and became increasingly concentrated among a small number of preferred customers.[5] Argentine economist Adolfo Canitrot studied the behavior of interest rates and industrial production between 1976 and 1980 and uncovered an inverse relationship. New industrial investment generally declined as interest rates rose, partly because the state abandoned its previous role in creating and channeling forced savings toward industry.[6] The 1977 financial reforms were designed to transfer this function to the private sector. State-owned banks gave up promoting government-defined priority activities in industry and agriculture. Their share of total financial system deposits shrank from 50 percent in 1975 to 34 percent in 1979.[7]

Even Brazil did not escape the regional pattern of growth in short-term financial activity detracting from long-term industrial financing. As in other Latin American countries, Brazil's pattern was due to a combination of government policy and international financial market conditions. Although Brazil experienced its most far-reaching financial reform in the 1960s, some key changes in financial policy were made in the 1970s, concomitant with the internationalization of capital markets. In 1976, as part of an effort to control inflation and promote foreign borrowing, the Brazilian government freed interest rates, while Central Bank Resolution 432 encouraged firms to borrow abroad by reducing the potential exchange risk. Law 4131 and Resolution 63, passed in the late 1960s, also deliberately encouraged direct foreign borrowing by private-sector firms and state-owned enterprises. The Second National Development Plan (NDP II), announced in 1985, advocated financial mergers to create conglomerates that could compete internationally.

As in Argentina and Mexico, the interaction of international financial integration and governmental monetary and financial policy engendered growth and concentration among private sector financial institutions in Brazil. The number of commercial banks fell from 328 in 1964 to 111 in 1980.[8] There is also an indication that, as in other cases, centralization and concentration in the private financial market allowed private-sector financiers to at least temporarily wrest some control over financial flows from public-sector institutions. For example, the profits of the former grew three times faster than those of the latter.[9]

In the face of increasingly internationalized capital and money markets, Brazilian financial policy followed the general trend of discouraging long-term productive investment. Interest rates on agricultural credits provided by the Bank of Brazil were negative, and state industrial credits also carried low or negative interest rates. Borrowers with access to subsidized credits could thus invest them in indexed government bonds, making large profits. As this form of intermarket financial arbitrage caught on, the average holding period for these government bonds fell from 11.4 days in 1973 to 1.8 days in 1979.[10] Brazilians called this arbitrage between financial market segments the *ciranda financeira,* or financial "ring around the rosy." "The role of internal debt was totally perverted," writes Brazilian economist José Serra. "Instead of providing development financing or permitting monetary control, it came to represent a base for . . . speculation."[11]

Industrial Concentration

Concentration within the industrial sector was the third major consequence of debt-led growth. In Mexico, the market for business finance was segmented between the relatively low-cost internationally integrated market and the relatively high-cost national market. Large-scale enterprises with access to foreign loans benefited in several ways. They could finance investment, enjoy the benefits of foreign exchange speculation, and profit as creditors from the high cost of peso financing. Uneven access to dollar financing created a dualism within the Mexican industrial sector, with small and medium-sized businesses excluded from the cheaper internationalized segment of the Mexican financial market. This contributed to industrial concentration, which in turn led to a crescendo of complaints about the expense of credit between 1979 and 1982. The president of the Credit Union for Small and Medium-Sized Business complained in 1982 that "credit is exceptionally expensive and our industries have little access." "Most of the credit," added one of his associates, "is channeled to large companies."[12] At the same time, large-scale industry had privileged access to credit for productive activity, as well as the opportunity to put profits to work in highly lucrative financial activities and conglomerate expansion.

Channeling low-cost credit to the large private conglomerates and high-cost loans to small and medium-sized entrepreneurs involved a complex relationship among the industrial-commercial conglomerates (*grupos*), the private banking sector, and the Central Bank. To expand the supply of domestic credit, the Central Bank encouraged private banks and industrialists to borrow abroad. Through a variety of mechanisms, the Central Bank accepted dollars that the private banks had borrowed on the international market and changed them into pesos with a guaranteed exchange rate.[13] The banks then loaned these pesos at differential rates, depending on the borrower's relationship with the bank. The system of borrowing dollars cheaply, and relending in pesos at high nominal interest rates to small and medium-sized borrowers who had no access to international loans, worked as long as the government guaranteed exchange stability and free exchange convertibility.

Banks reserved cheap dollar financing for their privileged customers. As a consequence, dollar financing by private banks to private-sector borrowers was concentrated in a few large, internationally-linked conglomerates. Ten Mexican conglomerates contracted 34 percent of private sector external debt. Three of them alone, the Monterrey-based Alfa, Vitro, and Visa, accounted for 20 percent of total private foreign borrowing. Foreign borrowing was also concentrated by company size. "Gigantic" companies had 52 percent of their total liabilities in foreign debt, while the corresponding amount for the smallest companies was 3 percent.[14] A 1982 survey by Banamex (a leading Mexican bank) revealed four sectors receiving between 25 percent and 45 percent of their financing from foreign loans: automobiles and automobile parts; construction and construction materials; chemicals and pharmaceuticals; and food, beer, and tobacco.[15] Construction and food and beverages are two traditional *grupo* strongholds, while the other two sectors are characterized by subsidiaries of multinational corporations and joint ventures with national conglomerates.

In Argentina there was also a large differential between the cost of local and foreign currency-based loans. Opening the capital account of the balance of payments to large capital inflows was intended to bring domestic lending rates in line with international rates, but this did not occur. The foreign (dollar) interest rate, adjusted by the programmed peso devaluation, remained below the domestic rate. As in Mexico, the differential interest rate led to economic concentration. Firms that did not have access to foreign credit had to borrow at higher domestic rates. Only banks and a few large corporations had direct access to foreign loans. Small firms had to borrow from banks that converted their dollar loans into high-cost peso credits. Therefore, access to foreign finance was a considerable competitive advantage, and helps to explain the correlation between access to foreign loans and top ranking among Argentine industrial corporations.[16]

Intensified competition resulting from tariff reductions and differential access to relatively cheap foreign credit caused smaller enterprises to go bankrupt. Large industrial companies with access to foreign credits actively recycled foreign resources in the domestic financial system, using profits from this transaction to cover operating losses.[17] Banks used the profits they gained from intermediating between the international and domestic markets to buy up bankrupt enterprises and group them into financial-industrial-commercial conglomerates.[18]

In Brazil, the combination of government policy and international liquidity also contributed to industrial concentration. The high rates paid on government bonds attracted liquidity within the Brazilian financial system to the primary and secondary market for government bonds. Yet credit available in the commercial bank market (as opposed to the indexed bond market) became increasingly limited. Although data are scarce, it appears that the financing available in the commercial bank market and through foreign borrowing flowed toward a limited number of dynamic industrial sectors dominated by the larger, domestically-owned groups, as it did in other Latin American countries. Debt-to-equity ratios rose for most major Brazilian firms, especially in the capital goods sector. Summarizing the available data, Frieden concludes that "the more dynamic sectors and the larger firms have indeed been the more heavily indebted; they can borrow because of their size and dynamism, and their access to finance increases both."[19]

Policies stimulating the private financial sector and the resulting concentration in credit allocation accentuated market imperfections in the productive sector. Larger, more creditworthy firms used foreign funds to speculate in the Brazilian money market and in the more loosely organized curb market, which loaned to smaller, less creditworthy Brazilian firms. Smaller firms without access to subsidized credit or foreign loans were forced into this exorbitantly-priced curb market for credit.[20] Oligopolistic firms could use their market power to pass high domestic credit costs on to the consumer, whether they were forced to rely on high cost markets or not. Monetary and financial policies combined with increased foreign borrowing to "reinforce the oligopolistic tendency of production, regardless of production efficiency criteria," while the financial backing and the market power of the large firms put inflationary pressures on the economy.[21]

Debt-Led Growth and Domestic Business: Political Implications

The differential impact of indebtedness on various segments of local business politicized both intra-capitalist relations and relations between business and government. During the borrowing boom, when international interest rates were low and domestic rates high, there was strong antagonism between those entrepreneurs who were financially well-connected and those who were not. In Brazil and Argentina, industrialists opposed policies that favored financiers at their expense. As the boom turned bust, they began to think the military government was incapable of creating a stable economic environment, and they expressed their frustration with economic policy through opposition to the government and the regime. They hoped to attain more influence over economic policy as the political regime became more open. The industrialists' goal in opposing authoritarian government was not regime change but change in the procedure and substance of economic policy making. Support for political opening was a means to that end.

The distributional consequences of debt-led growth also had an impact on business support for the Mexican regime. The boom in short-term financial activity provoked the Mexican government to nationalize all private banks. This dealt the final blow to a forty-year government-business accord. In 1988 business opposition to the regime is often couched in terms of support for political opening, or democracy, but business opposition could just as easily push the PRI to become more repressive.

The Role of Business in the Argentine "Apertura"

Supported by heavy foreign borrowing, the Argentine dictatorship's laissez-faire policy lasted from 1976 to 1981. Although many large conglomerates had benefited during the boom (relative to small and medium-sized industrialists), the end of the borrowing binge pushed a significant number to the verge of bankruptcy. In 1981 industrialists owed between $4 and $8 billion in debt to Argentine banks and financial institutions that they could not pay due to high interest rates, the peso's devaluation, and severe import competition.[22] Even though their personal wealth was often safe in foreign banks, these industrialists still wanted government policies to help their enterprises through the crisis and ultimately strengthen industry.

General Viola began to dismantle the orthodox policies of Economics Minister Martínez de Hoz in response to the industrialists' situation, but Viola had no clear alternative policy. This lack of direction during an industrial crisis fueled business opposition to the military regime. The head of one provincial Chamber of Industry stated in 1981 that "companies are in a critical state because of unemployment, recession, financial usury, speculative indexation, and above all, enormous economic uncertainty."[23] The president of Ford's Argentine subsidiary was among the many prominent industrialists who were harshly critical of the Viola government. "The high interest rates, the most worrying factor, have been discussed at all levels within the government," he complained, "but still nothing has been done to stop them climbing. No industrialist in the world can work with interest rates in excess of 11 percent a month."[24] A National Businessmen's Assembly (CONAE) wrote an open letter to the government denouncing the perilous state of national industry. They were briefly placed under arrest when they called a press conference to publicize their complaints. Leaders of the Argentine Industrial Union, the country's largest employer association, threatened social upheaval unless solutions were quickly found for the industrialists' problems. Viola's Minister of Industry resigned in frustration over the government's inability and/or unwillingness to respond to the industrialists' problems. In sum, the vociferous complaints of industrial leaders in 1981 fueled the growing society-wide debate in Argentina over return to civilian rule.

Eventually, the military replaced General Viola. His successor, General Galtieri, tried to divert attention from the nation's domestic problems by invading the Falkland/Malvinas Islands in April 1982. Britain's victory and the unnecessary death of Argentine military personnel were the final nails in the coffin of one of history's most brutal dictatorships. Businesspeople looked forward to more influence over economic policy under civilian rule. Indeed, Raúl Alfonsín took office in December 1983 with promises of negotiation (*concertación*) among government, labor, and business, but the time was not ripe for building pluralist corporatism in Argentina. Labor adamantly refused wage restraints after enduring almost a decade of shrinking real wages. Business was divided and disorganized internally. The immediate pressures of the debt crisis led to a relatively closed, top-down pattern of economic policy making under the new democratic government.

For example, in early 1985 Alfonsín established ten committees composed of representatives from labor, industry, and the government to discuss key aspects of the national economic situation. Nevertheless, these committees had little to do with the design of the April 1985 "heterodox shock." In fact, the inspiration for Argentina's most important economic policy package to date came from abroad.[25] Business and labor complained that the heterodox shock, which included wage and price controls and the creation of a new currency, was developed and implemented in an authoritarian, technocratic manner.

Consolidation of civilian rule requires growth, and growth in Argentina depends on mobilizing private-sector investment. The public sector cannot lead investment, pay debt service, and cut public deficits all at the same time. In 1986 the Argentine government opted to lead investment. That year witnessed Argentina's first fixed investment increase in six years, fueled by a 37 percent expansion in public investment, but at the same time, private investment shrank by 10 percent.[26]

Businesspeople cite high interest rates and political instability as the key factors behind their reluctance to invest. Although they do not want a return to military rule, they are not yet ready to vote with their assets.

Business and Political Opening in Brazil

Business opposition to Brazil's military government began with the Second National Development Plan (NDP II), which extended Brazil's ambitious industrialization plan to the capital goods sector. It was made possible in large part by foreign loans. Industrialists producing consumer durables, including subsidiaries of multinational corporations and the local companies dependent on them, were wary of efforts to develop a local capital goods industry. They had been able to operate comfortably while relying on imported capital goods. Furthermore, the plan raised expectations among capital goods producers that the government of General Geisel (1974-1978) found difficult to fulfill.

As state intervention expanded in support of the NDP II's controversial development goals, the nature of economic decision making changed. It became "more centralized, arbitrary, and less subject to private sector input."[27] Some businesspeople became dissatisfied with the *ad hoc*, personalized system of business representation in the military regime's economic policy-making process. In this process, private entrepreneurs expressed their policy preferences in small, informal, policy-specific groups combining bureaucrats and businesspeople. These groups are sometimes called "bureaucratic rings;" in the 1970s there were probably hundreds forming and breaking up at any given time.[28] Under Geisel, businesspeople became increasingly disillusioned with this relatively unpredictable and often arbitrary system of business representation.

Discontent with both the substance and form of economic policy led to a chorus of industrialist demands for political opening and insistence on increased private sector participation in government decision making. In 1978, as public opposition continued to mount, a group of prominent industrial leaders issued a public declaration against authoritarianism.

By 1980 the Brazilian economy was beginning to seriously falter; industrialists' prospects were worse than they had been since 1964. Aiming to correct Brazil's deteriorating balance of payments, "Superminister" of the Economy Delfim Netto engineered a shift back to the recessionary policies followed in the late 1970s. Industrialists objected to the recessionary policies as well as to Delfim Netto's arrogant personal style. Their critique of the government became more pointed, as they accused the government of sacrificing the capital goods sector to achieve balanc- of-payments stability. In 1981 industrial leaders called for debt renegotiation without recourse to the International Monetary Fund (IMF). A majority of those leaders surveyed in March 1981 favored gradual political opening, hoping for more influence over economic policy. Looking toward the establishment of a strong congress, some business leaders became interested in techniques used by U.S.

business to lobby the legislature.

Recessionary policies, and high interest rates in particular, continued to push many industrial concerns toward bankruptcy. In early 1982 many industrialists hoped for a politically-motivated reflation in anticipation of the November elections. Instead, succumbing to pressure from international creditors, the government announced a new austerity program one month before those elections. The large Matorazzo Group, which had been in financial trouble for several years, explicitly attacked the government in its 1982 annual report. Other business leaders echoed their criticisms. José Diniz, president of a large capital goods firm, warned that the business community was planning a major revolt against government policies. Although the business community did not take the initiative in pushing for democratization, its weight in the coalition of social forces calling for democracy was crucial.

As the presidential campaign heated up in 1984, many industrialists broke with the tradition of staying out of public political debates. Domestic entrepreneurs surveyed in 1984 had little hope that the nation's economic ills could be cured before the political transition was over.[29] Paulo Salim Maluf, Partido Democrático Social (PDS) presidential candidate and a businessman himself, was perhaps a natural choice for business backing. He was outmaneuvered, however, by opposition candidate Tancredo Neves. As governor of the state of Minas Gerais, Neves had worked hard to win support from business groups that had been excluded from the ruling PDS bureaucracy and earlier from the military government. The president of the national Chamber of Commerce broke the traditional political silence of Brazilian business associations and announced his support for Neves. Robert Marinho, a prominent conservative entrepreneur who had been close to the military government throughout the 1970s, also campaigned publicly for Neves.

President Tancredo Neves did not live long enough to enjoy a honeymoon with his business supporters. His vice president and successor, José Sarney, quickly frustrated businesspeople with his administration's indecision over economic policy and debt renegotiation. Industrialists adamantly resisted IMF pressures, demanding concrete plans from Sarney rather than "more shows and speeches." During negotiations in 1985, the president of a leading São Paulo business association (FIESP) said, "The IMF can do whatever it wants, but we will do only what is feasible."[30] In part to placate Brazilian industrialists, Sarney appointed Dilson Funaro, a widely respected São Paulo businessman, as Finance Minister.

In early 1986 the Funaro team came up with its own version of the heterodox shock, known as the Cruzado Plan (explained in Pang's chapter in this volume). As in Argentina, policy formulation and implementation proceeded in a closed, elitist fashion. Although Sarney gained a temporary increase in business support and general political popularity, it did not last long. Business leaders attacked Sarney for delaying necessary adjustments in the heterodox plan for political reasons. The second Cruzado Plan, announced after the November 1986 elections, alienated business, the middle class, and labor. Cruzado II lifted price controls on cars, beverages, and tobacco, and raised prices for oil. Sarney's popularity plummeted, and street protests were evidence of popular discontent with the new economic plan. Industrialists found their profit margins squeezed by frozen prices and began a campaign of civil disobedience. They raised prices without permission, removed some products from the market, and repackaged others to seem like new products not subject to price controls or to contain less for the same price. Labor demanded a debt moratorium and restriction of price adjustments. By the end of 1986 Brazilian inflation was back to triple digits—an annual 170 percent for December.

Relations between Sarney and the business community have continued to deteriorate. Production-related investment, even in the government-supported export sector, has virtually dried up. Businesspeople have called for Sarney to define the rules of the game. They have attacked him personally for failing to stick to one course, complaining of "zigzagging economic policies." An incident in early 1987 demonstrates the current level of antagonism between Brazilian industrialists and the government. FIESP president Mario Armato sent a long telex to Sarney accusing him of losing control of the economy. Sarney responded by calling the FIESP leader an anarchist, a "Brazilian Bakunin." Armato, who is in the distilling business, registered the name "Bakunin" for a new vodka he was preparing to market! In a 1987 interview Armato attacked what he saw as a continuation of authoritarian and technocratic government: "We must return to simplicity and abandon the hermetic and complicated language of government technocrats who seek to reduce everything to formulas no one understands and that have never worked up until now."[31]

As in Argentina, Brazilian industrialists do not wish a return to military rule, but they are hesitant to support the new democratic government by investing, due to a lack of confidence in its policies. Without their investment, the fledgling democracy cannot become stronger. It is a vicious circle.

The Role of Business in Mexico's Political Future

In Mexico, the consequences of debt-led growth have contributed to the erosion of a fifty-year political regime characterized by corporatist, one-party rule. As Kaufman explains in his chapter, shifting government-business relations are one factor contributing to the potential for political change in Mexico today. This change could be a political opening, or increased instability engendering repression. The financial speculation fueled by government policy and international liquidity provoked hostility toward Mexican bankers from labor, small and medium-sized industrialists, and some government advisors.

In a September 1982 speech that shook the global financial community, President López Portillo called a temporary debt moratorium and nationalized Mexico's private banks. The bank nationalization was the final blow to an informal accord between government and business. According to this unwritten agreement, Mexican entrepreneurs stayed out of politics in exchange for the ruling party's guarantee of a profitable investment climate. Domestic entrepreneurs were consulted on government economic policies, and in many cases they exercised veto power. Thus business could legitimately pressure government, but it could not participate in party or electoral politics or in social mobilization.

The bank nationalization created economic uncertainty and rekindled tremendous business mistrust of the existing political regime. During the Echeverría administration in the early 1970s, entrepreneurs had begun to doubt whether the regime continued to represent their interests. This mistrust was temporarily assuaged by the oil and borrowing boom, only to resurge with a vengeance after the bank nationalization. In 1988 a majority of the Mexican business sector feels a need for change in government-business relations, but they disagree on tactics and strategy.

Small and medium-sized industrialists who depend on the state have discussed being formally incorporated into the ruling party (PRI) following the pattern of labor and peasant representation. Another group of industrialists and merchants based in Mexico City, who are organized in official business associations such as CONCANACO, want moderate change in the one-party democracy and have suggested pressuring the PRI from within. Northern industrialists and agro-exporters want to see radical change in the political system and call for a "democracy without adjectives." In a departure from their past behavior, these entrepreneurs have engaged in several different forms of political activity, including joining the right-wing opposition party (Partido Acción Nacional, or PAN), engaging in civic action and social mobilization to denounce vote fraud, and conducting media campaigns to improve the popular image of businesspeople.

Political mistrust and economic uncertainty translate into reluctance to invest. The Mexican government had hoped for an economic recovery in 1987 fueled by a 15 percent increase in private sector investment. Yet 80 to 90 percent of entrepreneurs questioned in a leading business magazine survey had no confidence in the government's capacity to manage the economy. Most said they were holding off on investment decisions until after the July 1988 presidential elections. As 1988 began, the Mexican economy was suffering from severe stagflation. Inflation rates were fast approaching the astronomical Southern Cone levels, and the Mexicans were contemplating their own version of the heterodox shock.

The investment decisions of domestic entrepreneurs are crucial determinants of Mexico's political future. Most Mexicans hold the government responsible for national economic performance as well as their own individual economic well-being. If stagflation continues, popular protest against the PRI will rise, and the PRI is likely to respond with increasing repression. The public sector lacks sufficient resources to be an engine of growth pulling the economy out of stagnation. Only private-sector investment can spur economic recovery and create an economic environment conducive to political opening rather than repression.

Conclusion

To varying degrees all over Latin America, internationalization increased the liquidity and segmentation of financial markets, spurring speculation and economic concentration. In the late 1970s government monetary policy fueled, rather than controlled, this speculation. Industrial and financial conglomerates profited heavily from short-term financial activity, and the incentive structure created by international financial integration and government policy drew resources away from industrial finance. Small and medium-sized industrialists without preferential access to credit markets were financially squeezed. The boom in profits of large corporations fueled mergers, so that wealth and financial resources became increasingly concentrated in the hands of a relatively small number of conglomerates. When the boom turned bust, the large companies and financial institutions that had access to international financial markets were caught with large nominal debts. Latin American governments bailed them out, while austerity programs shrank domestic purchasing power and undermined many small and medium-sized entrepreneurs.

The distributional impact of debt management on domestic entrepreneurs is one of several variables contributing to the shift in government-business relations in many Latin American countries in the late 1970s and 1980s. The frustration of Brazilian and Argentine industrialists with the military governments' economic policies led them to join the broader social movements calling for political opening in the two countries. The industrialists' shift from at least tacit support of military government to opposition reflected their hope that a new democratic regime would afford them greater voice in economy policy making. At the end of the 1980s these hopes are eroding, and government-business relations in Brazil and Argentina are still troubled.

In Mexico, debt management policies—including the dramatic 1982 bank nationalization and trade liberalization—are also contributing to a breakdown in government-business relations. Small and medium-sized industrialists, who face growing international competition and who cannot benefit from short-term financial activity, have begun to change their decades-old policy of unquestioning support for the ruling PRI. According to ex-bankers and large agribusinessmen from northern Mexico, the bank nationalization is an indication that the power of the presidency threatens private property rights. Breaking the traditional pattern of behind-the-scenes bargaining, they now campaign publicly for a democratic opening and refuse to make new long-term investments. Ironically, their investment strike undermines the chances for political opening; stagnant economies are not the natural habitat of fledgling democracies.

In the 1980s and 1990s, massive international debt relief and political reaccommodation between Latin American governments and domestic businesspeople are requisites for renewed entrepreneurial spirit. Debt relief and political reaccommodation would encourage Latin American entrepreneurs to invest in new industrial expansion. This in turn would improve the prognosis for a long-term democratic opening. Without growth in domestic private-sector investment, democracy will remain a dream for current and future generations of Latin Americans.

Notes

1. Assereto Antonio Amerlinck, "Perfil de las crisis recientes del sistema financiero mexicano," *Comercio Exterior* 34, no. 10 (October 1984): 962.

2. This is calculated from data in the annual reports of the Mexican Central Bank.

3. Adolfo Canitrot, "Discipline as the Central Objective of Economic Policy: An Essay on the Economic Programme of the Argentine Government since 1976," *World Development* 8, no. 11 (1980): 923.

4. World Bank, *Chile: An Economy in Transition* (Washington, DC: IBRD, 1979), 210.

5. See José Manuel Quijano, Hilda Sánchez, and Fernando Antía, *Desarrollo económico y penetración extranjera* (Puebla, México: Universidad Autónoma, 1985).

6. Adolfo Canitrot, "Teoría y práctica del liberalismo: política anti-inflacionaria y apertura económica en la Argentina, 1976-1981," *Estudios Cedes* 3, no. 10 (1980).

7. Aldo Ferrer, "El monetarismo en Argentina y Chile," *Comercio Exterior* 31, no. 1 (January 1981): 12.

8. Harry M. Makler, "Financial Conglomerates in Brazil and Mexico" (paper presented at the Annual Meeting of the Latin American Studies Association, Albuquerque, New Mexico, April 18-20, 1985).

9. Ibid.

10. José Serra, "Notas sobre el sistema financiero brasileño," *Economía de América Latina*, no. 7 (1981): 65.

11. Ibid., 61.

12. Confidential interviews in Mexico City, 1985.

13. Jorge Eduardo Uriarte Seldner, "La banca mexicana en los financiamientos internacionales," *Comercio Exterior* 33, no. 9 (1983).

14. José Manuel Quijano, *La banca: pasado y presente* (Mexico City: CIDE, 1983), 273.

15. *Expansión* (Mexico City), March 1982, 21.

16. David Felix, "El monetarismo latinoamericano en crisis," *Investigación Económica* (October-December 1984); Bernardo P. Kosacoff, "Industrialización y monetarismo en Argentina," *Economía de América Latina*, no. 12 (1984).

17. Aldo Ferrer, *¿Puede Argentina pagar su deuda externa?* (Buenos Aires: El Cid Editorial, 1982), 73.

18. Felix, "El monetarismo latinoamericano," 21.

19. Jeffry Frieden, "The Brazilian Borrowing Experience," *Latin American Research Review* 22, no. 2 (1987).

20. Some credit incentives were opened especially for smaller enterprises, but the overall effect was "too little, too late."

21. Christian Anglade, "The State and Capital Accumulation in Contemporary Brazil," in *The State and Capital Accumulation in Latin America*, ed. Christian Anglade and Carlos Fortín (London: Macmillan, 1985), 80.

22. *Quarterly Economic Review of Argentina*, First Quarter 1981.

23. *Latin America Regional Report-Southern Cone*, June 26, 1981.

24. *Latin America Regional Report-Southern Cone*, September 4, 1981.

25. The ideas behind the plan came from a report made by several West German economists visiting Argentina on a grant from West Germany's Ebert Foundation.

26. *Quarterly Economic Review of Argentina*, Fourth Quarter 1986.

27. Ben Ross Schneider, "Framing the State: Economic Policy and Political Representation in Post-Authoritarian Brazil," in *State and Society in Brazil: Continuities and Changes*, ed. John Wirth, Edson Nunes, and Thomas Bogenschild (Boulder, CO: Westview Press, 1987).

28. Fernando Henrique Cardoso, *Autoritarismo e democratização* (Rio de Janeiro: Paz e Terra, 1975).

29. Survey by *Exame* is summarized in *Latin America Regional Report-Brazil*, April 20, 1984.

30. *Latin America Regional Report-Brazil*, July 5, 1985.

31. *Latin America Regional Report-Brazil*, July 17, 1987.

Suggestions for Further Reading

Cardoso, Fernando H. "Entrepreneurs and the Transition Process: The Brazilian Case." In *Transitions from Authoritarian Rule*, ed. Guillermo O'Donnell, Philippe C. Schmitter, and Laurence Whitehead. Baltimore: Johns Hopkins University Press, 1986.

Lessard, Donald R., and John Williamson, eds. *Capital Flight and Third World Debt*. Washington, DC: Institute for International Economics, 1987.

Maxfield, Sylvia, and Ricardo Anzaldua, eds. *Government and Private Sector in Contemporary Mexico*. San Diego: Center for U.S.-Mexican Studies, University of California, San Diego, 1987.

Schneider, Ben Ross. "Framing the State: Economic Policy and Political Representation in Post-Authoritarian Brazil." In *State and Society in Brazil: Continuities and Changes*, ed. John Wirth, Edson Nunes, and Thomas Bogenschild. Boulder, CO: Westview Press, 1987.

6

Organized Labor:
A Major Victim of the Debt Crisis

Ian Roxborough

Organized labor in Latin America has been a major victim of the debt crisis of the 1980s. The general picture has been one of almost unrelieved gloom. Across the continent, wages and employment have dropped, often sharply, as the costs of adjustment have fallen on the poorer sections of the population. Labor has been unable to defend its real living standard in the face of very high rates of inflation and is everywhere in retreat. An overall view of the decline in real wages is given in Table 6.1 produced by the International Labor Office (ILO).

Looking at the summary data for Latin America as a whole, it can be seen that real industrial wages fell between 1983 and 1984, remained low in 1985 and then recovered somewhat in 1986. A large part of this recovery was due to the exceptional performance of real wages in Brazil in 1986, a trend that was sharply reversed in 1987. It will also be noted that the decline in Mexico has been particularly severe and sustained.

Unemployment data are broadly consonant with the information on wages. In economies with very little unemployment relief, open unemployment has historically been very low. Surplus labor has appeared primarily in the form of poorly-paid work with low productivity, generally known as underemployment. While this undoubtedly continues to be the case, the recession of the 1980s has been so severe that even open unemployment has increased markedly, as will be seen from Table 6.2. There is some indication that open unemployment was beginning to fall gradually in 1986 and 1987, although this may merely indicate the increasing ability of the completely unemployed to move into underemployment.

Given the diversity of national experiences, any attempt to generalize across the region would be fruitless. Instead, the remainder of this chapter will focus on the three large industrial countries of Argentina, Brazil, and Mexico. As will become apparent, the 1980s have seen dramatic changes, both in government policy towards organized labor and in the situation of the working class as a whole. In all three countries, to varying degrees, there has been an erosion of corporatist mechanisms of labor control in recent years. Governments face labor movements that have a greater measure of independence from immediate state control. This means that

Table 6.1
Trends of Real Industrial Wages, 1981-86 (1980=100)

Country	1981	1982	1983	1984	1985	1986
Argentina	89.7	80.3	103.9	126.3	102.9	107.8
Brazil	108.5	121.6	173.6	105.1	112.6	131.9
Colombia	100.2	104.0	109.8	117.4	113.4	118.9
Costa Rica	91.2	76.4	85.7	82.2	90.2	95.3
Chile	111.6	108.5	96.3	95.5	90.4	92.1
Mexico	103.0	101.5	74.5	71.9	72.1	66.1
Paraguay	106.4	103.3	93.0	92.4	89.6	86.0
Peru	94.7	95.9	78.4	65.2	61.3	65.5
Uruguay	106.7	103.5	82.1	80.2	97.6	103.3
Latin America	101.3	99.4	99.7	92.9	92.2	96.3

Source: *PREALC Newsletter*, no. 14, August 1987.

Table 6.2
Urban Unemployment, 1980-87 (%)

Country	1980	1981	1982	1983	1984	1985	1986	1987
Argentina	2.6	4.7	5.3	4.7	4.6	6.1	5.2	6.0
Bolivia	5.8	9.7	10.9	13.0	15.5	18.2	20.0	21.0
Brazil	6.2	7.9	6.3	6.7	7.1	5.3	3.6	3.6
Colombia	9.7	8.3	9.1	11.7	13.4	14.0	13.8	12.8
Chile	11.7	9.0	20.0	19.0	18.5	17.0	13.1	12.1
Guatemala	2.2	1.5	6.0	9.9	9.1	12.0	14.2	12.6
Mexico	4.5	4.2	4.2	6.6	5.7	4.4	4.3	4.2
Uruguay	7.4	6.7	11.9	15.5	14.0	13.1	10.7	9.5
Latin America	6.3	6.5	9.2	10.9	11.0	11.3	10.6	10.2

The 1987 figures are preliminary and partial. In some cases, they correspond to national averages; in others they represent the capital city or the principal cities. Nevertheless, they are generally comparable through time for each country.
Source: *PREALC Newsletter*, no. 15, December 1987.

support must be bargained for in some way, or the government must be prepared to overcome possible union opposition to its economic policies.

Several factors condition labor responses. Because they drive down real wages and push up unemployment, orthodox policies often generate widespread labor protest. To deal with such a challenge, each government has experimented with two basic choices—it has attempted to divide the unions politically, or it has sought some form of social pact. Each approach has had varying degrees of success, but the general story is one of "muddling through," rather than of a clear strategic plan to deal with labor. At the same time, high levels of unemployment are major impediments to worker protest. As the effects of the economic crisis have bitten deeper into the working class, labor's capacity to respond has also diminished.

In 1985 in Argentina and in 1986 in Brazil, there appeared to be a way out. It was thought that a heterodox shock could deal with inflation and get the economy growing again, thereby enabling real wages to rise. This would provide the material underpinning for union support of the government. With the unsatisfactory results of the Austral Plan in Argentina, and the disastrous collapse of the Cruzado Plan in Brazil, however, the heterodox shocks lost much of their appeal by 1987. Nevertheless, some Mexican policy makers were still toying with the idea of their own version.

Labor Relations under the Sarney Government in Brazil

When José Sarney assumed office April 17, 1985, there existed a widespread perception of crisis. The President-elect, Tancredo Neves, had died before assuming office; and Vice President Sarney, the next in line, had been chosen from among those who had previously supported the military government in order to balance the ticket. His legitimacy was in some doubt, and his showing in the polls was far from reassuring.[1]

In June Sarney began discussions with businessmen concerning a possible social pact, and later that month met with the more moderate unions, the Coordenação Nacional da Classe Trabalhadora, or CONCLAT (later renamed the Central Geral dos Trabalhadores, or CGT). These unions had previously operated within the official corporatist structures and were predisposed towards permanent cooperation with the government. Alongside these moderate unions, the last years of the military government had seen the rise of militant unions, particularly in the ABC region of greater São Paulo, organized into the Central Unica dos Trabalhadores (CUT) and affiliated with the Workers' Party (Partido dos Trabalhadores, or PT). Dealing with the CUT would be a difficult task and was initially set aside.

One key issue was reform of the corporatist labor legislation, largely intact since the late 1930s. Almir Pazzianotto, the new Minister of Labor and formerly a lawyer for the militant São Paulo unions, declared that he would cease the practice of official intervention in unions. He also reinstated the political rights of some union leaders, who had been barred from union activity by the previous regime. And he promised new labor legislation that eliminated the granting of exclusive jurisdiction to official unions and guaranteed freedom of association.

On this last issue, however, union opinion was seriously divided, since the elimination of state restrictions on association also implied the abolition of the obligatory syndical tax—a major source of union funding in the past. The Ministry of Labor estimated that only 500 of the 4,500 unions then existing in Brazil would be able to survive the abolition of this tax, and no action was taken on legislation as late as 1987.

In the meantime, prospects for a social pact on economic policy also rapidly disappeared. In the context of bitterly-fought strikes in the metalworking sector of São Paulo, one moderate union leader after another came out against the idea. Labor Minister Pazzianotto publicly lamented the unionists' widespread perception that a social pact would be nothing more than another wage cut, and this indeed seemed to be the heart of the problem: the government was seen as offering nothing concrete to unionists in exchange for their support. This failure of the government to offer any concrete *quid pro quo* would continue to mark discussions of a social pact throughout 1986 and 1987.

The Cruzado Plan

On February 28, 1986, the government announced a dramatic new stabilization program. The Cruzado Plan was based on a belief that inflation was largely inertial, and that a heterodox shock would dramatically reduce inflationary expectations.[2] Wages and prices were frozen overnight. The policy of freezing prices proved immensely popular. Sarney's ratings in the opinion polls shot up immediately to over 80 percent, and then held steady at around the 50 percent mark (with a slight tendency to decline over time).

To avoid a renewal of inflationary pressures, however, active support from both the unions and the general public for continuation of the policy had to be encouraged. In this regard, the government's failure to anticipate the inevitable shortages and black markets that would result from a price control policy was a major mistake. Government action in this area, as was so typical of the Sarney government as a whole, was largely improvised and often tardy. Possibly more important, the government's inability to win the support of the CUT meant that a significant and militant section of organized labor was likely to obstruct the continued successful implementation of a wage freeze. While most workers benefited from the Cruzado Plan, a significant number of unions, largely affiliated with the CUT, were about to have their contracts renewed, and the sudden wage freeze left them in a disadvantageous position.

The Cruzado Plan thus rapidly ran into problems. As suppressed inflationary pressures began to mount, the industrial relations scene began to deteriorate, and the government became increasingly alarmed by the strike movement. In August Sarney called members of his cabinet together to discuss the strikes. On October 2, the Army occupied the Volta Redonda steelworks to break a strike. The government maintained its efforts to suppress inflation until the elections of November 1986. It then freed many prices, and inflation began once again to eat into real wages. The CUT responded by calling for a general strike. Within a few days the CGT had joined forces with the CUT, and the strike was announced for December 12. In a typical piece of rhetorical exaggeration, Sarney declared that those who called for a general strike were "enemies," and repeated his call for a social pact.[3] In any event, the strike was a failure. It is difficult to estimate accurately the number of people who participated, but there is no doubt that the results were disappointing to the CUT and CGT, each of whom accused the other of being responsible for the failure. The Serviço Nacional de Informações (SNI) estimated that some 12 percent of workers went out on strike, although this may well be an underestimate.

The immediate result of the general strike's failure was to cause a rethinking of the unions' position. On December 14 both the CGT and the CUT announced that they were willing to discuss a social pact, but the CUT rapidly reverted to its original position. The following month, the CUT announced its rejection of a social pact, although saying that "conversations" were acceptable.[4]

While this was going on, the government was deeply divided over the appropriate economic policy to pursue in the wake of the Cruzado Plan's failure. Entrepreneurs pushing for a general lifting of the price freeze warned of widespread chaos in the economy if their counsel was not heeded. They said businessmen would take matters into their own hands and announce price increases even where this was prohibited. Sarney responded with a furious attack, accusing the entrepreneurs of being "anarchists."[5]

In this climate of uncertainty and confusion, the talks between the unions and the government finally broke down at the end of January 1987 and the CUT began preparations for another general strike. By now a sense of political crisis was emerging. In March the Navy occupied many of Brazil's ports to break a seamen's strike, and the Army occupied the oil refineries to prevent the oil workers from going out on strike. The international press published photographs of tanks and troops with fixed bayonets outside the refineries. In April, and again in June, the Brazilian press began to speculate openly about the possibility of an impending military coup.

In this context, the Sarney government's relations with the labor movement deteriorated even further. Sarney's standing in the opinion polls had dropped to around 10 percent; his bus had been stoned by demonstrators; and the country was hit by a number of massive strikes. In June, the new Finance Minister, Bresser Pereira, again attempted to use a wage/price freeze to halt inflation. In contrast to the first months of the Cruzado Plan, however, real wages dropped sharply and the economy moved into a recession. In August, the CUT and the CGT responded with another attempt at a general strike. Although the organizers did manage to mobilize significant contingents outside the São Paulo heartland, an important achievement, the overall results of the general strike proved even more disastrous than the one in December. Participation was minimal both in the city of São Paulo and in the adjacent ABC industrial region. Despite the failure of the general strike itself, the Brazilian economy continued to be plagued with massive sectoral stoppages, particularly in the public sector. By the end of 1987 the economy was out of control, the finance ministry had again changed hands, and rumors of an impending military coup persisted.

Obstacles to a Social Pact

Throughout this period, there was a widespread perception in Brazil that some form of a social pact would be advantageous. The press gave it extensive coverage during the first two and a half years of the Sarney government. A Gallup poll taken on May 3, 1987, asked respondents whether "the government should make entrepreneurs and workers enter into an accord to increase wages and prices by equal amounts." The answers were strikingly in favor of such an agreement, with 83 percent saying that it would be useful. Only 24 percent thought that it would be easy to obtain such an agreement, however, and 70 percent thought it would be difficult. Indeed, 33 percent of the respondents thought that such an accord would be impossible.[6] This poll expressed the dilemma in a nutshell: while a social pact might well be desirable, it would be difficult and perhaps impossible to organize.

Why was it so elusive? There are a number of factors to be considered. First, as we have seen, there was considerable resistance in union ranks to a social pact. The CUT's reluctance seems to have stemmed from two factors: its own history and its rivalry with the CGT. The CUT unions had come into being during a period of militant confrontation with the military government. Based in the metalworking unions, particularly the automobile industry in the ABC region, these new unions had sufficient muscle to take on the employers in a direct confrontation and win concessions, even with a government that was basically hostile to them. This "new" style of unionism contrasted markedly with the more usual type in Brazil, where union leaders would use their contacts with the government to elicit support for moderate demands. The CUT leaders were used to dealing directly with employers and, while not necessarily trusting them, were confident and aggressive in their dealings. The government, by contrast, was seen as a class enemy, which might intervene in the unions to weaken their leadership and break strikes.

The second factor making the CUT unfavorably disposed to an agreement with the government was its rivalry with the CGT. The relations between the two centrals have been complicated. They have engaged in joint actions (like the two general strikes), and there has been periodic talk of a merger of some kind, but each is engaged in an intense campaign to expand its influence at the expense of the other.

While the characteristics of Brazilian unions play some role in making a social pact difficult, a more important factor has been ineptness on the part of the government. One necessary condition for a social pact is that the government must offer something in exchange for union compliance. Nothing has been put on the table to induce the unions to participate in a social pact, which has been a major complaint of both the unions and the Minister of Labor. The discussions of a social pact do not seem to have been linked, for example, to reform of the labor law, also under continuous discussion during this period. And with the possible exception of the Cruzado Plan, the government has not proposed any economic package that would increase real wages.

A second precondition for a social pact is that there be a certain measure of trust

Figure 6.1
Strikes and Discussion of Social Pact in Brazil, 1985-87

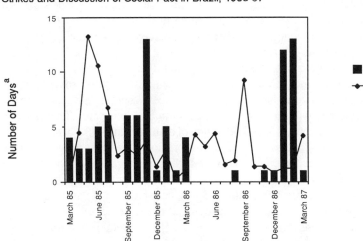

aStriker-days: Number of person-days per month lost to strikes (millions)
Social pact: Number of days per month pact discussed in local press

among the parties to the pact. In concrete terms, this amounts to whether the government is considered credible. There is a perception among union leaders that the government only calls for a social pact when it is in economic difficulty. The most frequent discussions of a social pact have been immediately following strike waves in mid-1985 and late 1986. There was no sustained discussion of the formation of a social pact during the period of the Cruzado Plan—precisely when the conditions for a pact were optimal. In Figure 6.1 it can clearly be seen that there is a two- to three-month time lag between the occurrence of a strike wave and increased intensity in discussion about a social pact.[7]

A Contradictory Policy?

This chapter began by asserting that a government faced with a strong and militant union movement had to co-opt that movement or seek to divide and weaken it. If it did neither, the unions would effectively destroy the government's ability to carry out a coherent economic program.[8] The irony of the Brazilian situation is that the Sarney government seems to have pursued both strategies simultaneously. On the one hand, the Ministry of Labor avoided interference in the unions and was in the forefront of attempts to articulate a social pact. On the other hand, the Presidency, the labor tribunals, the Minister of Justice, the military, and several other high-ranking government officials engaged in verbal and legal attacks on striking workers, laying much of the blame for political unrest on the CUT.

Simultaneous—though unwitting—pursuit of both strategies militated against the success of either. Almir Pazzianotto's renunciation of the right to intervene in unions meant that a powerful weapon was missing from the government's arsenal. Repression of the unions would be much more difficult. At the same time, the constant attacks on the unions, together with a perception that the government lacked seriousness in its call for a social pact (or that it wanted a social pact at the workers' expense), meant that the unions were not likely to cooperate.

There was nothing inevitable in this. A coherent policy by the government—along either strategy—would have stood some chance of success. With regard to the co-optation strategy, it was surely within the government's power to offer a *quid pro quo* to the unions in exchange for a moderation of demands and strike behavior. The irony of the Brazilian situation is that the basis for a social pact was provided by the Cruzado Plan. Of course, the effects on groups other than organized labor were also important. The Cruzado Plan was unlikely to succeed without some orthodox measures to reduce inflation being introduced at the same time. If these were not to reduce real wages, then the costs would have to be borne by other sectors of society. In any event, for reasons that are still the subject of considerable controversy, the Cruzado Plan collapsed and with it any realistic hope of a durable social pact.

Nonetheless, the government may well not face a serious challenge from the unions in the immediate future. By mid-1987 the Brazilian economy was rapidly heading into a serious recession. While labor grievances increased, the deterioration of the labor market weakened the unions' ability seriously to disrupt government policy, but the government was in no position to take advantage of labor's weakness. Obsessed with remaining in power and burdened by the reactionary inheritance of the military dictatorship, the Sarney government allowed programmatic content to disappear, losing whatever initiative it might initially have possessed.

The Labor Strategies of the Alfonsín Government in Argentina

When Raúl Alfonsín was elected in 1983, following the debacle of the Malvinas/Falklands War, he inherited an economy in crisis and a powerful and antagonistic labor movement identified with his political opponents, the Peronists. The internal politics of Argentine labor, however, have always been characterized by incessant factional fighting, reunifications, and new schisms. There is a basic division within the Peronist Confederación General de Trabajadores (CGT) between groups that seek some sort of accommodation with the government of the day, and those that try to use the industrial muscle of organized labor—in direct confrontation with the government if necessary—to achieve wage increases.[9] In the years following the 1983 election, the Peronist unions were severely fragmented, disoriented, and on the defensive. The most conciliatory faction was associated with Lorenzo Miguel and the "62 Organizations." The more militant wing was headed by Saúl Ubaldini, one of the main leaders of the street protests against the old military regime. By mid-January 1984 the two wings of the CGT had compromised on a transitory collective leadership.

In confronting this situation, Alfonsín tried at least three successive policies toward labor. He began with an attempt to undermine Peronist control over the unions through government intervention in union elections and an attempt at reforming the labor laws. When this failed he tried to organize a social pact, again without success. Alfonsín's third strategy, implicit in the Austral Plan, was basically an attempt to circumvent the unions. Finally, with the gradual collapse of the Austral Plan, government policy toward labor has become increasingly incoherent.

Attempts at Reform and Social Pact

During the initial phase, the Alfonsín government appears to have believed that with appropriate support and encouragement, non-Peronist elements within organized labor might mount a relatively successful challenge to the domination of the unions by Peronism. Nominating Aldo Mucci, a non-Peronist union leader, as his first Minister of Labor, Alfonsín began his attempt to displace the Peronist union oligarchs. One of the first government initiatives was an attempt to democratize Argentina's unions by proposing new regulations for internal elections. Behind this concern for union democracy was a belief that the power of the Peronist union bosses needed to be curbed, and that many workers would vote for more moderate union leaders.

Union reaction to the draft law for union reorganization was mixed. While most Peronists were opposed, some thirty leaders from the combative wing of Peronism and from the independent left supported it.[10] The new law was seen by dissident union currents as clearly beneficial to them. In March 1984, however, Peronists joined with other opposition politicians to defeat the union reorganization law in the Senate by a vote of 24 to 22. This marked the effective end of this first strategy of undermining the Peronists from within. In the Ministry of Labor, Mucci was replaced by J.M. Casella, and the stage was set for a new strategy of "*concertación*" (negotiating a social pact).

Early in May there was a closed meeting between the leadership of the CGT, the Ministers of Labor and Economics, and Bishop Bufano, a member of the bishops' social pastoral team. As an outcome of these talks, the government backed down on its proposals for amending union election procedures. Following this conciliatory move, the CGT appeared amenable to some form of *concertación*. Within a month, however, the CGT had hardened its position. One of its leaders, Jorge Triaca, asserted that "a general strike is inevitable unless there is an urgent rectification of economic and social policy... We know that what the country needs is a serious and responsible *concertación*."[11] Behind the series of proposals and counterproposals was a struggle between the government and the unions for control over the substantial funds generated by the unions for pensions, social benefits and vacations. The Alfonsín government wished to restrict the use of this financial power by the unions, but in the end the government had to admit defeat. The government and the unions came to an agreement on the administration of the unions' social and welfare programs, the *concertación* talks were resumed, and the strike plan was suspended. Nevertheless, the proposal for *concertación* continued to be a source of conflict and tension. By early July the unions were back on the offensive, demanding much higher government-decreed wage increases to offset inflation. Throughout this period, the CGT followed a policy of supporting *concertación*, while threatening to withdraw its support and call a general strike if government policy was unfavorable.

One effect of the fragmentation was to make any agreement between government and unions difficult to implement; there would always be some section of organized labor which would refuse to be bound by any agreement. By mid-1985, influential sectors within the government had come to the conclusion that the attempt at *concertación*, a largely symbolic operation, had failed. In this context, the government opted for the gamble of a heterodox stabilization policy.

The Austral Plan

The Austral Plan was announced in mid-June 1985. Prices were frozen and the wage increase of 22.6 percent agreed on for June was maintained, but thereafter wages would also be frozen. The effect on wages has been the subject of some debate.[12] Clearly, government workers bore the brunt of any deterioration in wages, whereas workers in the private sector may have benefited directly from the Austral Plan. In any event, the initial reaction of the CGT, which had not been consulted in advance, was divided. Lorenzo Miguel met with Alfonsín on June 26 and came away from the meeting saying that there was no alternative for the workers but to collaborate with the new policies.[13] On the other hand, most Argentine unionists were inclined to believe that real wages fell after the introduction of the Austral Plan, and the CGT officially demanded a 50 percent wage increase and measures to stop layoffs and dismissals.

By the beginning of 1986, as prices began to drift upward, the CGT began to mobilize a series of general protest strikes. Meanwhile, the major employers' confederations were also highly critical of the Austral Plan, urging a lowering of interest rates and an increase in credit. It thus looked as though an alliance of labor and employers versus the government might be shaping up. In February 1986, the government responded by resuming talks with the CGT over the possibility of a new wage policy based on an annual norm for wage increases and a maximum and minimum zone for such increases. During much of the rest of 1986, this resulted in a series of specific agreements with individual union federations. But significant sectors within the CGT continued to press for the dismantling of the Austral Plan and the dismissal of its most powerful backer, Finance Minister Juan V. Sourrouille.[14]

At the end of March 1987, a change in labor ministers improved considerably the prospects for a social pact. As a price for its collaboration, the CGT demanded a wage increase that would cover its losses since the beginning of the year. In the end, however, it was the employers who broke off negotiations. A number of clauses that would have greatly increased union power at the plant level (a certain amount of worker participation, opening "the books," and an increase in union delegates) were judged to be unacceptable.[15]

In July the government announced a further opening of Argentina to the international economy, provoking a hostile reaction from the CGT. Alfonsín replied in kind, accusing the CGT of adopting a "reactionary and anti-worker" position.[16] It was left to the Labor Minister to attempt to smooth over the troubled waters by noting that the President's remarks were "unfortunate." While the orthodox Peronists around Lorenzo Miguel were prepared to agree to a number of wage deals with the government, the renovationist current around Saúl Ubaldini was incensed by the continuing fall in real wages. One estimate suggested that real wages fell by nearly 23 percent during the first half of 1987.[17] Inflation began to rise again, and in October the government imposed an emergency wage-price freeze. After a lull in industrial action, the CGT returned to its strategy of general strikes in the second half of 1987. As 1988 began, the Alfonsín government had failed to bring inflation down to acceptable levels or to significantly reduce the power of the Peronist unions. For their part, the unions remained deeply divided and unable to adequately defend their members' interests.

The parallels with Brazil were striking. A combination of union divisions and government incompetence (or misfortune) had led to the possibility of the much-desired social pact being reduced to zero. As a result, neither government was able to establish the social foundations for an amelioration of escalating distributive conflicts. Here, however, the similarity ceased. In Argentina, the unions were linked with a political party that was a credible alternative government. This was not the case in Brazil, since the CUT was affiliated with the PT, which had no chance of becoming a governing party, and the CGT was loosely associated with the PMDB, already part of the governing coalition. The result was that the political costs of losing labor support in Brazil were not as immediate and direct as they were in Argentina.

Widespread dissatisfaction with the government's economic policy seems to have been a significant factor in the improved electoral performance of the Peronists in the local elections of September 1987, and further restricted the government's room for maneuver. In the absence of either political or economic solutions, Argentina remained locked in a familiar standoff. Whether this situation will continue depends to some extent on a number of factors not considered in this chapter, such as the long-run decline in the unionized sector of the Argentine economy,[18] a growing sense that it would be suicidal to repeat the conflicts of the past, the burgeoning importance of reformist forces among the Peronists, and an increasing conviction that the military must remain in the barracks. These trends clearly exist. The extent to which they will dominate the future will depend, at least in part, on a resumption of economic growth and on an abatement of the distributive zero-sum conflicts associated with inflation, which have had such deleterious effects on Argentine society in the past.

The PRI and Labor in Mexico

The debt crisis of 1982 was a severe shock to the Mexican economy. Among other effects, both employment and real wages fell dramatically. According to official ILO figures, average industrial wages dropped by 37.5 percent between May 1982 and November 1985. Over the same period industrial employment dropped from 597,000 to 522,000. At the end of 1987 prospects for a substantial reactivation of the Mexican economy were uncertain, and both analysts and political decision makers seemed to have few clear and agreed upon solutions to the crisis. Inflation continued at an unacceptably high rate, and capital flight remained a serious problem. With the de la Madrid administration about to come to its end, and with the U.S. presidential election in the offing, the political dimension of the crisis also loomed large.

The Historic Social Pact

Mexico is strikingly different from both Argentina and Brazil in that for most of its recent history a form of permanent social pact has been in operation. Since World War II, organized labor in Mexico has acted as one of the principal pillars—if not *the* principal pillar—of the regime. On the one hand, it has provided the regime with a substantial political clientele. In terms of sheer numbers, this has been less important than the role of peasant organizations, but it has not been insignificant. On the other hand, organized labor has behaved in a way that made the Mexican "miracle" possible. By allowing wages to rise in line with, or slightly below, the rate of productivity increase, the official unions removed a major source of cost-push inflation from the system. The impressive growth of the Mexican economy during most of the postwar period enabled both profits and wages to increase steadily. This favorable economic setting was further enhanced by a low incidence of industrial conflict, which helped create a propitious climate for foreign investment.

One reason for the relative absence of overt industrial conflict in Mexico during the "miracle" period was the combination of oligarchic union leadership unresponsive to the rank and file, and the co-optation of the top union leadership into the ranks of the ruling Partido Revolucionario Institucional (PRI). Mexican union confederations formed part of the corporatist structure of the PRI, and many labor leaders were rewarded with legislative seats and a variety of other perquisites. Foremost among Mexican union confederations, the Confederación de Trabajadores de México (CTM) enjoyed a reputation for unconditionally supporting the government. For many analysts, these captive unions acted to restrain wage demands by means of coercion and corruption.[19] The absence of any meaningful union democracy, together with the intervention of the state in the selection of union leaders, meant that the rank and file were in no position to exert pressure on employers for substantial wage increases.

Although the Mexican political system had as one of its focal points a form of corporatist social pact, the 1970s saw the development of a "new unionism," with an increasing number of militant union movements breaking away from direct state tutelage. At the end of the decade, some observers saw this as the beginning of a breakdown in the historic social pact. In a sense this happened. The social pact did suffer serious erosion in the next decade, but it did so in a totally unforeseen fashion.

The Response to the Debt Crisis

Unlike Argentina and Brazil, Mexico adopted a totally orthodox approach to the debt problem after the 1982 collapse. It consistently maintained the stance of a "good debtor," accepting IMF recommendations on stabilization measures and meeting its debt payments. This was in marked contrast to the more aggressive stance on debt payments in Brazil and Argentina, and the willingness of both of those countries to experiment with heterodox policy measures. By maintaining a posture of complete orthodoxy, the Mexican government severely restricted its room for maneuver.

To a large extent, the Mexican political system could weather the discontent generated by these stabilization measures because it confronted neither democratic pressures nor a serious prospect of military intervention. Whereas the governments of Raúl Alfonsín and José Sarney had to look both to their electoral popularity and restive military establishments, Mexican President Miguel de la Madrid had only minor worries on these scores. He could not entirely neglect popular discontent (particularly after the emergence of the Democratic Current within the PRI led by Cuauhtémoc Cárdenas), and the possibility of a military intervention could never be completely ruled out. Nevertheless, compared with the situation in Argentina and Brazil, these were problems of a quite different order.

As a result, de la Madrid took a tough stance vis-à-vis organized labor. The historic social pact was abandoned in favor of a two-pronged strategy. Since real wages had fallen massively, union leaders could no longer claim to be "delivering the goods," and there was little point in continuing to seek labor support. Changed labor market conditions would suffice to discipline the working class. This was the first element of the de la Madrid strategy. The second was to distance the regime from the CTM and lend support to its rival confederations, in particular the CROC and the CROM.

The economic crisis also created the conditions for a widespread managerial push for increased productivity in both the private and the public sectors. In part this meant the closure of inefficient plants and relocation of production to newer establishments, particularly in the north and along the border. It also meant a rollback of union gains in terms of working practices. In the 1970s, the more militant unions had achieved a considerable measure of control over hiring and firing, the operation of internal labor markets, and working conditions and line speeds. Some unions had managed to unionize lower level supervisory staff. Managerial attacks on such practices seem to have been thoroughly under way by 1986.[20]

The de la Madrid administration made a major commitment to increasing efficiency in the state sector. Initially, the government made a serious effort to rationalize PEMEX, the strategic state oil company, which automatically brought the government into conflict with the powerful petroleum workers' union. Despite considerable overstaffing in the industry, the government made little progress in its efforts to break the power of the union. It then turned to the steel industry and closed a major plant, Fundidora Monterrey, which resulted in a direct and indirect loss of 15,000 jobs.

The extent of industrial reorganization in the private sector has also been dramatic. Between 25,000 and 40,000 workers in the automobile industry have been laid off. Massive layoffs have been accompanied by major technological change and dramatic increases in productivity. The Ford plant installed just outside Mexico City in the early 1970s produced 80 engines per worker; the new Ford plant in Chihuahua produced 333 engines per worker. After the earthquake, modernization of the Mexican telephone system was accelerated. In 1976, 22,000 workers operated a system of three million telephones; by 1986 40,000 workers were operating a system of seven million telephones.[21]

Wage Policy and Inter-Union Rivalry

The de la Madrid term has been marked from the beginning by tensions between the CTM and the President. In the presidential succession of 1982, the CTM had opposed the candidacy of Miguel de la Madrid, and the initial period of his administration was marked by a certain verbal distancing between the government and the CTM. Nevertheless, the confederation was initially willing to support the government's efforts to deal with the economic crisis.

The CTM proposed a wage-price freeze, but this was rejected by the government. President de la Madrid declared, "I will not allow myself to be pressured by old styles of negotiation and claims to power."[22] The CTM was to be punished for its failure to support de la Madrid, and its power was to be reduced. Minister of Labor Arsenio Farrell announced that the CROC "was destined to be the vanguard of the proletariat in Mexico . . . the great workers' organization." Both the CROC and to a lesser extent the CROM were given official support, and a number of unions switched to these confederations.[23] Relations between the CTM and the government deteriorated.

Immediately after the onset of the 1982 crisis, the CTM continued its traditional dual policy of offering support for the government's economic policies and engaging in mass strikes in support of wage increases. In June 1983, unions affiliated with the CTM struck for a 50 percent wage increase. Some three thousand strikes were registered in the second week of June. The militant unions of university workers and nuclear industry workers went out on strike at the same time, while other official union confederations, the CROC and the CROM, remained aloof. The CTM unions reached a series of accords with their respective employers, but the university and nuclear workers met with an intransigent response from the government and were forced to return to work without a settlement. Clearly the government had taken the opportunity to weaken the more militant and independent unions. Later, the CTM switched tactics and proposed the creation of more worker-owned enterprises and a series of measures to strengthen the social sector of the economy. In July 1986, the PRI unionists proposed a reorientation of economic policy based on wage increases and a reactivation of the internal market. Payment of the foreign debt would take second place to domestic necessities. These proposals were rejected out of hand.

The leadership crisis in the CTM, simmering for some years, was exacerbated by the economic problems, and tensions between the CTM and the other union confederations increased. Relations between the CTM's Fidel Velázquez and the petroleum workers' boss deteriorated considerably. There have been incidents of union gangsterism in the northern industrial zone of Mexico City as rival groups dispute control of the labor force.[24]

Within the ranks of PRI labor, the more militant unions attempted to take on the government and failed. The attempted strike by the electricity workers' union in March 1987 and by the telephone workers in April were both decisively defeated when the government used legal powers to requisition the parastatals. Across the board, trade unions have emerged defeated in their confrontations with employers and the government.

Efforts at broadening the struggle have met with only partial success. A number of coordinating organizations have been formed, within the union sector as well as in the peasant and popular residential sectors. The Coordinadora Nacional del Movimiento Urbano Popular (CONAMUP) organized a relatively successful demonstration in October 1983, and there have been a variety of actions since. The potential of such organizations, however, is by no means clear. A more serious challenge to existing government policy was that mounted within the PRI by the Democratic Current. Picking up the reformist and nationalist traditions within the PRI, the Democratic Current came out as an open faction in 1986, but was met with massive hostility by the mainstream political bureaucracy. By the beginning of 1988, this led a number of activists, headed by Cuauhtémoc Cárdenas, to split from the PRI and mount an opposition challenge in the presidential election. [25]

Managing Without a Social Pact?

One of the striking features of the de la Madrid administration and its approach to the debt crisis was the way it displaced the CTM from the center of the political system and deemphasized the importance of negotiation with organized labor as a central element in Mexico's political economy. By all accounts Mexico's next President, Carlos Salinas de Gortari, looked as if he would continue in the orthodox conservative path laid down by Miguel de la Madrid. Nevertheless, Mexico's political system has often shown a capacity to produce sudden and dramatic policy shifts.

There are, in fact, good reasons why the costs of marginalizing the CTM may be seen as unacceptably high. All relatively developed industrial economies display tendencies towards institutionalized bargaining with labor, and the Mexican economy is no exception in this regard. As two of the most astute observers of contemporary Mexican labor argue, ". . . it is quite probable that these differences will continue to be aired with greater or lesser belligerence, but always under the umbrella of what we have called the historic alliance. It doesn't seem to us that we are on the verge of any spectacular rupture."[26] There have been other moments when the historic alliance of organized labor and the state appeared on the verge of collapse, but it would be risky to project on that basis that no change will occur now.

There are also purely political reasons for the PRI to be concerned about the good will of organized labor. While Mexico can hardly claim to be a democracy, it would be naive in the extreme to underestimate the government's concern about political support. The high and increasing electoral abstentionism must seriously erode the regime's claim to legitimacy and render its response to the growing challenge of the right and the left increasingly problematic. The loss of the urban working class vote would be a serious political blow to the PRI. Combined with the sort of internal challenge represented by the Democratic Current, these considerations may push the PRI once more in the direction of inclusionary corporatism. Given its present policies, however, it is far from clear what the government can offer organized labor in exchange for electoral support, since the previous *raison d'être* of this alliance may now be absent.

Conclusion

By reason of its magnitude, the debt crisis of the 1980s is likely to produce significant changes in the forms of working class organization and the systems of national industrial relations in many Latin American countries. These will have a variety of direct and indirect effects on the stability of the political system and on prospects for the maintenance and extension of democracy. As a brief look at the three large industrial economies of Argentina, Brazil and Mexico indicates, these effects are likely to vary from country to country, depending on government policy and the historical alignments of organized labor.

Governments have tried a variety of policies toward labor. In Argentina and Brazil, these have oscillated between attempting to organize some form of social pact and adopting a policy of divide and rule. In Mexico, the trend seems to have been more in the opposite direction, from a reliance on a social pact to an attempt to use the labor market to discipline the unions. In all cases, except possibly during brief periods when heterodox policies appeared to be working, governments have had little success in their efforts. Overall, what characterizes labor policy in all three countries is a painful form of "muddling through." Buffeted by the gales of the debt crisis, and beset by declining popularity and a truculent military, both the Argentine and Brazilian governments appeared at the end of 1987 to be lapsing into political stagnation. Despite much greater control over the political system, the PRI had also come under severe strain, and its ability to manage Mexico's political system (much less to respond positively to growing demands for moves in the direction of a more open political system) appeared increasingly problematic.

At the same time, and largely as a result of deteriorating economic conditions, organized labor in these countries has been on the defensive. It has been deeply divided over what strategy to pursue and has switched rapidly from one strategy to another as circumstances changed, and as one or another tendency within the labor movement gained temporary ascendancy.

Overall, the picture has hardly been an edifying one. Under the impact of the debt crisis, the ability of political actors in Latin America to resolve conflicts over growth and distribution has sharply deteriorated. The result—particularly in Argentina and Brazil—has been an increase in conflict over wages, employment and inflation, an upsurge in working class mobilization, and widespread bitterness and disillusionment. This does not bode well for the future of democracy.

Notes

1. Sarney had a popularity rating of between 35 and 45 percent in opinion polls published regularly in the *Folha de São Paulo*.

2. José Marcio Rego, *Inflação inercial, teorias sobre inflação e o plano cruzado* (Rio de Janeiro: Paz e Terra, 1986).

3. *Folha de São Paulo*, December 12, 1987.

4. Ibid., January 6, 1987.

5. Ibid., January 10, 1987.

6. It should be kept in mind that this poll was taken after the failure of the Cruzado Plan. There was still considerable support for a new price freeze. A DataFolha poll on April 26, 1987, asked whether respondents "would approve a new freeze on prices and incomes." Just over a quarter (27 percent) were opposed. A third (35 percent) were in favor, and another 34 percent were in favor of a price freeze without a corresponding income freeze. A month later a DataFolha poll found 56 percent in favor of a price freeze and 34 percent opposed. *Folha de São Paulo*, May 3 and April 26, 1987.

7. I have used a very crude measure of discussion of social pact: I have simply counted the number of days per month on which there was some report dealing with a social pact in the newspapers. Clearly, more sophisticated measures would be desirable, although it remains to be seen whether the results would be substantially different.

8. It is obviously a matter of judgment as to how strong the Brazilian union movement was at the beginning of the Sarney government; the position taken here is that it was sufficiently strong to pose a serious threat to the government's economic policy.

9. The two wings of Argentine unionism roughly parallel the division between the CGT and the CUT in Brazil.

10. *El Bimestre Político y Económico*, no. 12 (November-December 1983).

11. *El Bimestre Político y Económico*, no. 15 (May-June 1984).

12. Roberto Frenkel, "Heterodox Theory and Policy: The Plan Austral in Argentina," *Journal of Development Economics* 27, nos. 1-2 (October 1987).

13. *El Bimestre Político y Económico*, no. 21 (May-June 1985).

14. *El Bimestre Político y Económico*, no. 25 (January-February 1986).

15. *El Bimestre Político y Económico*, no. 32 (March-April 1987).

16. *El Bimestre Político y Económico*, no. 34 (July-August 1987).

17. *Financial Times*, October 23, 1987.

18. Peter Ranis, "The Dilemmas of Democracy in Argentina," *Current History* (January 1986): 32.

19. For a discussion and critique of this view of Mexican unionism, see Ian Roxborough, *Unions and Politics in Mexico* (Cambridge: Cambridge University Press, 1984).

20. *Proceso*, March 10, 1986.

21. *Proceso*, April 6, 1987; E. de la Garza Toledo et al., "Crisis y reestructuración productiva en México" (typescript, 1986).

22. Quoted in R.A. Garavito Elías, "El sindicalismo oficial ante la crisis actual," in CLACSO, *El sindicalismo latinoamericano en los ochenta* (Santiago: CLACSO, 1985), 161.

23. *Proceso*, December 22, 1986 and February 2, 1987.

24. *Proceso*, December 29, 1986, May 25, 1987 and May 11, 1987; R. Trejo and J. Woldenberg, "Sindicatos y proyecto nacional en la crisis de hoy," in *México: presente y futuro*, ed. J. Alcocer (Mexico City: Ediciones de Cultura Popular, 1985).

25. At the end of December 1987, the press reported that the Mexican government might be about to introduce a heterodox shock policy. This speculation came in view of accelerating inflation and a threatened general strike. The government began with a devaluation of the peso, and allowed prices of gasoline, electricity, telephone calls, sugar and fertilizers to rise by 79 percent. It then announced an "economic solidarity pact," involving wage increases of some 35 percent and a promise to index both wages and prices. Although the government claimed that the indexation would be "temporary and unexceptional," in early 1988 it was unclear what would happen. At all events, these announcements hinted at a possible revival of a social pact approach to labor and possible sweeping policy changes. (See *New York Times*, December 16 and 22, 1987.)

26. Trejo and Woldenberg, "Sindicatos y proyecto nacional."

Suggestions for Further Reading

Epstein, Edward. "Trade Unions and Austerity." In *Austerity Policies in Latin America*, ed. William Canak. Boulder, CO: Westview Press, 1988.

Flynn, Peter. "Brazil: The Politics of the Cruzado Plan." *Third World Quarterly*, October 1986.

Manzetti, Luigi, and Marco Dell'Aquila. "Economic Stabilization in Argentina: The Austral Plan." *Journal of Latin American Studies* 20 (May 1988).

Monteón, Michael. "Can Argentina's Democracy Survive Economic Disaster?" In *From Military Rule to Liberal Democracy in Argentina*, ed. Monica Peralta-Ramos and Carlos Waisman. Boulder, CO: Westview Press, 1987.

Phillip, George, ed. *The Mexican Economy*. London: Croom Helm, 1988.

PART III

Case Studies of Debt and Democracy

7

Economic Orthodoxy and Political Change in Mexico: The Stabilization and Adjustment Policies of the de la Madrid Administration

Robert R. Kaufman

Ever since the 1940s, the stability of the Mexican political system has rested on a synthesis of two seemingly contradictory historical legacies. One of these, an outgrowth of the civil war and social reforms of the period between 1910 and 1940, has been the capacity of the Partido Revolucionario Institucional (PRI) and allied sectoral organizations to dominate the electoral arena and mediate class relations. For over sixty years, the legitimation provided by the dominant party allowed the governmental elite to combine highly concentrated executive authority with considerable tolerance for public debate and political dissent. The second legacy, originating at the end of the turbulent 1930s, derives from attempts by successive presidential administrations to curb reformist impulses, establish collaborative ties with the emerging private sector, and build a cooperative relationship with the United States. Throughout the post-World War II era, this provided the foundation for the material base of the system—an expanding economy that generated both patronage resources for the regime's popular base and extraordinary profits for strategically placed private sector groups.

The political system that emerged from these historical experiences, with its complex mixture of authoritarian and democratic features, provides a unique setting for an examination of the relationship between political regimes and economic adjustment during the 1980s. On the one hand, compared to the new, still fragile democracies discussed elsewhere in this volume, policy makers in Mexico were highly insulated from short-term popular pressures by the control of the apparatus of the ruling party and the executive bureaucracy. During the presidential term of Miguel de la Madrid (1982-88), this insulation permitted conservative technocrats to implement a collaborative approach toward external creditors and comparatively orthodox economic policies at home. At the same time, because of the PRI's hegemony within the system, Mexican authorities were able to impose such policies without recourse to the kind of exclusionary repression characteristic of, say, the military-backed Pinochet regime in Chile.

Nevertheless, the unprecedented economic and political challenges of the 1980s have posed major threats to the historic capacity of the Mexican system to manage social conflict. Under de la Madrid's tough austerity program, living standards deteriorated more severely than at any time since the Great Depression of the 1930s. This was a dangerous situation for a regime that relied heavily on material rewards to sustain its popular support. And although levels of social protest remained remarkably low for most of de la Madrid's term, the political costs of his economic adjustment strategy became highly visible during the presidential transition of 1988. Even according to the official vote count, approximately half the electorate voted for the candidates opposing Carlos Salinas of the PRI— the first time the ruling party had ever won less than 70 percent of the vote. If the PRI's overwhelming political hegemony has ended, we will see major political changes in the next decade, either toward a much more open political regime or a more repressive one.

In this chapter, we focus on the economic policy choices leading up to this point, and on the political forces that shaped them. Whatever the wisdom of the economic course followed under de la Madrid, it was one that many other governments in the region had attempted to evade. What impelled the Mexican regime to run such high political risks? The first section sketches the political and economic struggles of earlier decades—particularly the way the reformist policies of the 1970s altered the political balances established during Mexico's long era of "stabilizing development" (roughly from the early 1950s to the late 1960s). In the next two sections, we first describe the main policy changes implemented under de la Madrid and then discuss some conflicting interpretations of the political relations underlying them. In the conclusion, finally, we offer some brief reflections on the long-term effects of these policies on the political system.

Background: The Stabilizing Development Model and the Reforms of the 1970s

We turn first to the rise and demise of the stabilizing development era of the 1950s and 1960s. As in most other large Latin American countries during those decades, the Mexican government relied on state-stimulated import substitution to drive economic expansion. To implement this strategy, however, governmental authorities relied heavily on relatively orthodox technocrats within the powerful Central Bank and Treasury Department. These, in turn, placed special emphasis on conservative exchange and interest rate policies aimed at attracting external financing, mobilizing domestic savings, and allocating credit toward priority public and private investments. Neglect of the rural poor and growing disparities in income were important components of this controversial model.[1] Nevertheless, within the expanding world economy of the early post-war era, these policies facilitated one of the highest rates of industrial growth in the region and, compared to other import-substituting economies, one of the lowest rates of domestic inflation.

Although a full discussion of this period is well beyond the scope of this paper, the underlying political balances reflected by these policies constitute an essential point of departure for understanding the unique synthesis discussed in the introduction, and the way this began to change in the 1970s and 1980s.[2] For our purposes, four sets of tacit "understandings" were particularly important:

1. Macroeconomic policy authority would be concentrated in the hands of technocrats in the Central Bank and the Treasury. In the aftermath of the civil wars of the 1910s, these institutions had been established as pivotal components of the state apparatus, with strong traditions of financial orthodoxy. Their mission in the 1950s and 1960s was to insure a suitable investment climate for both domestic and foreign business interests.

2. In exchange, business groups—especially the conservative northern interests that had frequently opposed pre-1940 reform initiatives—would sustain a relatively low profile in national political life, relying on informal contacts and formal consultations conducted through officially-recognized associational groups for political access.

3. The heads of the Confederación de Trabajadores Mexicanos (CTM) and other allied groups of unionized workers, the key base of organized support for the PRI, would be provided with an expanding material resource base to distribute to their members. Real wage levels, which had deteriorated badly in the 1940s, began to rise by the mid-1950s and continued to do so until the end of the 1970s.

4. The government would deal with resource constraints by shifting spending priorities and attention away from social services and distributive activities aimed at the PRI's traditional peasant constituency, linked to the Confederación Nacional de Campesinos (CNC), and at the unorganized underclasses within the Mexican population.

From the perspective of much of the Mexican elite, interested in the stability of the system as a whole, such trade-offs must have appeared well worth making. By the end of the 1960s, however, there were growing signs that at least some significant changes in the strategy were unavoidable. In the first place, the rapid growth of preceding decades had itself generated accumulating infrastructural and capital goods bottlenecks that required urgent attention if expansion was to be maintained in the future. At about the same time, the system began to encounter signs of deteriorating political legitimacy: bitter student protests, a sharp decline in electoral turnout, and, perhaps most threatening, an upsurge in rural land seizures and guerrilla activity.

For Mexican elites, these developments indicated quite strongly that significant changes in the prevailing political and economic model were unavoidable. The turn in more reformist directions—the dominant trend under both the flamboyant Luis Echeverría and the more moderate José López Portillo—can be understood primarily as an attempt to address these issues from above. Among the most significant reforms undertaken during this period were an acceleration of the land reform in the early 1970s; increased investment in health and education; greater latitude for independent unions not directly linked to the CTM; a shift to the left in foreign policy; and a reform of the electoral system aimed at providing greater representation for opposition parties of the left and right.

Notwithstanding bitter controversies that flared up at various points in the 1970s, these reformist efforts were at least partially successful in accomplishing their purpose. Without jeopardizing the essential structures of PRI domination, the political spaces opened under Echeverría and López Portillo helped to deflect or co-opt more radical pressures on the system, but these achievements came at the cost of upsetting the arrangements that had contributed to the stability of the earlier period. For our purposes, three developments are particularly relevant to the crisis of the 1980s.

Fiscal Pressures Associated with Growth of the State Enterprise Sector

Although public investment grew steadily throughout the stabilizing development period, a new "shared development" strategy announced under Echeverría in the early 1970s marked an important shift in emphasis on the state's role in the accumulation process, inaugurating a trend that continued throughout the decade. The overall level of public expenditure, comparatively low in 1970, became one of the highest in the region by 1982. The state's share of all fixed capital formation, about one third in the 1950s and 40 percent in the 1960s, had risen to over 50 percent by the early 1980s, with particular emphasis on petroleum, electricity and steel.[3]

The revenue side of this equation, however, constituted a serious weakness for the model as a whole. Initiatives to increase Mexico's low tax rates, an important component of the earlier stabilizing development model, were blocked under Echeverría by strong behind-the-scenes pressure from business elites. Thus, continued high rates of expansion were increasingly accompanied by resurgent inflation and growing fiscal and external accounts deficits, which were in turn covered by a ballooning of the foreign debt. In 1975-76, a speculative run on the peso triggered a major economic crisis, forcing the outgoing Echeverría administration into an International Monetary Fund (IMF) stabilization agreement and Mexico's first devaluation since 1954. Although the onset of the oil boom in 1978 rather quickly dissolved the immediate crisis, the underlying structural problems were essentially the same as those contributing to the post-1982 collapse.

Decline in the Influence of Central Bank and Treasury Technocrats

The onset of the Echeverría period also brought a major shift in the correlation of factional forces within the state apparatus and the PRI leadership. Although Bank and Treasury officials remained extremely powerful players in the policy process, under both Echeverría and López Portillo they lost the hegemony they had previously exercised. Conversely, structuralist and neo-Keynesian economists, who played a major role in shaping the shared development doctrines of the early

1970s, continued to have a significant policy-making influence until the advent of de la Madrid. Bank and Treasury influence was also diminished by the emergence of new bureaucratic centers of power in the cabinet and within the state enterprise sector. One of the most important of such developments was the formation in 1977 of the Secretaría de Programación y Presupuesto (SPP), a new superministry with responsibilities for investment planning and public expenditures.[4] Although conservative technocrats often controlled this agency, it nevertheless tended to tilt in more expansionist directions than the Bank and the Treasury, and on occasion it provided an important foothold for economists with less orthodox perspectives.

Breakdown of the Social Contract with Business

Finally, as an important corollary of the developments just described, major new uncertainties were introduced into the relations between the state and large business groups that had grown increasingly powerful during previous decades.[5] To be sure, the private sector was itself deeply divided over such issues as trade policy and foreign investment, and reactions to specific government initiatives were far from monolithic. Many industrialists profited substantially, for example, from the subsidized inputs and lucrative contracts provided by the expanding state enterprise sector. But business interests in general were uneasy about the new populist directions assumed by the governments of the 1970s, particularly at a moment when the decline of the Bank and Treasury technocrats seemed to be reducing their most important point of access. The central tendency among these groups was thus to expand their political and organizational resources in ways that would reduce their dependence on the good will of governmental authorities.

Special note must be taken at this point of the role played by powerful industrial-financial elites based along the northern border with the United States. With economic and political antecedents that predated the 1910 Revolution, this group stood out as the most orthodox and politically active component of the private sector, more extensively linked than most other Mexican business groups to U.S. capital and export markets and in a reasonably good position to profit from the liberalization of trade and capital flows. Particularly after the mid-1970s, they also provided the cutting edge to business demands for greater political power, spearheading publicity campaigns, sponsoring the formation of a major new peak association (the Consejo Coordinador Empresarial, or CCE), and providing increasing financial backing for the right-wing Partido Acción Nacional (PAN) opposition party.

Confrontations between these hardline groups and the government fluctuated considerably under Echeverría and López Portillo. They reached a high point during Echeverría's land reform in the mid-1970s, then subsided for most of López Portillo's term, and resurged after the 1982 decision to nationalize the private banking sector. Even during the quiet periods, however, it was clear that there would be no return to the norms of the stabilizing development era. By the onset of the

1980s, the state-business relationship had become irreversibly politicized.

The Crisis of the 1980s

Toward the end of 1980, a sharp rise in U.S. interest rates and a decline in the price of Mexican oil exports marked the onset of developments that eventually led to the crisis of 1982. For our purposes, it is not necessary to weigh precisely the relative importance of external and internal causes; clearly, both were important. The tightening of U.S. monetary policy—the most immediate source of Mexico's debt-service squeeze—was obviously well beyond the control of the Mexican government, as was the subsequent evolution of U.S. trade, fiscal and monetary policies. But Mexican fiscal and trade policies compounded the vulnerability of the system to such shocks, particularly after oil prices began to slump in 1980-81. In an attempt to sustain the expansion of the late 1970s, the government stepped up external borrowing activity, relying on expanding the volume of short-term credits to finance the growing fiscal and trade deficits, and allowing the peso to become increasingly overvalued.

In 1982, speculative pressures on the peso intensified, and the government began to engage in increasingly desperate efforts to stem the outflow of capital. In February, the Central Bank allowed the dollar price of the peso to double in an attempt to halt foreign exchange speculation. Next came the establishment of a two-tier exchange market that instituted a fixed peso/dollar rate for priority transactions, but an unregulated rate for all others. When such measures proved ineffective, the crisis broke into the open. In August, the government fired the shot heard round the world, announcing that it could not meet interest payments due within the next few days, and initiating negotiations for bridge loans and rescheduling agreements with the U.S. Treasury, the IMF, and the private commercial banks. In September, during the final months of the presidential transition period, continued speculation against the peso triggered the controversial decision to nationalize the domestic banking system, which evoked another sharp wave of private sector protest. The year ended, finally, with the conclusion of an IMF agreement in November and the inauguration of de la Madrid in December. By early 1983, with the negotiation of a $10 billion "rescue package" from the private banks, the immediate sense of emergency at last began to subside, and the stage was set for the new administration to confront the more enduring problems of stabilization and adjustment.

Economic Adjustment Strategies under de la Madrid

The inauguration of the de la Madrid administration marked a significant change in the balance of forces within the governmental elite: a strong political resurgence of the technocratic factions associated with the Treasury and the Central Bank, a sharply diminished role for *políticos* connected with the PRI and the labor movement, and the virtual elimination of structuralist and neo-Keynesian economists from top levels of government. Holding an M.A. from Harvard, de la Madrid had based his own career in the Treasury/Bank network, as had 13 of his 18 initial cabinet appointees and a large number of undersecretaries and governors.[6] The most important of these were the men who filled the three main command centers of the economic bureaucracy, all powerful figures with strong commitments to economic orthodoxy. The Treasury position went to Jesús Silva Herzog, a Yale Ph.D. in economics, initially appointed during the last months of the López Portillo administration. Miguel Mancera, another prominent orthodox economist, was reappointed as head of the Central Bank, after having resigned in protest over the nationalization decree. Finally, Carlos Salinas, whose background had also been in the Treasury, was appointed as head of the SPP.

Since the politics of the presidential succession were, as is customary, shrouded in secrecy, we can only speculate about the calculations that produced this transfer of power. Nevertheless, it seems clear that the designation of de la Madrid as president, announced as economic pressures began to intensify in late 1981, already reflected a shift of elite priorities toward an emphasis on economic liberalization and private investment. By 1982, as the crisis deepened and the broader decision-making team was assembled, it was also clear that the new administration had come to office prepared to institute tough austerity measures and committed to an agenda of far-reaching economic restructuring. The recovery strategy elaborated in the course of the presidential transition envisioned a two-step process. The first, to be completed in 1983, was to impose an orthodox IMF-backed package aimed at reducing inflation and realigning the exchange rate. This, it was hoped, would quickly establish conditions for an orderly rescheduling of the debt and a rapid reopening of access to international credit markets. The second step was to lower trade barriers, diversify exports, and reduce the scope of the public enterprise sector, measures that were expected to produce a significant resumption of growth by 1984 or 1985.[7]

The actual course of economic events fell substantially short of initial hopes and expectations. Mexico's austerity program of 1983 did eliminate the massive trade deficit, but at the cost of a precipitous decline in imports and a crushing domestic recession. Moreover, although these measures won praise from international bankers, there was no resumption of voluntary private lending. And by 1986-87, after a very brief recovery, the Mexican economy had again entered a new round of crises, characterized by inflation, recession, and severe balance-of-payments pressure.

Although these disappointments forced some adjustments in the government's policy and diagnostic assumptions, the de la Madrid administration continued to follow a course that was more or less consistent with its original project. We shall deal with some of the implications of this persistence in the last section of this chapter. First, however, we must review some of the principal policy developments with respect to stabilization, the liberalization of trade and investment, and external financing.

Stabilization Policies

Efforts to reduce inflation and balance-of-payments deficits went through several specific phases:

1. Until the middle of 1984, the administration stayed very close to the goals of the IMF agreement signed at the end of 1982. This featured highly restrictive fiscal and monetary policies and a substantial lag of wages behind inflation.

2. Between mid-1984 and the northern municipal and gubernatorial elections of July 1985, fiscal and monetary controls were relaxed somewhat and the economy experienced a slight recovery. Concern over the growing fiscal deficit, however, prompted the IMF to announce in September 1985 that it would suspend disbursement of the last installment of the loan signed in late 1982.

3. From mid-1985 to mid-1986, as oil prices collapsed, external accounts deficits widened and the administration again reimposed an austerity package, relying on a highly restrictive interest rate policy that virtually froze new credit to the private sector. During this twelve-month period, the Mexican economy reentered a period of contraction and inflation, comparable in severity to that experienced in 1982-83.

4. Finally, in late 1986, after wresting some important concessions in new agreements with the IMF and the private banks, the government began an attempt to ease the economy out of recession with a cautious relaxation of credit to the private sector. Again, however, the recovery was fragile and was quickly wiped out after the U.S. stock market crash of October 1987.

Table 7.1 depicts the principal macroeconomic trends of the period as a whole. Although there were some bright spots not depicted in the data (for example, a substantial upsurge in non-traditional exports), the overall picture was of economic stagnation and unrelieved deterioration in wage levels. Meanwhile, the inflation rate, which had dipped only slightly during the years of greatest fiscal orthodoxy (1983-84), began to surge again during the recession years of 1985 and 1986, and climbed even more in 1987.

What had gone wrong? A key issue of debate regarding efforts to stabilize prices and reactivate the economy was the apparently technical question of how to measure and assess the size of the fiscal deficit. As measured in conventional terms, it had begun to grow again from a comparatively acceptable 6 percent of GDP in 1984 to over 18 percent by 1987. On the one hand, most orthodox economists argued that the inability to contain the widening budget gap accounted both for the high interest rates that inhibited private investment and for the continuing problems of inflation. Most Mexican officials, on the other hand, argued that the deficits were being driven up by the high nominal interest rates required to place government bonds in private financial markets. That is, they said that the deficit was a reflection, rather than a cause, of inertial inflationary pressures. When nominal interest charges were deleted from the calculations, they argued, "operating" budget figures actually showed a slight surplus in 1985 and only a modest deficit in 1986. Finally, they suggested that external debt service obligations had also placed a major strain on

Table 7.1
Mexican Economic Performance Indicators, 1981-87

	1981	1982	1983	1984	1985	1986	1987
GDP Growth Rate (%)	8.0	-0.6	-4.2	3.6	2.6	-4.0	1.0
Consumer Prices (%)	28.7	98.8	80.8	59.2	63.7	105.7	143.6
Urban Minimum Wage (1980=100)	101.9	92.7	76.6	72.3	71.1	64.9	55.9
Interest Payments on External Debt (% of exports)	29.0	47.2	37.5	39.0	36.0	37.9	27.9
Fiscal Deficit[a] (% of GDP)	14.8	17.7	8.9	8.7	10.0	16.3	n.a.
Current Account ($ billion)	-12.5	-6.2	5.3	4.2	1.2	-1.3	n.a.
Gross Fixed Capital Formation (% of GDP)	25.7	22.3	17.3	18.0	n.a.	n.a.	n.a.
Private	14.5	12.4	10.1	10.9			
Public	11.2	9.9	7.2	7.1			

[a]Financial deficit
Sources: U.N. Economic Commission for Latin America and the Caribbean (ECLAC), *Preliminary Overview of the Latin American Economy, 1987*, and Eduard F. Buffie and Alan Sangines Krauss, "Economic Policy and Foreign Debt in Mexico," in *Developing Country Debt,* ed. Jeffrey Sachs (Washington, DC: National Bureau of Economic Research Conference Report, 1987).

public revenues, which implied that effective deficit reduction would have to be tied to significant debt relief.

Public controversy over this issue reached a particularly acrimonious level during the crisis of 1985-86. The 1985 IMF decision to suspend the payment on its previous Extended Fund Facility (EFF) agreement, announced on the very day a major earthquake devastated large portions of downtown Mexico City, set into motion a bitter round of negotiations that lasted for most of the next year. Although the debate subsided somewhat after a new IMF agreement in 1986—one that reflected an easing of the Fund's previous position—the "fiscal question" continued to be the major issue of stabilization policy during the last part of the de la Madrid term.

Despite strong political pressure to pump up the domestic economy, it should be emphasized that the administration stuck quite closely to other key aspects of its initial stabilization strategy. Private sector credit remained extremely tight, even in the face of a new round of gubernatorial elections in July 1986. The general thrust of exchange rate policy was toward prolonged and painful increases in the dollar price of the peso. And wage policy remained particularly tough throughout the presidential term, with the PRI-controlled tripartite bargaining commissions setting wage levels well behind the escalating rates of inflation, reversing the general tendency toward improvement set into motion in the mid-1950s. Overall, real wages dropped by around 40 percent during the 1980s, a record roughly comparable to the "shock treatments" imposed in the Southern Cone during the late 1970s.[8]

Reforms of Economic Structures including Trade Liberalization and Privatization

Although the government moved more slowly than anticipated in its original plans for structural adjustment, there were significant changes in this area as well. Several important foundation stones, aimed at restoring private sector confidence and strengthening private capital markets, were set into place during the first year of de la Madrid's term. The government rapidly settled on compensation for the private bank nationalization of 1982, and it offered private firms the opportunity to service dollar debts at favorable rates of exchange. It also permitted the establishment of private brokerage houses with wide latitude for financing transactions in domestic capital markets, and by 1987 (until the October crash), these measures had laid the groundwork for the first significant stock market in Mexican history.

With the de la Madrid administration initially facing a severe foreign exchange shortage, it hesitated in 1983 to lower trade restrictions. Nevertheless, in subsequent years, import authorizations were relaxed substantially, and there was significant progress in replacing the cumbersome import licensing system with a more generalized tariff system. By 1985, the proportion of imports covered by licensing requirements had been reduced from 75 to only 38 percent.[9] In 1986, the government signed the General Agreement on Tariffs and Trade (GATT) treaty, ending more than a decade of bitter debate over whether to accept the liberal trade provisions embodied in that system of agreements,[10] and in 1987 it agreed to a major liberalization of bilateral trade relations with the United States. In the meantime, and perhaps most significantly in terms of structural changes in the Mexican economy, the peso devaluations of the preceding years had led to a significant expansion of non-oil exports, led by rapidly growing investments in the assembly (*maquiladora*) plants along the northern border.

Progress was more limited in the public enterprise sector, where the giant firms proved highly resistant to rationalization or reduction. Within PEMEX, for example, the government could not carry through its plans to reduce the powerful oil workers' union control over contracting and subcontracting. Nevertheless, by 1987 the government had managed to sell or close a substantial number of medium and smaller public firms, and at least in some areas it had proved itself willing to confront powerful vested interests. Over the intense protest from the steel workers' union, it closed Fundidora, the oldest steel complex in the country, and at various points it used unusually strict interpretations of the labor code to crack down on striking electrical workers, teachers, and steel workers in Altos Hornos. As was the case in many other parts of the world, the absence of private buyers was probably a more important impediment to reducing the size of the state enterprise sector than was the opposition of the unions.

Bargaining with External Creditors

At the onset of the debt crisis in 1982-83, two assumptions governed the negotiating stance that the Mexican regime adopted toward external creditors. The first was that the risks of confrontation were higher than those implied by an orderly rescheduling of the debt, a view that continued to guide government policy throughout de la Madrid's term. The second major assumption was that a rapid resumption of private voluntary lending would allow the economy to grow out of its debt burden. As the Mexican economy began to enter a new round of crises in 1985-86, this second assumption became increasingly untenable. Indeed, the total debt burden had actually increased as a percentage of GDP during that period (from 70 to 83.8 percent), while external interest payments continued to absorb nearly 37 percent of total exports.[11] From about 1985 onward, therefore, Mexico's relations with its creditors began to reflect the tensions between its continued adherence to the first assumption and its changing views on the second. On the one hand, during 1986-87 this implied increasing demands for concessions and relief, extracted in difficult, often acrimonious rounds of bargaining with creditors. On the other hand, although the government sometimes appeared to approach the brink of a moratorium during these negotiations, it invariably stopped short of stepping over the edge.

The IMF and commercial bank agreements reached in 1986 are illustrative of the general process. During 1985 and 1986, the long stalemate that preceded these agreements triggered an extensive debate within the Mexican government over the possibilities of a more radical approach to the debt. In March 1986, an internal report prepared under Council of Economic Advisors head, Leopoldo Solís, argued that neither the exchange rate nor domestic inflation would be controllable as long as inconclusive negotiations with the IMF and the banks encouraged speculation against the peso. The report suggested that the government consider bypassing the IMF and taking unilateral action on debt relief if it could not reach agreements with the banks. Treasury Secretary Silva Herzog, ousted in June 1986 during a fierce political rivalry with Carlos Salinas, also began to advocate a much tougher bargaining stance in the months prior to his dismissal.

A confrontation with creditors was finally averted by the conclusion of a new IMF agreement in July 1986, followed by a rescheduling agreement with the banks a few months later. The specific terms of both agreements involved some unprecedented concessions on the part of the creditors. The IMF, under strong U.S. pressure to head off a crisis, acquiesced to Mexican interpretations of its fiscal budget deficits, and in an even more novel step, agreed to peg lending levels to fluctuations in the price of oil.[12] Likewise, in agreements with the commercial banks, the government obtained rescheduling at unusually low interest rates and a commitment for additional lending if the economy fell below growth levels targeted for the coming year.

Within the parameters of the existing international "rules of the game," such concessions represented important victories for the Mexican negotiators. Nevertheless, the still unanswered question was whether they would be sufficient to permit the economy to do more than tread water during the remaining years of the decade. Even with the agreements described above, Mexico remained a net exporter of capital. By 1986-87, therefore, a growing number of Mexican and U.S. economists, including many with highly orthodox perspectives, had begun to advocate even more extensive forms of debt relief.[13] Thus, although the government had shown great skill in playing the game, the issue remained whether it had not already reached a point where the risks of a still more radical bargaining position might have been worth taking.

Changes in Political Alignments

This brings us to a more direct examination of the political factors influencing the way the Mexican system responded to the crisis of the 1980s. Our analysis of this issue is organized around three long-standing interpretive hypotheses about the historical capacity of the Mexican system to manage social conflict. One view, often held by close observers of day-to-day Mexican politics, is that despite the appearance of executive power, economic policy making has actually been immobilized by cross pressures from competing business and popular-sector interests.[14] A second perspective emphasizes the autonomy of executive decision makers from such conflicts.[15] Finally, there is a third view which stresses more asymmetric patterns of state autonomy and vulnerability: a high capacity to deflect pressures from the regime's popular constituency, but considerable vulnerability to pressures from key segments of the Mexican business elite and their allies within the creditor countries.[16]

Political Stalemate: Popular Resistance to Economic Orthodoxy?

During the 1980s, this image was advanced primarily by conservative U.S. and domestic critics of the de la Madrid administration. In particular, they argued that the fragility of the economic recovery under de la Madrid was attributable to actual or anticipated resistance of the PRI's electoral and union base to the government's stabilization and adjustment program—which prevented the government from sustaining its fiscal austerity and from opening the economy more completely to market forces. Various aspects of our discussion above do provide some support for this view: for example, the capacity of the oil workers' unions to block the rationalization of PEMEX, and the relaxation of budget constraints in the months preceding the 1985 gubernatorial elections. More broadly, it is likely that the traditional legitimation concerns of the Mexican elite helped to deter a full-scale "shock treatment" that might have opened the economy to market forces at a single stroke.

Even after taking such "backsliding" into account, however, it is important to emphasize that the de la Madrid administration moved toward its orthodox objectives with a sustained consistency that during the decade of the 1980s had few parallels in the rest of Latin America. What is particularly striking in this context, moreover, is the extent to which the government was willing to deploy its organizational resources to impose costs on the PRI's popular bases. The deterioration of wages and salaries, including those of "privileged" blue-collar and public-sector workers, sharply reversed the upward trend of the past three decades, with one of the worst periods coming on the eve of the 1986 gubernatorial elections. In conflicts with powerful steel and electrical workers' unions, which had gained considerable bargaining leverage in the 1970s, the government also proved willing to implement the provisions of the labor code with unusual strictness. It virtually ignored public CTM demands for a change in economic strategy in 1985-86. And at the end of de la Madrid's term, it forced both the CTM and the PRI left wing to swallow the designation of Carlos Salinas, the most orthodox of the leading contenders, as de la Madrid's successor.[17] In 1988 these circumstances impelled Cuauhtémoc Cárdenas to split away from the PRI and assume the leadership of the strongest left-wing electoral challenge in the PRI's history.

Finally, it is important to note that although popular political pressures may have played some role in moderating the implementation of the restructuring program, in several important policy areas the principal impediment was often not popular opposition but division among industrial and financial groups themselves. The most effective resistance to entry into the GATT, for example, came from import-substituting firms associated with the official industrial association CONACIN-TRA (Cámera Nacional de la Industria de Transformación).[18] Growing fiscal deficits, similarly, were attributable at least in part to the debt-servicing demands of external creditors and to the capacity of powerful private financial groups to insist on high interest rates for government bonds.[19]

State Autonomy?

A diametrically opposite hypothesis emphasizes the power of the state vis-à-vis all segments of civil society. In many respects, this perspective seems to provide a more plausible basis for understanding the capacity of the de la Madrid administration to sustain such an unpopular policy course. Despite their internal political and institutional rivalries, the technocrats under de la Madrid did constitute a remarkably cohesive decision-making elite. They shared deep interests in the maintenance and modernization of the Mexican system. They were generally committed to an orthodox strategy of economic recovery. And they could deploy extraordinarily strong bureaucratic and political resources against opponents. In at least some respects, it should be noted, these resources could be used against business groups as well as the popular sectors—as evidenced, for example, in the decision to enter GATT, or in the extremely severe credit restrictions imposed on the private sector as a whole.

But to what extent were state executives actually free to pursue a course fully consistent with their general interest in shoring up the economic and political foundations of the Mexican system? The puzzle left partially unresolved by the autonomy hypothesis is why the administration was so persistent in pursuing such a politically-costly policy course that was producing such disappointing results. Part of the answer may lie in the deeply orthodox convictions that appeared to govern official perceptions, along with the weakness of the feedback mechanisms inherent in a system of concentrated executive authority. By 1985-86, however, many officials had themselves tacitly changed some of the key assumptions that originally guided their selection of strategies. The inertial source of fiscal deficits, for example, was widely acknowledged within official circles, as was the severe constraint that debt service burdens placed on domestic stabilization and adjustment.

Moreover, although orthodox policies may still have been the best of the unattractive choices available to the elite, other plausible alternatives were already on the drawing board by the mid-1980s. One possibility was Argentine-style price controls aimed at halting the inertial inflationary spirals. Such controls finally were applied in 1988, but only after several years of hesitation in the face of steadily rising prices. Another alternative—a position which, as noted, was eventually associated with Jesús Silva Herzog—might have been to combine fiscal austerity at home with a much harder-line stance toward servicing the external debt. Each of these possible adjustments was at least partially consistent with the changing assumptions of the administration itself; for that reason, it is doubtful that (mis)perceptions alone can explain the delays and non-decisions. To understand these fully, we must move beyond the autonomy hypothesis to consider the way the government's interest in maintaining the political system interacted with the need to acknowledge the reactions and perceptions of local and international business forces.

The State and Business

To an important extent, the initial designation of de la Madrid as president was motivated by a concern for providing reassurances to increasingly independent and militant business groups. Although such groups were frequently divided over major policy issues, the orthodox northern financial-industrial sector was a particularly important constituency. Well before the beginning of the de la Madrid administration, the bitter polarization of the mid-1970s had already given considerable momentum to their demands for economic liberalization and changes in the political system. After the post-1982 crisis closed in, however, several additional factors tended to augment the weight of the hardliners even more, and to increase their capacity to deter the de la Madrid government from straying too far from its initial policy course.

The first was the September 1982 bank nationalization.[20] Although compensation issues were quickly settled under de la Madrid, the nationalization decree reinforced the hardline thesis that the PRI-dominated system could not be trusted to refrain from taking arbitrary and "demagogic" initiatives. This was the second time since the land reform of the mid-1970s, the business radicals argued, that there had been a major assault on private property. Even though many moderate business sectors did not answer the ensuing summons for a united front with the hardliners, this argument clearly left the moderates in a weaker position than before. Even after the immediate crisis had passed, the nationalization episode placed special pressure on de la Madrid to demonstrate that there would be no more surprises in his term and that his administration would work consistently to guarantee a safe and predictable investment climate.

More generally, the international financial crisis itself tended to shift the balance of power within the Mexican business community and to increase the leverage that orthodox hardliners could use against the state. On the one hand, interruption of the external credit flow weakened the state enterprise sector's capacity to deliver subsidies and public contracts to business groups closely associated with the PRI-dominated system. On the other hand, although most northern sectors had also fed at the public trough, their control over liquid assets and their links to foreign markets placed them in a better position to ride out the credit austerity, to capitalize on peso devaluations or, if necessary, to get their money out of the country entirely.[21]

Under these circumstances, the hardline groups had relatively little to lose and a great deal to gain by keeping the heat on the administration to maintain its orthodox course. Leaders of the northern-dominated interest associations, while offering some praise for the government's good intentions, generally sustained a steady drumbeat of criticism against indecision and populist backsliding. In the meantime, the PAN—with sympathetic coverage from much of the U.S. press—mobilized more direct challenges against the PRI itself. Particularly severe confrontations came after the local elections of 1985 and 1986, when PAN supporters occupied bridges, closed stores, and issued angry denunciations of dictatorship and electoral fraud. Although these broad challenges did not deal specifically with economic policy issues, they nevertheless served to reinforce a point already made in 1975-76 and in the early 1980s: militant business groups were capable of mobilizing considerable domestic and foreign support against a government that threatened their interests.

From the perspective of Mexican decision makers, this did not leave a great deal of room for maneuver. On the one hand, the hardliners' capacity for political disruption was high. On the other hand, their economic collaboration appeared crucial to the administration's hopes for economic recovery. At a minimum, this meant that a higher priority than before had to be attached to interest rate and exchange policies that would coax the investment resources controlled by these groups back into the country. For good or ill, it also implied avoiding sudden changes in orthodox domestic policy or open confrontations with international creditors. Were there better solutions? Although it is hard to say for sure, the threat of a right-wing business backlash provided a strong deterrent against exploring the possibilities.

Conclusion: Some Questions About Feedback and
the Long-Term Adaptation of the Mexican System

What do the orthodox choices described above imply about the long-term evolution of the Mexican system? In advocating such orthodoxy, neoclassical economists have frequently distinguished between short-term "political logic" that attempts to avoid immediate popular protest, and a more far-sighted "economic rationality" that might lay the groundwork for future growth and the foundations for a more stable and legitimate political system. Is this the process that has been at work in Mexico during the past decade?

Despite the disappointments of the de la Madrid period, it is conceivable that this is the case—or at least that the choices made by the Mexican government were the best of the options available. More heterodox policies could, after all, have exacerbated political and economic difficulties. And for all the frustrations associated with the economic stabilization program, the measures taken under de la Madrid did leave the Mexican economy in a better position to compete in world markets. In the longer-run, finally, it is not inconceivable that a more stable and pluralistic political system could emerge from the current opposition challenge to the hegemony of the PRI—depending, of course, on the leadership provided by the heads of the competing political sectors.

Although this scenario is possible, at the moment it does not seem especially likely to materialize. Indeed, for several reasons, it is difficult to see how existing political structures in Mexico can be reformed or democratized without significant changes in the government's domestic policies and in its relations to creditors. In the first place, it is misleading to assume that the policies followed under de la Madrid were driven exclusively by considerations of long-term economic rationality. Rather, as the preceding pages suggest, it is more useful to view the administration as having made a choice between competing political logics, both rather short-term in character: whether to appeal to the popular-sector base of the PRI, or to avert the sort of capital flight and business protest that had posed such difficulties for the system from the mid-1970s onward. Given the control mechanisms available for containing popular-sector opposition, it is not difficult to understand why authorities might have considered business protest the more immediate danger. But this did not imply either the long time horizons or the "technical" neutrality sometimes claimed for orthodox approaches.

Despite the extraordinary sacrifices imposed on Mexican society, moreover, this approach has not (so far) produced a sustained economic recovery. On the contrary, in terms of growth and wage levels, Mexico actually did worse than countries like Brazil and Argentina, that followed more heterodox economic policies. To some extent, this reflected factors beyond the control of Mexican authorities, as well as cross-national differences in domestic economic structures. Even so, as in the 1930s, the rapidly changing world environment of the 1980s appears to call for significant changes in conventional economic wisdom. For the incoming Salinas administration, it may well be more far-sighted to adopt more flexible economic policies that attach a higher priority to rebuilding the popular legitimacy of the system.

Finally, even if there is a return to high growth rates in Mexico, we must not assume that this will lead automatically to a reconsolidation of the PRI's popular support and/or to the democratization of the political system. To contribute to either (or both) objectives, the economic policies pursued under the next administration will have to be grounded in a more extensive renegotiation of the understanding that once regulated conflict within the Mexican society. This involves a major, often contradictory set of challenges: establishing a new framework of understandings with the private sector that either neutralizes or accommodates its most radical components; reestablishing a stable framework for trade and credit relations with the U.S. government; and shoring up the regime's deteriorating mechanism of legitimation by broadening access to political power and material resources. A new wave of economic expansion will not in itself resolve such challenges. Indeed, in the absence of attention to the political dimensions of recovery, it could well compound them by raising expectations, shifting the balance among social forces, and altering distributive shares.

Notes

1. Roger Hansen, *The Politics of Mexican Development* (Baltimore: Johns Hopkins University Press, 1971); John K. Thompson, *Inflation, Financial Markets and Economic Development: The Experience of Mexico* (Greenwich, CT: JAI Press, 1979).

2. For a more extended discussion, see Robert R. Kaufman, *Heterodoxy and Orthodoxy: Economic Stabilization and Adjustment in Argentina, Brazil and Mexico* (Berkeley: Institute of International Studies, University of California, forthcoming).

3. E.V.K. FitzGerald, "The State and Capital Accumulation in Mexico," *Journal of Latin American Studies* 10, no. 2 (November 1978): 277.

4. John J. Bailey, "Public Budgeting in Mexico, 1970-1982," *Public Budgeting and Finance* (Spring 1984) and "Presidency, Bureaucracy and Administrative Reform in Mexico: The Secretariat of Programming and Budget," *Interamerican Economic Affairs* 34, no. 1 (Summer 1980).

5. Sylvia Maxfield and Ricardo Anzaldua Montoya, eds., *Government and Private Sector in Contemporary Mexico* (San Diego: Center for U.S.-Mexican Studies, University of California, 1987).

6. Oscar Hinojosa, "Banco de México y Hacienda, manantiales de los hombres del presidente," *Proceso*, no. 507, July 21, 1986.

7. Jaime Ros and Nora Lustig, *Stabilization and Adjustment Policies and Programmes, Country Study: Mexico* (Helsinki: WIDER, 1987).

8. See Roxborough data in this volume.

9. Ros and Lustig, *Stabilization*.

10. Dale Story, *Industry, the State, and Public Policy in Mexico* (Austin: University of Texas Press, 1986).

11. World Bank, *World Debt Tables*.

12. *Wall Street Journal*, July 23, 1986.

13. See Dornbush chapter in this volume. In December 1987, the Mexican government announced a new agreement, worked out in the U.S. Treasury and Morgan Guaranty Trust, in which existing Mexican debt was to be auctioned at a discount for new Mexican bonds backed by zero-coupon Treasury notes. Although it was initially hoped that this device might pare as much as $20 billion from the total Mexican debt, the major commercial banks proved unwilling to accept large discounts. The total value of the bids accepted was only $3.67 billion, which reduced Mexico's foreign debt by only $1.1 billion. See *New York Times*, March 4, 1988.

14. Raymond Vernon, *The Dilemma of Mexico's Development* (Cambridge: Harvard University Press, 1965).

15. Susan Kaufman Purcell, "Decision Making in an Authoritarian Regime: Theoretical Implications for a Mexican Case Study, " *World Politics* 26, no. 1 (October 1973) and *The Mexican Profit Sharing Decision: Politics and Economic Change in an Authoritarian Regime* (Berkeley: University of California Press, 1975).

16. Nora Hamilton, *The Limits of State Autonomy* (Princeton: Princeton University Press, 1982).

17. See Roxborough chapter in this volume.

18. Dale Story, *Industry, the State, and Public Policy*.

19. See Dornbush chapter in this volume.

20. Matilde Luna, Ricardo Tirado and Francisco Valdés, "Businessmen and Politics in Mexico, 1982-1986," in *Government and Private Sector*, ed. Maxfield and Anzaldua.

21. See chapters by Frieden and Maxfield in this volume.

Suggestions for Further Reading

Buffie, Edward F. and Allen Sangines Kress. "Economic Policy and Foreign Debt in Mexico." In *Developing Country Debt*, ed. Jeffrey Sachs. Chicago: University of Chicago Press, forthcoming 1989.

FitzGerald, E.V.K. "The State and Capital Accumulation in Mexico." *Journal of Latin American Studies* 10, no. 2 (November 1978).

Hansen, Roger D. *The Politics of Mexican Development*. Baltimore: Johns Hopkins University Press, 1971.

Maxfield, Sylvia and Ricardo Anzaldua M., eds. *Government and Private Sector in Contemporary Mexico*. San Diego: Center for U.S.- Mexican Studies, University of California, 1987.

Reyna, José Luis and Richard S. Weinert, eds. *Authoritarianism in Mexico*. Philadelphia: Institute for the Study of Human Issues, 1977.

Rivera Ríos, Miguel Angel. *Crisis y reorganización del capitalismo mexicano: 1960-1985*. Mexico City: Ediciones Era SA, 1985.

Solís, Leopoldo. *Economic Policy Reform in Mexico: A Case Study for Developing Countries*. Elmsford, New York: Pergamon, 1981.

Vernon, Raymond. *The Dilemma of Mexico's Development: The Roles of the Private and Public Sectors*. Cambridge: Harvard University Press, 1965.

Villarreal, René. *La contrarevolución monetarista: teoría, política económica, e ideología del neoliberalismo*. Mexico City: Ediciones Oceano SA, 1984.

8

Debt, Adjustment, and
Democratic Cacophony in Brazil

Eul-Soo Pang

Since the founding of the New Republic in March 1985, efforts to find a solution to Brazil's debt crisis have taken place within the context of debates over organizing and consolidating a new constitutional system. Despite Brazil's giant economy (the world's eighth largest in terms of gross domestic product, or GDP) and enormous potential, the political experiment has not been fruitful. A new constituent assembly, in session since 1987, has not been able to overcome a myriad of divisive ideological interests. President José Sarney has become increasingly preoccupied with preventing the assembly from shortening his term in office and defending the prerogatives of the executive branch against proposals to establish a parliamentary system.

The unfortunate consequences of these conflicts have been a paralysis of the presidential system, utter chaos in the economy, a collapse of party discipline, and the resurgence of the armed forces as a powerful voice in political and economic matters. Sarney has changed his cabinet four times since March 1985, when he was thrust forward to assume the presidential mantle. Under Finance Minister Dilson Funaro, Sarney experimented with the bold inflation-bashing Cruzado Plan in 1986. By the end of the year, however, it became clear that the monetary reform plan had fallen short of its intended objectives, further debilitating the Sarney presidency and nearly forcing Brazil into an economic abyss. In February 1987, Sarney took a step that no self-respecting political conservative would take: a moratorium on interest payments on Brazil's $67 billion commercial bank debt. Within the next twelve months, Sarney had appointed two more finance ministers (Luiz Carlos Bresser Pereira and Mailson Pereira da Nóbrega). Early in March 1988 he succumbed to international banking community pressure by settling up the arrears in interest so that Brazil could "return" to the international financial market.

These problems are deeper than imprudence or lack of will on the part of specific leaders. Indecision and politically-convenient policy choices have prolonged Brazil's business recession and pushed the country into social upheaval. Brazil lacks a constructive political culture in which each politician, economic technocrat, businessman, academic, and private citizen has a role in the new democracy. The

127

lack of a clearly perceived role for civil society has compounded the economic crisis, for the state failed to institute workable—albeit politically unpalatable—recovery measures. Brazil will not be able to consolidate democracy unless it can agree on its economic, social, and political goals. The country first needs to go through a series of preliminary steps, such as direct election of a president who can rally the country, a new constitution that can set the tone for the long-term development of Brazil's immense natural resources, and a new debt strategy that will satisfy both Brazilians and the international financial community.

The Etiology of Debt

By mid-1988, Third World debt had reached an all-time high of $1.15 trillion. Brazil's share was roughly $118 billion, or 10.3 percent. When the military took power in April 1964, the country's external debt was only $3.5 billion; when they returned to the barracks in March 1985 it had risen to $100 billion. Thus the debt had increased 29-fold over the period, while per capita income had only gone up 2.3-fold, from $832 to $1,924.[1] Debt-servicing obligations, combined with the host of austerity measures that Brazil adopted at the recommendation of the International Monetary Fund (IMF) between 1983 and 1985, led to a decline of personal income and GDP. In 1982, Brazil's GDP stood at $296 billion, while two years later it was only $226 billion.[2] One serious problem has been the lack of new loans at the same time that the country has paid over $39 billion in interest since 1983, making it the world's largest capital exporter after Japan.[3]

Such massive indebtedness can be explained in terms of Brazil's historic propensity over the past five decades to borrow externally for economic development. Brazilians have associated direct investment with the process of "denationalization," or foreign control of their economy. The social and political drawbacks of such a process seemed to outweigh the benefits.[4] Since the multinational corporations often defined spending priorities, they thus acquired a key role in national economic planning. The opposition to MNC power led to xenophobic nationalism on both the right and left. In fact, these were the very arguments that precipitated the political debates preceding the coup of 1964.

The alternative to seeking direct investment was external borrowing. In order to finance massive economic development projects, the Brazilian government made two basic decisions. First, it would borrow on its own account, rather than raising taxes or relying too heavily on private domestic savings. Second, it would provide state guarantees for public enterprises and private companies seeking foreign loans. In 1967, the national treasury became the guarantor of all public loans transacted at home and overseas. Aviso GB-588 empowered the Bank of Brazil to meet all "obligations with the guarantee from the national treasury or from any other official financial institution" in the event that a state-owned corporation failed to meet its payments. By mid-1985, GB-588 was costing the Ministry of Finance over $6 million per month, backing public firms that failed to honor their debt obligations.[5]

Even given Brazil's preference for obtaining foreign capital through loans, we still need to explain the "overborrowing" that occurred. Three explanations focus on events related to the international economy. First, the two oil price rises in 1973-74 and 1979 were very detrimental to a country importing most of its petroleum. Between 1973 and 1983, the price of oil went from $2.54 to $33 per barrel. A simultaneous fall in the price of many of Brazil's primary export products caught the country in a serious terms-of-trade squeeze. Second, partially as a result of the oil price rise, an international recession in the early 1980s further blocked Brazil's ability to earn foreign exchange through exports. The economic problem was exacerbated by its political concomitant—increased protectionism in the advanced industrial countries. Third, international interest rates went up sharply in this period. Since much of Brazil's debt was priced through "floating" interest rates, a general rise in interest rates meant higher payments for Brazil.

All three international factors led to increased deficits on the current account of the balance of payments. Another blow was dealt when the international banks that had been lending to Brazil suddenly stopped lending in late 1982 because of the debt crisis in Mexico. When the Mexican government announced that it could not continue meeting the payments on its debt, a "contagion" effect spread throughout the region, until no Latin American government could get money. A combination of these factors led the Brazilian government to seek the first of many debt reschedulings in early 1983.[6]

Beyond these external problems over which Brazil had little control, there were also some domestic factors that provide complementary explanations for the debt build-up in the 1960s and 1970s. Since the Great Depression of the 1930s, Brazil and the rest of Latin America have embarked on a public sector expansionist policy, whereby the state has become the nation's major financier, manufacturer, planner of development projects, regulator of private business, and even distributor of goods and services. A key feature of this process was the creation of a large number of publicly-owned and managed corporations.

In Brazil, these corporations more than quadrupled in number during the years of military rule. From the 180 public firms extant when the military took over in 1964, the number grew to 683 in 1982, and then declined to 646 when the military relinquished power in 1985. There are now 632 such firms.[7] The slight decrease has been the result of the privatization program initiated by the last military president, José Figueiredo, and continued by Sarney as a way of reducing expenditures. Despite their decline in numbers, the economic power and political clout of the parastatals have not diminished. Of the Fortune 500 international corporations, Brazil can claim seven. Five of them are state firms—Petrobrás (oil); Companhia Vale do Rio Doce (iron ore); and Siderbrás, Usiminas, and Cosipa (all steel manufacturers).

These companies are also the country's major debtors. Brazil's public firms as a whole hold over 70 percent of the country's external debt.[8] Thus we can see the relationship between the development strategy—which relied on state firms, assigned them massive projects to carry out, and sent them to the international capital markets to seek funding—and the build-up of Brazil's huge debt. In relative terms, Brazil used its borrowed resources much more productively than other Latin American nations. A much larger percentage went for investment than consumption. Likewise, Brazil made a greater effort to increase its exports to make debt service possible. But clearly not enough control was maintained to match the maturity of loans with the time necessary to get the projects underway and generate the foreign exchange revenue to repay the loans. Consequently, once the adverse international shocks struck, Brazil was forced to borrow money just to pay interest, and the positive impact of the debt ceased. Thus these internal processes were combined with the external factors to create the debt crisis that has nearly paralyzed the country for the last half decade.

Reviving Democracy and Adjustment Policies

In the early 1980s, as external lending contracted, Brazil was hit by a major economic crisis. This crisis, and the Figueiredo administration's response to it, played a crucial role in the transition to civilian rule in 1985. The austerity programs that the IMF and the Figueiredo government adopted in early 1983 involved drastic cuts in public spending, devaluation of the cruzeiro, reduction of subsidies and subsidized credit, modifications of wage policy (freeze), and a curb on state firms' voracious appetite for borrowing. In 1983, Brazil experienced a 4 percent drop in GDP and a 211 percent rise in inflation; the real wage declined by 12 percent. Business recession provoked urban food riots by the unemployed and the poor. In 1984, over 900 riots in Rio de Janeiro, São Paulo, and other urban centers were directed against the IMF, the country's alleged source of social and economic woes.[9] Both the left and right raised nationalist objections to the periodic visits by IMF economists, who appeared to subject ministers and their aides to humiliating confrontations. More serious was the Brazilian layperson's perception that these visits deepened their country's ongoing economic difficulties, especially the unemployment situation.

Meanwhile, as Figueiredo's term neared its end, the question of the presidential succession loomed larger on the agenda. In the electoral college charged with selecting the next president, the pro-military party, the Partido Democrático Social (PDS), controlled 359 out of 680 votes, while the largest opposition party, the Partido Movimento Democrático Brasileiro (PMDB), only controlled 269. If all PDS delegates backed the official candidate, therefore, he was guaranteed a victory, but this was not to be.

There were four PDS frontrunners: Figueiredo's vice president Aureliano Chaves, Federal Deputy Paulo Maluf, Minister of the Interior David Andreazza, and Federal Senator Marco Maciel. While these figures and others jockeyed for the nomination in the years preceding the election, Figueiredo remained on the sidelines. One reason for his reticence was the plummeting popularity of his government, due to the austerity measures introduced by the IMF-Brazil accord. Throughout 1984, moreover, a series of major and minor illnesses increased the President's reluctance to become involved in naming his successor. In the meantime, opposition leaders, academics, and union chiefs increased the pressure on the government. A "direct elections now" campaign mobilized millions of demonstrators in Brazil's major cities. In April 1984, a direct election bill, initiated over military opposition, was defeated in the Congress only after the federal capital was sealed off by government troops and placed under martial law.

In the context of these economic and political pressures, the PDS split apart. With Figueiredo unwilling to arbitrate internal party politics, the nomination went to Paulo Maluf, a politician with considerable opposition in both the PDS and the military. To block Maluf, Sarney, Chaves, and many other PDS chiefs broke away to form a dissident party, the Liberal Front (PFL). In the electoral college, the PFL joined forces with the PMDB to nominate Tancredo Neves, governor of Minas Gerais, for president. In the January 1985 electoral college vote, this opposition slate handily defeated the official party ticket.

This was not the end of the story, however, since Tancredo Neves fell fatally ill the day before his inauguration and was unable to assume office. Ironically, after all the sound and fury of mobilizing opposition and maneuvering in the electoral college, his replacement was Vice-President-elect José Sarney, a man who only months earlier had been a staunch PDS supporter of the military regime! Twice governor of Maranhão during the military rule, federal deputy, federal senator, and finally president of the official party, Sarney was seen as an excellent choice by the conservatives and especially by the armed forces. Thus, as Sarney began his presidency, he was ideologically suspect to the majority of PMDB politicians and Brazil's center-left. This mutual distrust between the President and PMDB chieftains still lingers and has sowed social, economic, and political unrest.

Struggles over patronage provided one important basis for this conflict. The PMDB, cut off from federal perks for over two decades, was anxious to expand its presence in the federal executive. Yet, as one study showed, during Sarney's first year in office only 15 percent of 4,565 federal appointments were first-time officials without prior ties to the military.[10] To make matters worse, PFL politicians had gained important cabinet positions in the electoral college compromise with the PMDB. In part, the PMDB's early support for parliamentarism resulted from their frustration over this situation.

During his initial years in office, however, Sarney could not stray far from the ambitious socio-economic agenda worked out under Neves and the PMDB. For Neves himself, the primary objective was to create jobs. The debt problem and an IMF accord were both to be subordinated to that priority. Within the PMDB, there were many who wanted to go even farther and declare a moratorium. With Tancredo Neves gone and a right-wing politician serving as President, the PMDB was determined to press expansionary objectives on the executive branch.

Within the executive itself, finally, the cabinet bequeathed by Tancredo Neves to Sarney was also deeply divided. The main rivalry was between the moderately orthodox Finance Minister Francisco Dornelles (Tancredo Neves' nephew), and Minister of Planning João Sayad, an academic economist selected by the left wing of the PMDB. The critical issues at stake were Brazil's debt renegotiation strategy, increasing federal revenues to pay for social obligations, and resuming economic growth. Dornelles was in favor of working with the IMF, but on Brazilian terms. In an orthodox attempt to revive the country's economy, Dornelles pushed for a tax increase, a reduction in public spending (including the parastatals), and a rollover of much of Brazil's external debt. Sayad adopted a more expansionary approach. Dornelles was too conservative for the PMDB and was forced to resign before the end of 1985.

The Cruzado Plans

With Dornelles out of the way, the government turned to more expansionary fiscal and credit policies to revive the economy. Dilson Funaro, Dornelles' successor in the Ministry of Finance, immediately broke off relations with the IMF and sought to negotiate directly with bankers and key industrial governments to secure a long-term rollover at a moderate interest rate. Bypassing the IMF was politically popular, but bankers balked at the Brazilian strategy. Yet Funaro claimed that his debt adjustment policy would create 1.5 million new jobs and that inflation and the public deficit would fall.[11]

The government broached the idea of a "social pact," such as Felipe González of Spain had devised, but Sarney never succeeded in forging labor, management, and other sectors into such an alliance. Political bickering within the left was part of the problem, and there was also strong resistance from much of the right, which regarded Sarney as a turncoat. Sarney did form a "Political Council" as a way of broadening his power base and consulting PMDB and PFL congressional leadership on key policy issues, but the council died of neglect by the end of Sarney's first year. The increasing mutual criticism between Sarney and the PMDB did not help.

The second year of Sarney's administration thus began on a pessimistic note. Despite Funaro's predictions, inflation climbed from 230 percent in 1985 to an annual rate of over 500 percent by February 1986. No viable solution to the debt was in sight. Each day Sarney was forced to spend more, partly as a payoff to political supporters, and partly to fund employment-generating public investment. The dismal result was to push the public deficit into the stratosphere. To distance himself from the Figueiredo regime, of which he had been part until July 1985, Sarney had no choice but to gamble on a new policy. Foreign bankers would have to wait.

The Cruzado Plan, also known as the "Economic Stabilization Plan" and "Inflation Zero," had been discussed by academic economists as early as 1984. Its origin has been widely attributed to three economists—André Lara Resende, Pérsio Arida, and Francisco Lopes, all U.S.-trained professors at the Catholic University of Rio—

who concluded that the escalating inflationary spiral was a result of indexing all wage, price, and interest rate levels to the inflation rate of the preceding contract period. In such a system, they suggested, major price increases in any one sector of the economy would quickly be reflected in all of the others. This in turn reinforced the perception of businessmen and other economic actors that, in the Brazilian economy, nothing was permanent and everything was adjustable. A new mentality had to prevail if Brazil was to build a new economy.

Sarney was presented with a plan that would introduce a new currency, deindex the economy and, most important, freeze wages and prices. As inflation rates climbed in mid-February, the Brazilian intelligence agency (SNI) alerted Sarney that his government was being "devoured" politically by increasing PMDB opposition (especially from its left wing) and the radical Workers' Party (PT). If present economic conditions persisted, Sarney was warned that he would be abandoned by every conceivable group. Worse, his own PFL could implode. For an economic reform plan to have an impact, it had to be introduced quickly—before early March, when the PMDB-dominated Congress would be back in session.[12] Although Sarney's decision to bypass his Political Council might seem reminiscent of the behavior of the past military regimes it seemed to be the best way to minimize repercussions. The President knew only too well the advantage of this blitzkrieg strategy. Under military rule, unpopular decree-laws were often announced while Congress was in recess or after it was closed by the armed forces. By late February, Sarney authorized his economic team to unveil the stabilization plan, adding "I am going to pray!" At this point, no one was concerned with the external debt handling.

The "heterodox" Cruzado Plan had five essential components: (a) the deindexation of the economy by eliminating monetary correction for wages, contracts, prices, and so forth; (b) the imposition of a freeze on all prices and on the value of federal treasury notes, known as Readjustable National Treasury Obligations or ORTN (the term "readjustable" was dropped after March 1); (c) the prohibition of indexed contracts for periods of less than a year, except savings accounts, retirement pensions, and other related funds; (d) a wage freeze, with an adjustment allowed every six months according to government-approved price indices; and (e) a new monetary unit, the cruzado, to replace the debased cruzeiro, with Cr$1000 becoming Cz$1.[13]

The plan turned out to be extremely difficult to enforce. First, left-wing PMDB politicians and economists complained that they had not been sufficiently consulted by Sarney and his economic team in the planning stages. The critics included Ulysses Guimarães, PMDB president, speaker of the Chamber of Deputies, and Sarney's leading political rival. Moreover, the overnight freeze on all goods and services increased the value of the cruzado (and of wages), and the general public began to indulge in an orgy of consumption. Hordes of women, self-appointed "Sarney's inspectors," denounced the markups of goods in supermarkets, boutiques, and other stores. When caught and fined, retailers blamed wholesalers, who in turn blamed raw materials suppliers and farmers for violating government-set prices. Within months of the start of the Cruzado Plan, consumer fraud became a fact of life. The terms "new" and "improved" were frequently used in repackaging old products, allowing manufacturers to raise prices legally. A new car (whose price was frozen) cost less than a used car, if one could be had. A shortage of components from suppliers forced GM, Ford, Volkswagen, and other automotive manufacturers to lay off workers. By August and September of 1986, inventories in all items were critically low. Some 140,000 bank tellers and clerical staff were laid off, as profits began to plummet. When demand continued to outstrip supply, there were shortages of consumer durables and even basic necessities.

The most vocal opposition to the freeze came from the agricultural and industrial sectors, which clamored for an upward adjustment in prices. Agricultural and ranching interests, the backbone of Brazil's export economy and cozy beneficiaries of the government subsidies, refused to support the Cruzado Plan. They withheld various products from market, shipped cattle to Paraguay, and even played shell games by moving cattle and grain from place to place. The government reacted forcefully. It permitted the importing of beef, milk, and other products from the United States, Europe, and Argentina, as a way of pressuring Brazilian producers to return to the market. Interminable bureaucratic procedures delayed the release of the imported foods, however, so the government was unable to respond quickly to the rising domestic demand. To encourage the flow of products to market, the Sarney administration reduced the sales tax (merchandise circulation tax) on meat from 12 percent to 1 percent in order to raise profit margins, but this too failed to lure Brazilian producers back to the market. By the end of the year Brazil was importing 30,000 tons of meat products per month, still far short of the estimated consumption of 2.4 million tons per year.[14]

In spite of these problems, Sarney and Funaro remained extremely popular with the public throughout 1986. But with congressional and gubernatorial elections approaching, neither they nor the PMDB leadership were willing to impose the fiscal and monetary restraint necessary to regain control of the situation. In July, as a partial attempt to dampen the consumption binge, the government introduced surcharges on new and used cars, fuel, overseas trips, and dollars sold to Brazilians going abroad. PMDB chieftains, fearing an electoral backlash, quickly distanced themselves from this package, as did several of Sarney's own ministers. Nevertheless, the "Cruzadinho" (or little Cruzado) fell short of the demand-reduction measures urged by many of Sarney's key economic advisors.

By October 1986, the cornucopian vision of Brazil's economic prosperity was all but gone. As the prospect of a crash loomed ever larger, Sarney's economic advisors again called for drastic steps to adjust the program: major cuts in public expenditures, an end to price freezes on selected items, and a rise in interest rates. Such steps were still politically too hot for Sarney to consider, however, and PMDB leaders would not hear of them. Consequently, no adjustment was attempted until after the November election.

Several factors prevented more timely action. First and foremost, Sarney lacked a strong power base to enforce the plan. Even after it was implemented, the government had its share of detractors. Sarney's ministers failed to rally around him, his economists argued among themselves, and the government never produced a consensus. In fact, Finance, Planning, and Central Bank officials (political appointees, but not all PMDB militants) never agreed on how to fine-tune the rules of adjustment. Each reflected a particular view point on economic theory as well as the policy priorities of his political patron.

Second, due to persistent political resistance from the President and PMDB leadership, the planners of the stabilization program never prevailed in carrying out their ideas. A suggestion to cut the federal deficit by laying off as many as 300,000 functionaries terrified Sarney and his political advisers. It was difficult for Sarney to comprehend that the Cruzado Plan was not designed to implement both anti-inflationary budget-cutting and expansionist money-guzzling growth policies at the same time.

Third, as we have seen, PMDB leaders were insistent on "playing politics" by postponing price, wage, and interest rate adjustment plans until after the November election. Sarney went along, hoping that the delay would ensure the victory of the PMDB and would in the process raise his political capital with the dominant party. Both the PMDB and the President had political motives, albeit different ones, in postponing corrective measures before the November election.

The Cruzado Plan II of late November 1986 was unveiled as the early vote count indicated a PMDB landslide. By this time, however, it was too late. In three months (December 1986 to February 1987), an unprecedented stampede to reprice goods and services took place throughout the country, defying the logic of all economic laws and pushing the country to the brink of hyperinflation. The state firms, especially Petrobrás, were forced into deficits, as the freeze drastically diminished their profit margins through much of 1986. The less profit the state firms made, the more treasury relief was required. Hence, the public deficit remained high. By February 1987, both the Cruzado Plans I and II were defunct. Inflation galloped to an annual rate of 400 percent by January. Sarney was ready to fire his economics ministers.

The economy grew by more than 8 percent in 1986. Exports fell, as Brazilians voraciously consumed. The trade surplus, originally projected as high as $15 billion, plummeted during the second half of 1986. It was only $9.5 billion, one third less than the projected figure. The external debt rose by another $5.5 billion in 1986, while direct foreign investment dropped to a negative figure. Net foreign reserves were less than $4 billion. In 1985, the real minimum wage increased by 12.2 percent, while for 1986 (the year of the Cruzado Plan), it increased only 0.1 percent.[15]

Sarney's Moratorium and the Bresser Plan

In early 1987, debt policy began to take center stage. As early as 1983, many PMDB politicians and economists pushed for a moratorium. Funaro's two top advisers even wrote a book, rationally explaining why a moratorium was an absolute necessity for the country's economic growth: Brazil could not (and still cannot) pay an average of $10 billion per year to bankers and sustain the growth rate of 6 to 7 percent that it needs to create employment for new entrants to the labor market.[16] Minister of Finance Funaro, after taking office in August 1985, toughened Brazil's position by declaring that interest payments should not exceed 2.5 percent of GDP, and by seeking support from other Latin American debtors for the possibility of a moratorium. Funaro also sought to secure lower interest rates and multi-year rescheduling. He deplored the treatment Argentina and Mexico received from the bankers, and he argued that instead of being a passive recipient, Brazil should take a proactive role in debt renegotiation.[17]

As the Cruzado Plans squandered Sarney's political capital, the President saw an opportunity to tie the five-year mandate to the debt issue. Warding off his detractors (the proponents of four-year tenure) required a dramatic political gesture to recover some of the popularity that Sarney had enjoyed in the midst of Cruzado I. In hindsight, it is plausible that the five-year mandate was also on Sarney's mind when he decreeed the Cruzado Plan in February 1986. Now a year later, Sarney tried another ploy, this time targeting the politically less dangerous international commercial banks. Many of Funaro's aides now claim that Sarney was using the moratorium to green his political pasture. They claim that Sarney and Funaro had in fact agreed to declare a moratorium on the debt when Brazil's foreign reserves sank below the mark of $5 billion. How and against whom had not been decided. By February 1987, with reserves at $3.8 billion, Brazil had no choice but to suspend interest payments.[18] Sarney met with three of the Finance Minister's top aides to determine "how" and "against whom." Funaro was not invited; by then he was a political liability. From the outset of the meeting, a comprehensive moratorium on all debts (owed to multilateral agencies, foreign governments, and private banks) was viewed as too dangerous and hence out of the question. Funaro's aides reminded Sarney that debt policy should be designed to maximize Brazil's financial resources. This ruled out a moratorium on industrial governments, for their export-import banks could retaliate by denying Brazil credit. Since the 1986 trade surplus had dropped substantially over previous years, this was a risk that could not be run. Also ruled out was a moratorium on multilateral lending institutions such as the IMF and the World Bank. Despite the fact that since 1983, Brazil had paid far more in interest to these institutions than it had received in credit, the government hoped to receive loans for future infrastructural investment. Debts to direct industrial investors and Brazil's customers overseas were also honored. This left the international commercial banks as the most vulnerable of the lot. The United States had steadily refused to deal with the debt through government-to-government negotiations and had insisted that Brazil deal directly with the banks. Thus, a moratorium against historically unpopular institutions (banks) might provoke little wrath among industrial governments; it seemed to be a gamble worth taking. Hence, medium- and long-term private bank debt ($67 billion in February 1987) was chosen to test the waters.

In hindsight, Funaro's two aides concluded that Sarney's political need to restore PMDB support for his five-year mandate outweighed any economic repercussions from overseas creditors in the moratorium decision. The fateful speech on "Sarney's moratorium" was peppered with uncharacteristic toughness. The President called critics of his government "traitors;" he refused to "pay the debt with the hunger of the people" (borrowing a line from a Tancredo Neves speech); and he described his decision as "responsible patriotism."[19] As it turned out, it was good theater.

Contrary to his own expectations, the world did not tremble. U.S., Canadian, Japanese, and European banks responded by raising their reserves for Third World debt, thus warding off any future spread of moratoria led by Brazil. The U.S. and European governments toughened their posture by making it clear that Brazil's action was tantamount to withdrawal from the international financial community. Funaro was sternly lectured by officials and bankers on three continents. Unknown to Funaro and his staff, Sarney secretly dispatched an emissary to Washington to fathom the depth of the U.S. reaction. It was reported as "not good." To no one's amazement, Sarney reversed his position by softpedalling the moratorium. By April, a month and a half after the February 21 moratorium was declared, Funaro was banished from the Ministry of Finance.

Luiz Carlos Bresser Pereira, Sarney's third Finance Minister, was a militant PMDB activist. Professor of economics and business administration and president of the state bank of São Paulo (BANESPA) before the appointment, Bresser was a known quantity to Brazilian politicians. By June, the Bresser Plan, a domestic adjustment package, was ready to be introduced. The immediate needs were to slow down the double-digit monthly inflation (which hovered at 27 percent in May), to reduce the public deficit without creating a recession and unemployment, and to bring down skyrocketing interest rates (as high as 2,000 percent). In São Paulo, which contributed 40 percent of federal revenues, nearly 500 companies went bankrupt in April.[20] The plan imposed a 90-day freeze on prices and wages, the elimination of the automatic wage adjustment known as the "trigger," and an accelerated devaluation of the cruzado to stimulate exports. The Bresser Plan also allowed the return of indexation (though limited in application) and a gradual increase in prices and wages. Bresser even talked optimistically about ending the freeze in 45 days.

For a short time, the plan did bring down inflation, but Bresser soon began to encounter crippling difficulties on a number of fronts. As before, Sarney refused to back efforts to cut the fiscal deficit by reducing expenditures. Workers and middle-class wage earners complained loudly about the plan. Industrialists again opposed the price controls, challenging government restrictions both in the courts and

No compto (handwritten margin note)

unilaterally. And the business sector as a whole mounted fierce resistance to proposed tax increases. Within a few months, the anti-inflationary package had become unravelled.

In his strategy of dealing with international bankers, Bresser adopted a moderate approach and avoided the confrontational style that Funaro preferred. Nevertheless, the stalemate with creditors continued. Both Washington and the banking community rejected his proposal to convert about half the commercial debt into bonds that would be sold to the banks at the current market price (about 45-50 cents to the dollar). Bresser also failed to persuade commercial bank creditors to reschedule the debt prior to an IMF agreement.

Frustrated by this lack of progress on all fronts, Sarney fired Bresser in December 1987, recanted his moratorium mistakes, and appointed a conservative career bureaucrat, Mailson Pereira da Nóbrega, as his fourth Minister of Finance. He also did a public "mea culpa" on the moratorium decision to smooth the path for Brazil's return to the global banking centers. Under the new Finance Minister's guidance, Brazil paid $510 million in back interest to commercial bankers, effectively ending the 1987 moratorium. Brazil was welcomed back to the international financial marketplace by bankers and industrial governments. Bankers agreed to loan Brazil $5.4 billion, about half the amount that Brazil had requested. It is clear that Brazil is now facing the very situation that Sarney had sought to avoid under PMDB pressure: the need to bring order to public finance, devise viable ways to implement debt-equity swaps, privatize state firms, and reopen Brazil for direct foreign investment.

The Constituent Assembly and Political Cacophony

Well before the constituent assembly met, the public assumed that democracy, especially a parliamentary democracy, could be the most effective way of dealing with Brazil's critical economic questions, such as the external debt, unemployment, and the state role in the economy. Such an attitude was born partly of the logical reaction against the two decades of authoritarianism and partly from the conviction that all major decisions of national importance should be subject to public scrutiny. Sarney's track record as a conservative politician further shored up the support for a parliamentary system.

In the national constituent assembly, the PMDB had 307 of the 559 delegates, while the PFL had 133 delegates. In theory, the two parties of the Democratic Alliance, first forged in August 1985 and working as partners in the government, gave Sarney an impressive margin with which to push any constitution that the alliance desired. But between the PMDB and the PFL, there was acrimony rather than harmony and rivalry rather than cooperation. During the first three months of operation, no fewer than 9,456 proposals (*emendas*) were filed in the constituent assembly; the final tally by November 1987, when the fourth draft was forged, reached over 12,000. Interestingly enough, the assembly decided to postpone public hearings on the external debt until *after* the constitution was approved. In fact, the assembly digressed from all external economic issues and concentrated on domestic problems.

The proponents of parliamentarism came from the left wing of the PMDB, but they had considerable support from all anti-Sarney politicians. Although it was argued that a parliamentary system of government would ensure democratic decision making for the country, many critics pointed out that Brazil had no viable party system to support this form of government. Parties in Brazil, except for some on the left, do not espouse ideologies. Many former supporters of the military regime in PDS switched to the PDMB shortly before the 1986 election. The ruling PMDB party hence lacks ideological cohesion, and is fragmented by the conflicts among many strong personalities, as well as by regional divisions. In brief, the support for parliamentarism in São Paulo and Rio began to erode. The erosion was helped along by the Sarney government's aid to cash-strapped states whose representatives agreed to oppose the parliamentary option.

Between the months of January and February 1988, Sarney was buoyed by the emergence of the Centrão, a center-right coalition of all parties in the assembly. It was able to contain the PMDB left wing and eagerly pushed for a five-year presidential mandate. Skillfully maneuvering his followers in the assembly and making a few concessions, Ulysses Guimarães sought to break up the Centrão. For example, he offered the hardcore right of the Centrão a compromise on the controversial agrarian reform articles originally proposed by the left. For a time, such tactics held the Centrão at bay.

But by late March, the political map of the constituent assembly was reshaped again. This time, an overwhelming majority (344 for, 212 against, and 3 abstentions) voted to retain the presidential system and a five-year term for Sarney. It was a victory for the Centrão and for Sarney. The proposed articles for the parliamentary system and its accompanying restrictions on the president no longer stood in the way of Sarney's pursuit of political goals. It is a moot question if parliamentarism could serve Brazil better in finding solutions to the economic problems, especially the external debt. What is clear is that the constituent assembly was not capable of dealing with the debt-related questions.

Debt and Democracy

Viable alternatives for creditors and debtors are limited in number. The political "see-saw" games that the left and the right have been playing since 1985 have considerably weakened Brazil's chances for implanting firm roots of democratic stability. To grow, Brazil needs funds. For the first three years of the Third World debt crisis, the country transferred $38.6 billion to the rich countries, yet Brazil received no new capital investment or fresh credit during this time.[21] The country must grow economically at an annual rate of 6 to 7 percent per year to keep pace with new job seekers coming onto the labor market. Brazil needs to restructure its export sector, including review of the current subsidies and incentive programs that cost as much as $6 billion per year. The country needs to expand exports without subsidies. Brazil's exports account for only 8-10 percent of its GDP, while Japan, the United States, and Western European countries export between 15 and 50 percent of their GDP.[22]

The level of debt servicing has bled Brazil; it should be renegotiated to allow the country's economy to grow and the banks to make a profit. This will require political participation of industrial governments, multilateral institutions, and the Brazilian government. The latter will have to find policies that are both economically viable and politically acceptable. Up until now, the exigencies of the Sarney government, the President's own hidden political agenda, and the priorities of the constituent assembly have collided mercilessly, turning Brazil into a rudderless ship. The trouble with the current democratic process is that the President has power but no legitimacy; the constituent assembly has legitimacy but no power. Hence a national consensus is hard to come by. This political stalemate and the economic drift have made Brazil vulnerable to international bankers and weakened the national resolve in search of solutions. Until Brazil finds this consensus, whether it be of the PMDB left or of the right-wing Centrão, the restoration of democracy will not be an easy process. Without a strong democratic regime in power, Brazil will not be able to negotiate successfully with its creditors.

Notes

1. *International Financial Statistics* and *World Debt Tables*, various issues. Per capita GDP figures are in 1980 dollars. See also Harold Lever, "The Debt Threat," *The New York Review of Books*, June 28, 1984 and Norman Gall, "Brazil and the Bankers: The Games Bankers Play," *Forbes*, December 5, 1983.

2. Inter-American Development Bank, *Annual Report 1986*; Banco Central do Brasil, *Brazil: Economic Program, International and External Adjustment*, 1984.

3. Ministério da Fazenda, *The Financing of Economic Development in the Period 1987-1991*, 1987, 3-4.

4. Similar concerns for foreign takeover of U.S. industries, real estate, and other assets have been rising. See, for example, *Wall Street Journal*, February 24, 1988.

5. SEPLAN/SEST, *Legislação básica*, 1984, 521. Also see Decreto No. 80.827 of November 28, 1977, "Programa do investimentos das empresas governamentais," *Diário Oficial da União*, November 29, 1977; *Correio Brasiliense*, July 26, 1985.

6. See Dornbusch chapter in this volume.

7. *Visão: quem é quem na economia brasileira-1987* (São Paulo: Visão, 1987), 369.

8. *O Estado de São Paulo*, January 8, 1985; "The International 500," *Fortune*, August 20, 1984; Bela Balassa, Gerardo M. Bueno, Pedro-Pablo Kuczynski, and Mário Henrique Simonsen, *Toward Renewed Economic Growth in Latin America* (Washington, DC: Institute for International Economics, 1986), 17-20.

9. *New York Times*, March 11, 1984; Eul-Soo Pang and Laura Jarnagin, "Brazilian Democracy and the Foreign Debt," *Current History* (February 1984).

10. Eder Sader, "A nova retórica da Nova República," in *Constituinte, economia e política da Nova República*, ed. Antônio Kandir (São Paulo: Cortez Editora, 1986), 52-53.

11. Carlos Alberto Sardenberg, *Aventura e agonia: nos bastidores do cruzado* (São Paulo: Editora Schwarcz, 1987), 188-89. Statement made before a Chamber of Deputies hearing.

12. Ibid., 225. Ironically, the idea of bypassing Congress came from the academic economists, not from Sarney.

13. "O Brasil da moeda forte," *Conjuntura Econômica* (March 1986), 11; Pérsio Arida et al., *Brasil, Argentina, Israel: inflação zero*, 12th ed. (Rio de Janeiro: Paz e Terra, 1986), 9-35; Francisco Lopes, *O Choque heterodoxo: combate a inflação e reforma monetária* (Rio: Editora Campus, 1986); *Correio Brasiliense*, August 17, 1986; "Prova da força," *Isto é*, July 30, 1986.

14. João Sayad, SEPLAN chief who eventually lost power struggle to his rival Funaro, complained that Finance officials had too much power over the importation. André Lara Resende et al., *Os país do cruzado contam por que não deu certo*, 2nd ed. (Rio de Janeiro: L&PM, 1987), 32. *Veja*, September 24, 1986, published a long article on the interim evaluation of the Cruzado Plan.

15. IADB, *Economic and Social Progress in Latin America 1987*, 246-248.

16. João Manuel Cardoso de Mello and Luiz Gonzaga de Mello Belluzzo, "Introdução," in *FMI x Brasil: a armadilha da recessão*, ed. Adroaldo Moura da Silva et al. (São Paulo: Forum Gazeta Mercantil, 1983).

17. *Jornal do Brasil*, December 14, 1986. As opposed to Funaro's 2.5 percent of GDP, Roberto Macedo, director of the Economics Faculty at the University of São Paulo and an influential PMDB politician, called for 2 percent of GDP as payment for the external debt interest. In 1986, Brazil was paying about 4 percent of GDP as debt service.

18. "Sarney sabia de tudo," *Senhor*, February 15, 1988.

19. Ibid.

20. *Folha de São Paulo*, May 30, 1987.

21. Ministério da Fazenda, *The Financing of Economic Development*, 3-4.

22. Câmara dos Deputados. Comissão de Inquírito Parlamentar (CD/CIP), *Dívida externa e FMI-Brasil Acordo*, testimony of Carlos Viacava, April 3, 1984. Viacava was the director of Cacex, Bank of Brazil, a division in charge of Brazil's foreign trade.

Suggestions for Further Reading

Baer, Werner. *Industrialization and Economic Development in Brazil*. Homewood, IL: The Economic Growth Center, Yale University, 1965.

Cardoso, Eliana, and Albert Fishlow. "The Macroeconomics of the Brazilian External Debt." In *Developing Country Debt*, ed. Jeffrey Sachs. Chicago: University of Chicago Press, forthcoming 1989.

Cardoso, Fernando Henrique. *Autoritarismo e democratização*. Rio de Janeiro: Editora Paz e Terra, 1975.

Evans, Peter. *Dependent Development: The Alliance of Multinational, State, and Local Capital in Brazil*. Princeton: Princeton University Press, 1979.

Frieden, Jeffry A. "The Brazilian Borrowing Experience: From Miracle to Debacle and Back." *Latin American Research Review* 22, no. 1 (1987).

Furtado, Celso. *The Economic Growth of Brazil: A Survey from Colonial to Modern Times.* Berkeley: University of California Press, 1971.

Lopes, Francisco Lafaiete. *O choque heterodoxo, combate a inflação e reforma monetaria.* Rio de Janeiro: Editoria Campus Ltda., 1986.

Skidmore, Thomas E. *The Politics of Military Rule in Brazil, 1964-1985.* New York: Oxford University Press, 1988.

Stepan, Alfred, ed. *Democratizing Brazil: Problems of Transition and Consolidation.* New York: Oxford University Press, forthcoming 1989.

9

Crisis Management, Economic Reform and Costa Rican Democracy

Joan M. Nelson

Among the countries considered in this volume, only Costa Rica is an established and stable competitive democracy. Every election since 1948 save two, has shifted power between major parties or coalitions. Free media, high voting participation, and myriad organized interest groups assure that the system is not only competitive but broadly inclusive.

Costa Rica is also small (2.7 million in 1988) and highly trade-dependent. The external shocks of the debt crisis struck Costa Rica early and with force. Terms of trade sank by one third between 1977 and 1981, while the volume of exports dwindled by 8 percent. Interest on commercial debt ballooned from $60 million in 1977 to $290 million in 1981 and $510 million in 1982. The economy stalled, then contracted. Gross domestic product (GDP) figured in constant 1980 colones was 14 percent lower in 1982 than in 1979.[1] The economic decline was unprecedented in living memory. Frightened Costa Ricans saw not only their welfare but their cherished democratic values and institutions threatened. The immediate crisis was contained by late 1983, but Costa Rica continues to carry a debt burden among the highest in the world relative to the size of its economy.

This chapter explores the interaction between the debt crisis and Costa Rican democracy: the effects of democratic institutions and values on the ability to cope with economic crisis, and the impact of the crisis and its aftermath on those same institutions and values. Costa Rica's adjustment efforts moved through three phases between 1978 and 1988: an initial period of unsuccessful crisis management from 1979 to mid-1982; a successful short-run stabilization effort during the first year and a half of the Monge government through the end of 1983; and the period from 1984 to the present, characterized by a continued need for tight macroeconomic management combined with efforts at more far-reaching economic reform. The discussion first describes and analyzes the two early phases, and assesses the role of Costa Rican democracy in the initial failure and subsequent economic success. It then turns to the way the system has dealt with longer term structural and debt management problems. The chapter concludes that Costa Rican democracy proved stronger than the challenge of the acute crisis period, but has yet to prove itself flexible enough to make the longer-term economic reforms crucial for its own self-preservation.

Crisis Management and Costa Rican Democracy

Economic Disintegration under Carazo, 1978-1982

In 1978, the mood in Costa Rica was buoyant. Extremely high coffee prices in 1976 and 1977 had lifted national income to a record level. The boom capped roughly fifteen years of brisk growth. With the exception of 1975, from the early 1960s to the late 1970s real GDP had grown between 5 and 7 percent per year. Moreover, the fruits of growth had been widely shared. "No other Latin American country registered so large a decrease in inequality nor so low a level of inequality as Costa Rica."[2]

The price of coffee was dropping, however, even as Rodrigo Carazo took office in spring 1978. Coffee revenues dwindled from a record $319 million in 1977 to $248 million in 1980. Meanwhile, the nation's oil bill rose from $83 to $186 million. Revolution in Nicaragua blocked trucks carrying exports to the Central American Common Market, while regional turmoil cut demand. The trade deficit grew 250 percent between 1977 and 1979 while, as already noted, interest payments soared.[3]

Rodrigo Carazo—businessman and economist, stock breeder and landowner—won the 1978 elections backed by a four-party Unity coalition with strong business support. His campaign stressed conservative fiscal management plus longer term reforms to open the economy and reduce state intervention. Yet confronted with the abrupt shift in external conditions, the government first attempted compensatory fiscal expansion, including heavy infrastructure investment. In contrast to the rally experienced after the first oil shock, coffee prices did not conveniently swing up. Moreover, the legislature refused to approve a proposed tax reform. The 1979 public sector deficit exceeded 12 percent of GDP. Inflation jumped from 6 to 9.2 percent, real interest rates became rapidly more negative, and public-sector borrowing crowded out private-sector credit.

Efforts to tighten economic management in 1980 were not enough to prevent the immediate collapse of an attempted standby agreement with the International Monetary Fund (IMF). Frightened businessmen moved capital out of the country at a quickened pace. By mid-1980, reserves covered only one week's imports, and the government began to increase arrears on debt service to protect remaining reserves. Despite extreme reluctance to devalue, by autumn 1980 a *de facto* dual exchange rate went into effect. At the end of the year the colón was floated, dropping rapidly from an official rate of 8.6 colones to the U.S. dollar to about 20 to 1.

Meanwhile the Minister of Finance, convinced that the crisis demanded both austerity measures and more basic shifts in incentives, pressed the IMF for a three-year Extended Fund Facility. The IMF was reluctant, especially in view of the recent

Unicameral legislature

aborted agreement, but by late 1980 it agreed to funding equivalent to 450 percent of Costa Rica's quota, contingent on stiff preconditions. Resistance within the government was as much or more of an obstacle than skepticism in the IMF. Nevertheless, by February 1981 a package of decrees meeting the preconditions was announced; briefly it appeared as if the government might take control. But in April, as Minister of Finance Hernando Sáenz concluded a European tour seeking further financial support, the entire effort collapsed. The Chambers of Industry and Commerce held a large public meeting in San José to protest the new decrees, particularly the requirement that business purchase foreign exchange on the free market to repay obligations incurred at the earlier official rate of exchange. President Carazo revoked the key decrees, and Sáenz promptly resigned.

Any semblance of coherent economic policy disintegrated during the remaining year of the Carazo government. In July 1981 the Supreme Court ruled unconstitutional the government's December 1980 decision to float the colón. The foreign exchange market was thrown into chaos. Carazo turned to the Assembly to approve a new fixed value for the colón, but political maneuvering within the legislature postponed action until November, and by then the newly-legislated official value was half the free rate. In September 1981 a moratorium was declared on servicing external debt; actual payments had ceased earlier. By autumn 1981 external agencies and Costa Ricans despaired of action from the Carazo government and turned their attention to the elections scheduled for February 1982.[4]

Stabilization under Monge, 1982-1983

To no one's surprise, the elections brought a resounding mandate for new economic management. National Liberation Party (PLN) candidate Alberto Monge Alvarez won 58 percent of the popular vote and his party took nearly a two-to-one majority in the unicameral legislature. By summer 1982 the new economic team launched a decisive stabilization program, seeking above all to restore a modicum of confidence in the government and the economy. The colón was appreciated from roughly 65 to 45 to the dollar. Strict foreign exchange controls were combined with measures designed to stabilize and eventually unify the official and free market rates. The fiscal deficit, which had reached 14.3 percent of GDP in 1981 and was headed higher when Monge took office, was slashed to 9 percent in 1982 and 3.4 percent in 1983, entailing drastic utility rate and tax increases. An IMF standby was arranged in late 1982, committing the government to continued wage restraint, further utility hikes, and increased interest rates (although considerably less than the IMF had originally urged). By December 1983 the exchange rate was unified, arrears were cleared, and prolonged negotiations with foreign commercial banks had produced agreement on rescheduled payments.[5]

The economy responded quickly, indeed much faster than anticipated (see Table 9.1). Inflation, which had neared 100 percent at the time of the elections, plunged to roughly 35 percent by late 1983. Real GDP had dropped 10 percent in 1982 but rebounded 4.6 percent in 1983. Unemployment declined (by one measure, to 6.2

Table 9.1
Costa Rican Economic Performance Indicators, 1979-86

	1979	1980	1981	1982	1983	1984	1985	1986
GDP Growth Rate (%)	4.9	0.8	-2.3	-7.3	2.9	8.0	1.0	4.0
Terms of Trade (1980=100)	110.5	100.0	92.5	92.7	95.9	94.5	94.8	104.3
Current Account (% of GDP)	-13.8	-13.7	-15.6	-10.4	-10.3	-7.0	-7.7	-4.4
Inflation[a] (%)	9.2	18.8	37.1	90.1	32.6	12.0	13.1	11.8
Budget Deficit (% of GDP)	-6.8	-7.4	-2.9	-0.9	-2.1	-0.7	-1.3	n.a.
Minimum Wage (1980=100)	98.5	100.0	90.4	85.9	99.3	104.4	112.2	119.0
Unemployment Rate (%)	4.9	5.9	8.7	9.4	8.6	6.6	6.7	6.7

[a]Consumer price index, year-end
Sources: IMF, *International Financial Statistics Yearbook*, 1987; World Bank, *World Tables*, 1988; U.N. Economic Commission for Latin America, *Preliminary Overview of the Latin American Economy*, 1987.

percent by as early as November 1982);[6] and imports increased. The immediate crisis had been contained.

Crisis Management Capacity and Costa Rican Democracy

What were the major causes for the Carazo government's inability to cope with the crisis? Were any of these causes inherent to democracies in general, or to Costa Rican democracy in particular? And what factors permitted the impressively successful short-term performance of the Monge government?

Some of the political obstacles to effective stabilization during the Carazo government obviously resulted from specific features of the domestic and international political situation of the late 1970s. The Unity coalition held only 27 of 55 seats in the unicameral Legislative Assembly, not enough of a margin to prevail over the PLN opposition without the cooperation of the four Marxist deputies. Moreover, the governing coalition rapidly disintegrated. At the close of the term, it had voted as a bloc only on the annual selections of Assembly officers. On the international side, Carazo entered office as the Nicaraguan revolution was fast accelerating, and he wished to support that revolution. Events across the northern border dominated the attention of the cabinet for much of the government's crucial first two years. As the economic situation worsened, Carazo's individual reaction was to withdraw and increasingly isolate himself.

The sheer speed with which the crisis unfolded also hampered an adequate response. Almost no one, in or outside of Costa Rica, had anticipated the seriousness of the situation, and it developed so swiftly that analysis constantly lagged behind reality. As in other countries, timely and adequate data on the extent of the debt, even in the public sector, did not exist.

Widespread attitudes and assumptions also affected economic policy choices, probably more strongly than in a less thoroughgoing democracy. The public could not have been less prepared for austerity. Real aggregate demand had expanded 25 percent between 1975 and 1977. "What clearly was an exceptional episode, in terms of improvement in real income, was rapidly accepted as the new norm."[7] Moreover, devaluation was associated in the public mind with economic mismanagement and was widely believed to benefit only exporters, above all the wealthy "coffee barons."

In addition to these situational and attitudinal obstacles, more durable structural and institutional features of Costa Rican democracy constrained the government's options. The Costa Rican presidency is unusually and deliberately weak. The president shares most significant powers with the cabinet or with the Legislative Assembly, as demonstrated by the unsuccessful effort to float the colón by decree. By the late 1970s some 130 autonomous public agencies had been created, over which the central government had little financial or administrative control. Moreover, the comparatively weak executive confronts well-organized and vocal interest groups. Thus the February 1981 package of measures, Carazo's most serious effort to contain the crisis, was destroyed by the protests of the Chamber of Industry and Commerce.

Constitutional provisions limiting the president to a single term, and preventing legislative deputies from serving consecutive terms, further impede executive control and party discipline. The president is a lame duck almost from the moment he announces the appointment of his cabinet. Even if his party ostensibly controls the Assembly, it shortly breaks into rival factions led by two or more contenders for the party's next presidential candidacy. Rivals for nomination, who often control sizable groups of deputies, are reluctant to offend any interest group that controls significant votes or money. (Public funding of campaigns covers some but far from all costs.) Party or coalition unity thus promptly shatters. The prohibition against deputies serving two consecutive terms further handicaps party discipline: party leaders cannot threaten to withhold endorsement in the next election since the current deputies cannot run.[8]

These same structural features confronted the Monge administration when it took office in April 1982. What had changed to permit the much more coherent and firm response? Most obviously, the Monge government was much stronger than its predecessor. Monge won 58 percent of the popular vote, while Unity won 33 percent; the comparable figures in 1978 had been just over 50 percent and 43 percent. In the Assembly, the PLN took 33 seats while Unity took 18, as compared to the government's two-vote margin over the PLN in 1978. And despite factional splits within the PLN, it was considerably more cohesive than the Unity coalition during Carazo's administration.

Clearly, there had been a radical shift in public mood. By mid-1982, all groups were paying dearly for an unplanned adjustment, and many were willing to acquiesce to any plausible policy that signalled the resumption of government control over the situation. The very fact that the government had so little room for maneuver dampened initial criticism; even left-wing critics agreed that there was no real alternative to an orthodox approach.[9] Monge and the PLN could also benefit from the classic new regime effect: Carazo was viewed as responsible for the nation's difficulties. At least initially, the new government was largely free of blame for painful policies.

The new government also had an advantage in dealing with Costa Rican unions, concentrated in the public sector and increasingly restive and bitter under Carazo. Not only the PLN as a party, but Monge personally, with his strong social democratic ties and long experience with national and international labor organizations, could better command union confidence and call for temporary sacrifice.

More arguably, some of the Costa Rican system's built-in obstacles to strong executive direction may have temporarily abated in response to crisis. The Assembly continued to balk—for instance, resisting approval of the new exchange rate arrangements—but it did pass crucial legislation. The crisis may also have muted the usual pattern of factional strife within the ruling party over candidacy for the next presidential election.

The political advantages of the Monge administration were powerfully reinforced by key economic factors. The worst impact of *de facto* devaluation had already occurred during the last half of the Carazo term. The Monge government did not have to impose further real devaluation. Indeed, as noted earlier, the government was convinced that the free market exchange rate had overshot, and substantially revalued the colón. By 1983, inflation had dropped dramatically and real wages, employment, and imports were all increasing. Tightly controlled current government expenditures remained the sole major austerity element of the program.

In certain ways, Costa Rican democracy greatly facilitated the rapid economic turnaround under Monge. The fact that Costa Rica was a bastion of democracy in a region of great turmoil prompted generous external assistance for the stabilization effort. The fundamental legitimacy of the system and renewed confidence in its long-run stability probably contributed to strong and rapid response of the business and financial sectors to the Monge government's stabilization program. In 1983 roughly $100 million in capital that had earlier fled the country was repatriated.[10] Traditional Costa Rican emphasis on equity and peaceful conflict resolution helped to minimize the political protest accompanying the stabilization effort.

In short, there is no simple answer to the question of how Costa Rican democracy affected the capacity to cope with economic crisis. Its initial effects were largely to obstruct appropriate policies, but other aspects of the system later facilitated adoption and pursuit of a highly effective program.

The question of interaction between crisis management and democracy can also be reversed: how did the crisis and its management affect Costa Rican democracy?

More precisely, how did the crisis itself and the efforts to cope with it affect stability, equity and legitimacy?

Economic crises trigger protest in all systems, and governments often hesitate to take vigorous stabilization measures because they fear the measures will provoke further instability. In Costa Rica the most obvious response to worsening conditions was labor unrest, intensifying under the Carazo government and continuing into the Monge administration. Draconian increases in utility rates also provoked protests and roadblocks across the nation in July 1983. But public protest was comparatively mild and violence was negligible, especially in view of the severity of economic deterioration. Several factors clearly contributed to the relatively limited protest. One of these was integral to democracy: as conditions deteriorated under Carazo, the certain prospect of elections and a new government was an important safety valve. A second factor was inherent in Costa Rican political culture but not necessarily in all democratic systems: a strong and widespread antipathy toward violence. A public opinion poll conducted shortly after the demonstrations of July 1983 found that a majority of those polled disapproved of using even so comparatively mild a tactic as roadblocks (although 35 percent of the respondents saw the barricades as warranted).[11]

The Monge government managed political pressures and the design of the stabilization program itself in a way that helped to limit protest. Union demands were handled with a mixture of firmness and concessions. A public sector wage freeze and a longer working day were announced almost immediately; the agreement with the IMF concluded late in 1982 reaffirmed the wage freeze. Several strikes were dissolved by threats of dismissal or use of the National Guard. From September 1982 on, however, wages were partly indexed through the device of a "basic basket" of commodities (the content of which was gradually expanded); wage adjustments compensated for increases in the absolute price of the basket. More fundamentally, wage increases outpaced inflation. Average real wages rose about 11 percent in 1983, and private-sector wages rose still more rapidly.[12]

Concern for social equity influenced the design of the program as a whole. Business, together with medium and large agricultural interests, bore sharp tax and utility increases. Wage increases were skewed in favor of lower-paid workers in both the public and private sectors. In the most trying period of adjustment, temporary public employment and food aid programs were helpful in reaching the unemployed or self-employed who could not benefit from wage increases. Perhaps one in every dozen families benefitted from short-term food aid. The real welfare impact on poorer families was still severe, but the key politically relevant fact was the widespread perception that Monge was making a serious effort to allocate the costs of adjustment equitably and to shield the most vulnerable groups.

In short, Costa Rican democracy emerged from its most severe crisis since the present system was established in 1948 with remarkably little damage to civic order and social harmony. Moreover, survey data for 1978, 1980 and 1983 suggest strongly that the fundamental legitimacy of the system was unimpaired, and even somewhat strengthened by 1983. Presumably, this reflects increased confidence and pride as a result of the system's demonstrated capacity to meet and master the crisis. Between 1978 and 1980, the proportion of respondents indicating high support for the system dropped from almost 80 to 70 percent,[13] but in 1983, the proportion of those affirming high support rebounded to over 93 percent.[14] The data for 1980 invite speculation on what might have happened had the new government taking office in 1982 proved less effective. But as events unfolded, democratic institutions and traditions proved sufficiently pliable to permit and even support effective short-term action, and the political system itself emerged largely unscathed.

Longer-Run Structural Change and Costa Rican Democracy

As 1984 began, the Monge government faced a triple challenge. It had to preserve, in the face of growing political pressures, the economic balance that had been so painfully restored. It also had to restore sustainable economic growth. That would require reforms to correct weaknesses in the economy predating, and in part responsible for, the debt crisis itself. Continued stability and growth were intertwined with each other and with a third challenge: management of an overwhelming external debt burden.

The Struggle to Preserve Economic Stability

Costa Rica's hard won modicum of economic stability encountered difficulties as soon as it was achieved. The government had early warned that recovery might take "at least four years."[15] By late 1983, however, perhaps spurred by the unexpected speed of initial recovery, the public mood was shifting from relief that the crisis had been brought under control to demands for rapid restoration of pre-crisis incomes and services. As originally submitted to the Assembly in late 1983, the 1984 budget had a deficit so large that the IMF insisted it be cut by legislative action. This was done through the Emergency Economic Law of February 1984. But by mid-1984 an unwisely generous loosening of credit restrictions caused imports to surge, reserves to dwindle, and arrears to begin to accumulate again.

A second standby agreement had almost been reached with the IMF by March 1984, but in light of the new trends, the IMF insisted on additional preconditions before granting final approval. At this point a lapse in economic leadership proved most costly. Central Bank Governor Carlos Manuel Castillo, the main architect of the stabilization effort of 1982-83, had resigned in February 1984 to seek nomination for the 1986 presidential election. The economic team was further shuffled later that spring, and a cohesive and respected team did not emerge until the autumn. Legislative reluctance to approve key legislation caused additional delay. The new standby was not finally approved until a whole year later, in March 1985. Agreements with the World Bank, the Paris Club, and the coordinating committee for those commercial banks to which Costa Rica was indebted all hinged on a completed standby with the IMF. Therefore the entire package of financial relief was not concluded until well into 1985. By that time election pressures had resulted in large budget increases. The central government deficit, pared to 1.3 percent of GDP in 1985, jumped to 4.6 percent in 1986.[16] As the Monge term drew to a close in April 1986, failure to meet agreed targets caused the second standby to expire with roughly half the funds undrawn.

Failure to meet fully the external agencies' or the government's own goals did not imply irresponsible economic management. The budget deficit was in fact kept low (and the combined public sector deficit cut back), inflation was contained within moderate bounds, and the exchange rate kept at realistic levels. Economic performance, however, was disappointing. After a solid increase of 6.1 percent in 1984, real per capita GNP was slightly negative in 1985 and barely recovered in 1986. Non-traditional exports to non-traditional markets were a bright spot, rising to almost one third of export earnings in 1986 and exceeding coffee earnings in 1987, but trade and current account balances continued to be negative.[17] Two factors accounted for the near stagnation. First, despite rescheduling and generous levels of concessional assistance, the debt overhang meant Costa Rica suffered large net financial outflows in 1983, 1984, and 1985. In good part due to the resource drain, investment lagged. Gross domestic investment for the four years from 1983 through 1986 averaged less than three quarters of the 1980 level, despite steady growth.[18] Second, the structural weaknesses of the economy were being addressed only to a limited degree.

The Need for Structural Reforms

Those weaknesses had begun to slow Costa Rica's economic growth even before the debt crisis began. One set of problems revolved around patterns of industrial development and foreign trade. During the 1960s and 1970s manufacturing expanded substantially, geared to domestic markets and to the Central American Common Market. The industries that emerged, however, were highly protected and for the most part not competitive in broader international markets. Moreover, imported inputs comprised an average of 60 percent of the value of the finished product. By the late 1970s, previously rapid expansion of manufactured exports was slowing and the trade deficit was steadily widening, while the economy remained vulnerable to swings in international prices for coffee and bananas.

A second set of issues grew out of the state's large and growing role in the economy. The PLN, the most durable of Costa Rica's parties, had long seen state-led growth in a mixed economy as Costa Rica's path to development. By 1978 the growing public sector accounted for 39 percent of investment, one quarter of GDP, and almost one fifth of employment. Slow growth of employment in industry increased political pressure on the public sector: two of every five new jobs generated in the late 1970s were public-sector jobs.[19]

Public-sector activities reflected strong and varied political demands. They included the vigorous educational, social, and infrastructure programs that had dramatically increased equity and well-being over three decades. But they also encompassed a rapidly growing range of public enterprises, many of which operated at a loss. A pervasive system of direct and indirect business and agriculture subsidies—sometimes described as "socialism for the rich"—sprouted in the 1970s, straining the budget and distorting investment incentives. Revenues did not keep pace, and the fiscal deficit widened throughout the 1970s. The growing trade and fiscal deficits were covered by domestic and foreign borrowing. Total external debt increased six-fold between 1970 and 1978.[20]

By then these trends were drawing increased attention. Costa Ricans drew anxious analogies to Uruguay, another small democracy where an expensive welfare system, overgrown bureaucracy, and low productivity had led to economic breakdown and military rule. Much of the public had begun to view parts of the public sector as corrupt and wasteful. The dominant newspaper, *La Nación*, and the National Association for Economic Development (ANFE), representing a small but elite circle of business leaders, politicians, civil servants and academics, vigorously pressed a conservative market-oriented critique. Even within the PLN itself, newer voices, including those of future presidents Monge and Arias, called for reassessing development strategy.[21]

Carazo's 1978 coalition, supported by an unusual alliance of manufacturing interests with traditional coffee, sugar and commercial groups, promised economic reform. Early in the Carazo administration, the National Plan for Development (1979-82) sketched guidelines for a new industrial policy. The thrust was not so much reducing the role of the state (despite Unity's free market rhetoric); rather, the Plan proposed shifting the emphasis of state incentives and support to favor new agroindustries oriented to a more open economy. The proposals failed to move much beyond rhetoric. The opposition of the unions and the PLN contingent in the Assembly, as well as fundamental conflicts between industrial and agro-industrial interests in Carazo's own coalition, produced an erratic course of measures announced and then diluted or withdrawn. As the economic crisis intensified, medium-term reforms were forced ever farther to the margins of political attention. Despite some early reform-oriented announcements, immediate stabilization issues necessarily dominated economic policy for the first eighteen months of Monge's government. Thus issues of national economic strategy and structural reform were in abeyance for roughly four years, from 1980 through 1983. The trends that had emerged during the 1970s remained unresolved. Meanwhile, Costa Rica's external debt had tripled, while sluggish growth and increasing protectionist sentiment in the advanced nations created a much more difficult international economic environment.

Structural Reforms during the Monge Administration

In late summer 1983 the U.S. Agency for International Development (AID) mission in San José, together with officials within the Monge government, saw in the approaching conclusion of the initial, successful stabilization drive an opportune moment to press for broader reforms. Partly or largely in response to AID encouragement, the government established an interministerial commission in September to prepare a "concepts paper on economic strategy" for the remaining thirty months of the Monge administration. The draft report highlighted nontraditional exports to markets outside of Central America as the key to restored income levels and sustainable growth, and spelled out an agenda of specific implementation measures. When the program was reviewed in the cabinet, however, conflicting views and political considerations gutted it. An initial proposal for a crawling peg, adjusted monthly, gave way to a vaguer commitment to a flexible exchange rate policy. The timetable attached to export promotion measures was eliminated. The original commitment to a thorough examination of price controls and agricultural support prices disappeared.[22] By the time the program was approved by the cabinet and presented to the press by President Monge on May 18, it was too vague to draw much attention. The episode was a preview of coming disagreements and conflicts.

The new economic team formed later in 1984 did produce significant reforms in the remaining two years of the Monge government, but progress was much slower and more partial than domestic and external reformers wished. Central Bank Governor Eduardo Lizano, a respected academic economist who had the confidence of the business sectors, was the most powerful and persistent advocate of reform within the government. Not surprisingly, two of the clearest areas of reform were those within his authority or influence: flexible exchange rate management and financial sector reform. Shortly after taking office in autumn 1984, Lizano replaced the semi-sacred fixed exchange rate with a system of biweekly mini-devaluations. There was barely a murmur of protest. With strong support from AID (which he used at one point to overcome Assembly resistance), Lizano also moved to loosen the monopoly of the state-owned commercial banks and to dismantle the elaborate system of credit categories that had increasingly been used to subsidize upper-income groups or to achieve political goals.

The need to stimulate and reorient exports was widely conceded, especially as Costa Rica's traditional markets in other Central American nations disintegrated. The high dependence on imported inputs, however, meant that competitive exports required reduced trade protection, a much more controversial prospect. Encouraged by the World Bank, Costa Rica collaborated with other Central American governments to rationalize and somewhat reduce the Common External Tariff, effective at the beginning of 1986. Steps toward full membership in the General Agreement on Tariffs and Trade (GATT) have followed, but protection remains substantial. The harshest battles to liberalize imports probably lie in the future.

Despite broad agreement that the state bureaucracy had become too cumbersome and expensive, there was little consensus on how to rationalize and reduce it. Three concrete issues became the focus of intense pressure from external donors during the Monge administration: the dismantling of the Costa Rican Development Corporation (CODESA); the reform of the National Production Council (CNP) charged with encouraging production and controlling distribution of basic grains; and the effort to contain the public-sector wage bill and cap the growth of public employment.

Established in the early 1970s, CODESA had mushroomed into a sprawling holding company for varied commercial, manufacturing and transport activities. It was widely viewed as corrupt, yet its original social democratic rationale remained convincing to many PLN legislators and much of the public. There was support for increased efficiency, but little enthusiasm for divestment. Moreover, there were few buyers for bankrupt parastatals. Therefore, many of CODESA's varied activities were transferred to central government ministries or to cooperatives, but only marginal parts of the empire were privatized.

Reform of the CNP involved different issues. One key question was rice policy: heavily subsidized producer prices had stimulated output on a scale that often exceeded local needs, and the CNP then sold the excess abroad at a heavy loss. Under strong external pressure, CNP losses were reduced by raising consumer prices, and limiting CNP purchases at high support prices to the level of domestic need. A new private entity was created to handle purchases for export, but efforts to reduce subsidies for rice farmers triggered roadblocks and demonstrations and a bitter power struggle in the cabinet. Many Costa Ricans strongly believe that the nation should produce as much as possible of its own food, justifying high support prices for rice. CNP support prices in general are also defended as aiding small farmers. Even though most rice is grown by a handful of large producers, they constitute an extraordinarily powerful lobby group that has successfully engaged the support of many smaller farmers who grow some rice.

Still more intense are the political pressures swirling around reduction of public-sector employment. Most of the articulate and organized middle classes are employed in the public sector, including three quarters of all professionals and over four fifths of the nation's technical personnel.[23] Moreover, public-sector employment is the best hope for the growing numbers of secondary school and university graduates produced each year, especially in the context of uncertain and slow overall economic growth. Perhaps equally important, the issue engages fundamental ideological conflicts regarding the role of the state. Although the economic braintrust of the PLN is convinced of the need to streamline and limit the state's economic role, the bulk of party cadres remain committed to the concept of state-led growth. Thus, growth of public employment has been slowed but not cut.[24]

Politics, Democracy, and Structural Reform

To what extent does this record of slow and partial reform reflect Costa Rican democracy? Structural reforms are difficult in any political system. Unlike austerity measures, which are expected to be temporary, structural reforms are explicitly permanent. A recognized national crisis can prompt acquiesence to temporary austerity measures, as it did in Costa Rica in 1982-83, but groups whose interests or convictions are threatened by proposed long-term reforms will mount strong and lasting resistance. Moreover, structural reforms are often complex measures carried out by many agencies in many stages, offering multiple opportunities for administrative or openly political delay and dilution.

Many of the political obstacles to economic liberalization in Costa Rica are similar to those in other countries, including authoritarian systems. Administrative weaknesses, vested interests, and statist ideologies are neither peculiar to, nor unusually marked in, democracies. In many systems, established parties rely substantially on patronage and favors, and therefore resist reforms that reduce public-sector jobs or shift resources such as credit from discretionary to market mechanisms. But democracies (and to some extent semi-authoritarian systems where elections serve important legitimizing functions) pose additional obstacles to economic reforms, especially those requiring a long-term outlook. Elections predictably swell public expenditures and prompt governments to postpone unpopular reforms. More broadly, the electoral cycle itself limits politicians' time horizons for planning reform strategy, particularly in fixed-term systems.

Particular features of Costa Rican democracy further hamper reform, such as the ban on re-election of the president mentioned earlier. The bar to legislators serving consecutive terms inhibits familiarity with the issues and technical expertise that might encourage constructive reform. Complex bureaucratic regulations protect individual rights (as well as the perquisites of public-sector workers), but hamstring policy implementation. More broadly, the habits of thought and the vested interests resisting reform in Costa Rica are the cumulative result of the choices of four decades of democracy.

Costa Rican emphasis on consultation and consensus slows reform, but also provides multiple channels for communication and education on policy issues. In both the Monge and Arias governments, key economic team members have spent a great deal of time and effort attempting to explain the rationale and need for reforms to cabinet members, legislators, public officials, and the public at large. The Unity Party has attempted for a decade to focus debate on the need for structural changes. Public views have almost surely shifted greatly in the last decade, from the widespread assumption (despite dissenting voices) that existing arrangements were basically sound, to the recognition that some major reforms are imperative to cope with change in Central America and the world. The leading economic analysts for both major parties agree on many issues, and are probably closer to each other than either group is to its own party's cadres.

Nevertheless, building consensus takes a great deal of time. A slow-motion race is under way in Costa Rica between the frustration and alienation produced by economic stagnation, and the unfolding struggle over the design, timing, and cost allocation of reforms needed to break out of stagnation. Vested interests are not likely to yield gracefully to broader national interests, nor will cogent economic analysis dissolve cherished ideologies. Reformers will have to chip away at established arrangements, making do with marginal consensus on specific issues, perhaps winning occasional larger victories where particularly clear links to economic growth can be demonstrated, or where coalitions can be built with newer, more externally-oriented interests. Broad public consensus on basic issues is more likely to validate cumulative changes already made, rather than provide the springboard for making them.

Debt, Democracy, and Economic Adjustment

Increasing imbalances and inefficiencies in Costa Rica's economic structure were slowing growth before the debt crisis erupted. Their solution would have challenged the flexibility and creativity of Costa Rican democracy in the 1980s and 1990s, even in the absence of the debt burden, but the debt has shaped the politics of reform in several ways.

Most obviously, for four years, from 1983 through mid-1986, the debt burden sharply reduced the resources available to restructure the economy and to ease welfare and political costs of restructuring. Relative to its economy, Costa Rica's debt is among the highest in the world. Table 9.2 indicates the strain of debt on the economy. Debt service to official and commercial creditors far outweighed the high levels of concessional aid provided by bilateral and multilateral donors after 1982.[25]

The Monge government initially took a conciliatory stance regarding external debt. To signal the government's good faith and improve the negotiating atmosphere, Costa Rica unilaterally resumed modest repayment ($40 million in 1982) to the banks, and pledged larger payments as increases in export earnings and capital inflow permitted, prior to working out formal agreements with the banks. Since Costa Rica's troubles predated the broader debt crisis, the commercial banks, initially blaming the situation wholly on Costa Rican mismanagement, took a very tough bargaining stance. The explosion of the crisis in Mexico and, a bit later, in Brazil and Argentina, cast a different and more sympathetic light on Costa Rica's problems, but raised new concerns about the effects of any agreement with Costa Rica on the banks' much larger stakes in other countries. Nevertheless, much of the commercial debt was finally rescheduled by September 1983. The banks later agreed to provide a modest new lending facility of $75 million as part of the larger financial package finally put together in 1985.

Costa Rica's ability to keep current on rescheduled debt service hinged on timely injections of foreign assistance. As the Monge administration drew to a close, officials and analysts were convinced that continued large net financial outflows

Table 9.2
Costa Rican Debt, Aid, and Resource Flows, 1982-86

	1982	1983	1984	1985	1986
Total Debt/GNP[a]	111.6	114.6	101.4	102.7	95.5
Public and Guaranteed Debt/GNP[b]	96.7	104.3	92.7	95.0	88.0
Total Debt Service/GNP	6.1	21.5	10.2	12.9	10.1
Total Debt Service/Exports of Goods and Services	12.5	50.6	27.9	39.8	26.3
Concessional Aid Per Capita (U.S. Dollars)[c]	32.0	100.8	86.0	107.7	n.a.
Net Resource Transfer/GNP[d]	2.9	4.0	-23.2	-35.9	37.5

[a]Includes long term debt, use of IMF credit and estimated short-term debt
[b]Includes public and publicly guaranteed long-term debt
[c]Net disbursements of aid from bilateral and multilateral sources
[d]Net long-term capital flows plus net short-term flows minus interest repayments
Sources: World Bank, *World Debt Tables, 1987-88*; World Bank, *World Development Report, 1987*; World Bank, *World Tables, 1988.*

were simply incompatible with resuming sustainable growth. In summer 1986, the new Arias government unilaterally decided to suspend two thirds of debt service due, exempting short-term credit. In September the government approached the coordinating committee of its creditor banks with a proposal that $1.4 billion in debt be rescheduled over 25 years at below-market rates of interest, with a cap on service in any one year of 1.5 percent of GDP. Initial angry reactions, including a threat by one bank to sue, cooled by early 1987. The commercial banks were well aware that Costa Rica could not honor its contractual terms of debt and resume healthy growth. Indeed, the Costa Rican proposal came three weeks after a senior Bank of America official, who was also chair of the coordinating committee for Costa Rica, stated in a speech to a Miami bankers' conference that Latin American debtors should receive interest relief. Further evidence of changing international attitudes came in October 1987, when a new standby agreement was concluded with the IMF despite continued arrears to the commercial banks. Disagreements among the creditor banks themselves and concern over jeopardizing concurrent negotiations with Brazil delayed rescheduling, but substantial debt relief is clearly in the cards. The extraordinary economic burden of the debt therefore will have been concentrated in the period from 1983 through mid-1986.

During that period, how did the debt affect the politics of reform and, more broadly, Costa Rican democracy? The debt itself did not become a hot political issue. After two years of heavy debt-service payments, a November 1985 poll asked respondents to name the country's most important problem; only 5 percent cited the external debt. More striking, in mid-1986, even as the new Arias government decided to suspend payments and seek radical rescheduling, survey data indicated that a majority of Costa Ricans favored paying the debt by increased production rather than by seeking relief.[26]

The main political impact of the debt burden has been indirect, via its effects on general economic conditions and its exposure of the country to external economic policy intervention. Economic stagnation has increased dissatisfaction and pessimism, which cannot fail to influence domestic politics, but the more specific and tangible effects of the debt burden on the politics of adjustment have taken the form of intense outsiders' involvement in specific reforms.

From 1983 through 1985, Costa Rica received net concessional development assistance averaging $93 per capita per year. The high aid levels were a direct reflection of the nation's special position as the sole stable and attractive democracy in turbulent Central America. As already noted, financing came with tight policy strings attached, including both short-run macroeconomic management, where the IMF took the lead, and medium-term structural reforms, pressed most vigorously by AID and the World Bank. The U.S. role in spurring reform was somewhat diluted by conflicting priorities. U.S. balance-of-payments support was used not only to support IMF-guided policies and to press for financial and public enterprise reform, but also to wring Costa Rican concessions vis-á-vis the Nicaraguan contras. Thus to some degree the debt did compromise Costa Rica's foreign policy autonomy, but the Arias government has strongly reasserted the nation's independence in this realm without incurring serious penalties.

How effective was aid and the accompanying dialogue and conditionality in promoting economic reform? The answers vary with different time perspectives and different levels of specificity. In the short run, and at the level of specific reforms, external intervention was quite effective. Many of the financial sector reforms, revised trade and tariff policies, and public enterprise reforms would not have taken place, or would have been greatly diluted, in the absence of external donor pressure. More broadly, policy dialogue shaped the agenda of public debate, and analyses done or sponsored by AID and the World Bank contributed to data availability and the sophistication of the debate. The need to respond to outside initiatives also prompted the government to strengthen its own interagency coordination and planning mechanisms, improving its ability to identify issues and design solutions of its own.

In some ways, however, external intervention impeded the very goals it sought to promote. The handful of key economic officials were so preoccupied with multiple donors' demands and schedules and the complexities of cross-conditionality that they had little time for longer-term planning and consensus building. External pressure also prompted strong resentment, particularly in the Assembly, diverting attention from the substance of the reforms.

More fundamentally, the assumption that large-scale aid would continue as long as necessary may well have diluted the general impetus for reform. Costa Ricans in and outside of the government count on their special relationship with the United

States. Indeed, they may see themselves as having considerable leverage, despite their small size and apparent dependence. Months before the 1986 elections, the press quoted Oscar Arias as saying, "As long as there are nine comandantes in Nicaragua, we will receive $200 million [a year from the United States] in aid. Hence we shall survive . . . If there were ten comandantes, we would get more."[27] The direct effects of aid and conditionality in supporting and promoting adjustment must be weighed against the diffuse impact of aid in diluting Costa Ricans' sense of responsibility for and control over their economic destiny.

In the future, long-term rescheduling and/or debt relief might well be followed by a sharp drop in U.S. bilateral aid, although larger events and trends in Central America will also affect U.S. aid to Costa Rica. In the 1990s, Costa Rica may be considerably less enmeshed with foreign economic aid and intervention, and much more reliant on domestic initiative and resources. The challenge to Costa Rican democracy will then be to replace outside pressure with internal commitment, this time not as a temporary rally against acute crisis but for a long-term, complex struggle.

Notes

Research on this paper was funded by the Ford and Rockefeller Foundations, as part of a grant with five other scholars for a larger study of the politics of economic adjustment. I would like to thank Eduardo Lizano and the Central Bank of Costa Rica for providing a hospitable temporary base in San José in autumn 1986. Thanks are also due to the Costa Rican officials, scholars, and politicians, and the staff members of AID in Washington and San José, the World Bank, and the IMF, who generously shared their information and perspectives. Needless to say, they are in no way responsible for the interpretations and views expressed here.

1. Terms of trade and GDP data from World Bank, *World Tables, 1987*; export volume from International Monetary Fund, *International Financial Statistics, 1987 Yearbook*; data on commercial debt service from Richard Feinberg, "Costa Rica: The End of the Fiesta," in *From Gunboats to Diplomacy*, ed. Richard Newfarmer (Baltimore: Johns Hopkins University Press, 1984), 103-105.

2. Gary S. Fields, "Employment and Growth in Costa Rica" (Agency for International Development, unpublished report, Washington, DC, February 1986), 17.

3. Feinberg, "End of Fiesta," 103-105; *World Tables*.

4. The preceding account of economic policy under Carazo draws on Claudio González-Vega, "Fear of Adjusting: The Social Costs of Economic Policies in Costa Rica in the 1970s," in *Revolution and Counter-Revolution in Central America and the Caribbean*, ed. Donald Schulz and Douglas H. Graham (Boulder, CO: Westview Press, 1984); Mitchell A. Seligson, "Costa Rica," in *Latin American and Caribbean Contemporary Record, Vol. I: 1981-1982*, ed. Abraham Lowenthal (New York: Holmes and Meier, 1983); *Latin America Political Report* and *Latin America Weekly Report*; and interviews.

5. For accounts of the initial stabilization effort, I have drawn on Carlos Manuel Castillo, "The Costa Rican Experience with the International Debt Crisis" (Paper prepared for the meeting of the Economic Group of the Interamerican Dialogue, CIEPLAN, Santiago, Chile,

March 17-18, 1985); Mitchell A. Seligson, "Costa Rica," in *Latin American and Caribbean Contemporary Record, Vol. II: 1982-83*, ed. Abraham Lowenthal (New York: Homes and Meier, 1984); U.S. AID economic analyses; and *Latin America Weekly Report* and *Latin America Regional Reports-Mexico and Central America*.

6. Seligson, "Costa Rica," Table 2, citing Dirección General de Estadística y Censos, *Indicadores Sociales y Económicos* 2, no. 2.

7. González-Vega, "Fear of Adjusting," 364.

8. This and the previous paragraph draw on Charles D. Ameringer, *Democracy in Costa Rica* (New York: Praeger Press, 1982), especially 40-42 and 49-52.

9. *Latin America Regional Reports-Mexico and Central America*, August 13, 1982.

10. Various U.S. Agency for International Development memoranda.

11. Consultoría Interdisciplinaria en Desarrollo, SA (CID), "Encuesta de opinión pública" (July 1983, mimeo). CID has conducted public opinion polls three times a year since 1979; the polls are Gallup-associated and well-respected.

12. U.N. Economic Commission for Latin America and the Caribbean, *Preliminary Overview of the Latin American Economy, 1987*, Table 6; Víctor Hugo Céspedes et al., *Costa Rica: estabilidad sin crecimiento* (San José: Academia de Centroamérica, 1984), 86. Céspedes calculated 1983 average real wage increases as a remarkable 19 percent.

13. Ameringer, *Democracy in Costa Rica*, 109. It is noteworthy that Costa Ricans gave no support to a proposal in late 1980 by former President Figueres that the constitution be suspended and an emergency government created including President Carazo, the four living ex-presidents, and the leading candidates for the presidency in 1982, with full powers to meet the crisis.

14. Mitchell A. Seligson and Edward N. Muller, "Democratic Stability and Economic Crises: Costa Rica, 1978-1983," *International Studies Quarterly* (September 1987): 318-320.

15. *Latin America Regional Reports-Mexico and Central America*, August 13, 1982.

16. *World Tables*.

17. *World Tables*. Data in Republic of Costa Rica Ministry of Finance and Central Bank, *Information Memorandum*, June 1987, give a similar picture.

18. *World Tables*.

19. González-Vega, "Fear of Adjusting," 358.

20. Republic of Costa Rica, *Information Memorandum*, Table 1. For a fuller discussion of Costa Rica's structural problems, see González-Vega, "Fear of Adjusting;" also Morris J. Blachman and Ronald G. Hellman, "Costa Rica," in *Confronting Revolution: Security through Diplomacy in Central America*, ed. Morris J. Blachman, William M. LeoGrande and Kenneth E. Sharpe (New York: Pantheon Books, 1986), 162-167.

21. Ameringer, *Democracy in Costa Rica*, 108, 127.

22. Robert W. Adler, "Policy Dialogue and Economic Recovery in Costa Rica: Leverage and Guile in a Democracy" (U.S. AID Memorandum, San José, December 10, 1984).

23. Blachman and Hellman, "Costa Rica," 161.

24. The preceding discussion of reform efforts is based on various AID and World Bank reports and on interviews with Costa Rican, U.S., and World Bank officials.

25. Data on debt relative to the economy from World Bank, *World Debt Tables, 1987-88*. By the Government of Costa Rica's own calculations, net resource transfers were negative from 1983 to 1986, totalling more than $600 million over the period, and equivalent to an

average of 4.2 percent of GDP each year. Republic of Costa Rica, *Information Memorandum.*
   26. CID polls, November 1985, July 1986.
   27. *Latin America Weekly Report,* May 22, 1985.

Suggestions for Further Reading

Ameringer, Charles D. *Democracy in Costa Rica.* New York: Praeger Press, 1982.

Blachman, Morris J., and Ronald G. Hellman. "Costa Rica." In *Confronting Revolution: Security through Diplomacy in Central America,* ed. Morris J. Blachman, William M. LeoGrande, and Kenneth E. Sharpe. New York: Pantheon Books, 1986.

González-Vega, Claudio. "Fear of Adjusting: The Social Costs of Economic Policies in Costa Rica in the 1970s." In *Revolution and Counter-Revolution in Central America and the Caribbean,* ed. Donald Schulz and Douglas H. Graham. Boulder, CO: Westview Press, 1984.

Reding, Andrew. "Costa Rica: Democratic Model in Jeopardy." *World Policy Journal* 1, no. 3 (Spring 1986).

Seligson, Mitchell A. "Costa Rica." In *Latin America and Caribbean Contemporary Record Vol. I: 1981-1982,* ed. Abraham Lowenthal. New York: Holmes and Meier, 1983.

_____. "Costa Rica." In *Latin America and Caribbean Contemporary Record Vol. II: 1982-1983,* ed. Abraham Lowenthal. New York: Holmes and Meier, 1984.

10

Democratization, Crisis, and the APRA's Modernization Project in Peru

Carol Wise

Peru stands out as a country out of step with its Latin American neighbors during most of the post war period. Government-sponsored import-substitution industrialization and populist social reforms were not seriously attempted until the 1960s, and they quickly ran up against the well-known limits of such policies by the end of the decade. The military intervention of 1968 departed from other predominantly authoritarian market-oriented coups of the time by undertaking a sweeping state capitalist reformist program. Peru joined ranks with the redemocratization trend of the 1980s, but the disappointing results of the military's state-fueled industrialization drive led to the election in 1980 of a center-right civilian coalition that embraced the same neoliberal economic program that had already been tried and failed in the Southern Cone. The negative outcomes of this policy, in both growth and distributional terms, combined with the political and economic pressures of the debt crisis, prompted another abrupt policy shift in 1985. Peru's current responses to the crisis stand out as perhaps the most unorthodox in the region.

The typical periodization for studying contemporary Peru includes the populist-developmentalist program of the first administration of Fernando Belaunde Terry from 1963-1968; the twelve-year reformist military experiment from 1968-1980; the electoral return of Belaunde and his Popular Action Party (AP) with a more economically orthodox platform in 1980; and the 1985 civilian transition that brought in Alan García Pérez and his American Popular Revolutionary Alliance (APRA) on a nationalist economic-reactivation ticket. Despite the usefulness of this periodization, three major themes have recurred across the four periods: development ideologies, development strategies, and the formation of political alliances to support the implementation of the strategies. Ideologically, the debate has swung back and forth between state and market approaches. The development strategies stemming from these ideologies have been import-substitution and the classic liberal primary-export model respectively. Efforts to support and legitimize the two approaches have centered on forging a "national project" to integrate one of the region's more socio-economically heterogeneous populations into an articulated multiclass alliance.

When comparing its progress with respect to these broad themes, Peru comes out behind the other major Latin American countries with which it is usually grouped. The ideological debate has been conducted in fairly black and white terms, with the liberal primary-exporter bias prevailing for most of this century. It was not until the throes of the economic crisis in the mid-1980s that the neostructuralist ideas concerning state intervention and inflation that had been circulating in other Latin American countries for some time began to infiltrate government circles in Peru. Likewise, a national industrial strategy that attempted to forge an explicit development pact between the state and domestic business and financial groups was not tried until the García administration after 1985. Various efforts to implement development strategy have been undermined by the lack of organizational and technical capacity within the state apparatus, and by the generally weak institutional structures of representative groups within the labor movement, the private sector, the peasantry, and political parties. Because of this chronic difficulty in channeling diverse multiclass interests toward constructive means, Peru has become best known in the 1980s for parallel underground expressions of such interests in the form of a burgeoning informal economy and the Sendero Luminoso (Shining Path) guerrilla movement.

If we step back from the usual periodization and look at Peruvian development patterns over the past two decades, it could be argued that Peru has undergone a more compressed version of what the rest of the region has experienced since the 1930s and 1940s. Some of the out-of-step characteristics of these patterns can be explained by the catching up attempted by successive regimes since the breakdown of the old oligarchic liberal-exporter model in the 1960s.[1] This chapter will explore this premise, as well as how this trend has been hastened by the advent of the debt crisis in the early 1980s. The following section will review the evolution of economic policy and the underlying political and institutional dynamics from the late 1960s up until the brink of the crisis. The remainder of the analysis focuses on the post-1983 period in Peru, particularly the opportunities for political alignment and a more coherent economic restructuring that resulted from the crisis and the challenges taken up by the García administration.

The crisis hit Peru at its most vulnerable point, when economic policy was almost entirely oriented toward a declining external sector and the ability of state elites to respond was quite low. Yet it also had a modernizing effect, in terms of promoting wider participation in a more sophisticated debate about the country's overwhelming problems and the possible solutions. The concomitant transition to constitutional democracy facilitated this process, as the 1983 nationwide municipal elections saw strong victories for the APRA and the six-party United Left (IU) coalition. The elections marked the formal opening of a new political space in Peru where the demands of groups, especially within the popular classes and the private sector, became more cohesive and were seriously taken up by the ascendant center-left political parties. But new alliances also meant new conflicts, and the combined effect of democratization and economic crisis made for more highly politicized relationships within and between state organizations and between the state and a broad range of groups in civil society. The new situation also revealed a considerable backwardness within the government bureaucracy, enshrouded in personalistic politics and petty patronage, which in the end has proved to be just as debilitating to the present government's program as the adverse international economic trends or the opposition of powerful domestic groups.

It is impossible to speak even minimally of a unified and autonomous state apparatus in Peru, capable of formulating and implementing collective policies generated from within the state. Rather, autonomy exists in the negative sense of loosely linked administrative structures constantly stampeded by particularistic public and private interest groups that frequently operate at cross purposes. It is helpful to keep this fragmentation in mind when attempting to understand past development shortcomings, as well as the formidable tasks that lie ahead in constructing a viable institutionally-based democracy from the fragile constitutional order that presently exists in Peru.

From Belaunde to Belaunde:
The Rise of the State and the Incapacity to Intervene

By the 1960s, Peru was very much a paradigm for the rapid population growth, intense urban migration, and socio-economic inequality that the Peruvian anthropologist José Matos Mar has called "desborde popular."[2] Matos speaks of a country divided by two separate logics: (1) the official Peru comprised of a highly centralized coastal bureaucracy serving as an umbrella for civilian institutions, the military, the church, banking, commerce, and the rest of the private sector; and (2) a marginal majority multi-ethnic Peru, divorced from officialdom and defending its political and economic interests through neighborhood associations, street vending, communal soup kitchens, and sporadic popular protest. Belaunde's earlier administration can be viewed as the first effort to bridge the deepening dualism between the modern and the traditional in Peru. He promoted an industrializing growth model meant simultaneously to allow emergent middle classes wider political expression, to promote greater economic integration of the traditional sector, and to break the historic hold of the oligarchic exporter class over the nation's politics and economy.

This modernizing spurt also stressed the importance to national integration of major public works projects in social and economic infrastructure, as well as the initiation of long overdue reforms in health, education, and the land tenure system. Even this limited statist program quickly brought to the fore the contradiction between the need for state intervention and the limited capacity of the Peruvian state—underdeveloped to a degree unusual even for Latin America—to contribute to development.[3] Peru's ability to thrive on a diverse primary export base through the 1950s greatly impeded the institution building and insulation of key parts of the state bureaucracy from clientelistic intrusion that have been crucial to the develop-

Peru has not developed planning agency or financial or competent bureaucracy.

ment strategies of some countries in the region. As a result, Peru has yet to produce a powerful planning or financial development agency capable of generating and realizing the state's policy goals, not to mention the competent cadre of state workers necessary to carry out such tasks.

Although Belaunde's platform recognized the need to cultivate technocratic expertise and coordinated planning, the bureaucracy remained unwieldy and chaotic to the point of putting Peru's incipient parliamentary democracy to the ultimate test. The National Planning Institute (INP) had been created just one year before Belaunde's election, and the national budget was still a formality that bore little relation to fiscal realities. Perhaps most telling was the delay until 1963 in creating the Banco de la Nación, the body that acts as revenue collector and treasurer for the state. These responsibilities had heretofore been in the hands of a private agency controlled by the commercial banks. Given this feeble institutional backup, the result of a large and rapid transfer of national resources to the public sector was predictable. Public decision making was quickly penetrated by private parties seeking tariff concessions and construction contracts, and the Popular Action functionaries, having assumed the role of state elites, became embroiled in widespread political patronage.

Belaunde's moderate populist program also faltered on its own grounds. Cooperación Popular, the main organization created to promote administrative decentralization and absorption of marginal labor, failed to capture sufficient state funds. The import-substitution emphasis had brought manufacturing's share of gross domestic product (GDP) up to 20 percent by 1968, yet most plants still served as assembly operations for imported products.[4] Executive power was greatly limited by a majority opposition in the legislature, representing the more traditional authoritarian populist strains of the APRA in coalition with the exporter oligarchy. Vehement battles over tax legislation to support state expansion ended in the familiar populist deadlock: no group or coalition was able to enforce its will, and the military stepped in. In addition, the 1960s provided a preview of how debt financing interacted with ongoing trends in the domestic political economy. First, as indicated in Table 10.1, the early access to international loans masked the beginning of a long-term structural stagnation in export volume and economic growth. Second, it permitted a relaxed tax effort and the postponement of political confrontation with private actors over the state's rapidly increasing revenue demands.

military stepped in

loans replaced tax effort

With its stress on more extensive distributional reforms and state investments in heavy industry, the military intervention led by General Juan Velasco Alvarado represented Peru's first serious attempt at political and economic transformation. This era broke with the past in important ways, such as the widespread agrarian reform and new laws governing private investment, worker ownership and job stability. Through increased investments, subsidies, nationalizations, and designation of new public enterprises, the state sector more than doubled between 1968 and 1980. Despite a ministerial overhaul and the multiplication of bureaucratic decrees to govern the new state-centered economic model, the accumulation process and

Table 10.1

Public Sector Behavior and Overall Economic Performance

Years	Govt Expend[a]	Govt Deficit[b]	Inflation Rate	GDP Growth	Foreign Debt[c]
1950-62	12.5%[d]	0.2%[d]	7.0%	5.3	$158 mn
1963-68	19.1[d]	-2.1[d]	11.6	4.4	737
1969-73	23.9	-2.6	7.0	7.2	1,491
1974-75	35.7	-8.4	20.2	4.6	3,066
1976-77	39.2	-9.8	35.7	1.5	4,311
1978-79	41.8	-3.6	62.7	1.2	5,764
1980-82	49.5	-6.6	66.2	2.3	6,908
1983-85	50.6	-7.4	30.8	-2.1	10,510

[a]Public sector current expenditure/GDP
[b]Public sector deficit/GDP
[c]Public sector long-term foreign debt
[d]Central government only
Source: Carlos Eduardo Paredes and Alberto Pasco-Font, *The Behavior of the Public Sector in Peru, 1970-1985: A Macroeconomic Approach* (Washington, DC: The World Bank, 1987).

underlying institutional logic displayed important continuities with the previous decade. The tax base narrowed, shifting further away from wealth and income taxes and toward more regressive and unpredictable indirect and foreign trade taxes, while primary products continued to account for 80 percent of export revenue. Foreign loans became increasingly important for state expansion, and the liquidity from these external savings temporarily smoothed over the usual battles between income redistribution and capital accumulation. By posting officers to key slots in the ministries and public enterprises, and by creating a poorly conceptualized corporatist network of state-dominated peak associations to mobilize support and mitigate opposition to the regime's policies, the military government mistook control for autonomy to implement its program.

The lack of a proper mix of macroeconomic policies and planning objectives to sustain this model led to a severe balance-of-payments crisis by 1975 and the need for debt rescheduling. The crisis, in turn, was largely responsible for a redefinition of state policy toward market approaches favoring privatization and orthodox stabilization. The privatization thrust, however, met with little success. On the one hand, it failed to recognize that state firms had come to play a major role in capital formation. On the other hand, the firms had become useful means for the private sector as well as high ranking military officers to get some of the economic spoils being generated.

The adjustment and stabilization policies implemented during this second military phase under General Francisco Morales Bermúdez (1975-1980) likewise met with resistance, as the combination of harsh austerity measures and the abandonment of explicit attempts at income redistribution unleashed fierce conflicts over who would bear the brunt of the economic downturn. It took three years for Peru to buckle down and successfully adhere to an IMF-sponsored stabilization program, at which point the 1979 mineral price boom hit. Having recently completed an oil pipeline and a major copper mine, the country was well-positioned to benefit from the dramatic 78 percent rise in the export price index between 1978 and 1980. This fortuitous timing of international trends had three major effects on domestic economic policy perceptions. First, it bolstered unwarranted optimism about prices on Peruvian primary-product exports.[5] Second, because the rapid comeback enabled the country to initiate another major round of external borrowing, it reinforced the perception that foreign loans would be in endless supply. Finally, coming on the heels of the stabilization program, the boom swayed policy preferences in favor of orthodox management approaches, ignoring the fact that much of the IMF's highly-touted budget balancing was due to increased revenues, while state spending actually continued to rise.

Orthodoxy had also been politically undermining, and it was largely the grassroots opposition to the severe impacts of austerity that led the military to convene a constituent assembly in 1978 and schedule elections for 1980. The debate over the new constitution expressed the need for a stronger executive and the protection of economic policy making from rampant politicking in order to avoid the pitfalls of the 1960s. Provisions allowing the legislative assembly to delegate presidential power to rule by decree for set periods of time were passed. Similar to the intentions guiding the governance of the U.S. Federal Reserve, the head of the Central Bank was to be appointed to a fixed five-year term to keep the office above political influence and fighting. The electoral campaign did not live up to this same concern for constructing a more flexible political framework. Belaunde, who refrained from participating in the constituent assembly, was voted back into office on a platform so vague that it offered something for everybody. After the fact, Belaunde's center-right Popular Action Party (AP) joined forces with the more conservative Popular Christian Party (PPC) in controlling Congress, and put forth an economic program that was a hybrid between the developmentalism of the 1960s and the orthodoxy of the late 1970s.

The market aspects of the program were geared toward dismantling the creations of the Velasco era and called for privatization, trade liberalization, and the reduction of government interference in pricing, marketing, and the financial system. Highly advantageous terms were offered to foreign and local private capital to promote raw material exports in the mining and oil sectors; industrialization was assigned low priority. On the developmentalist side, the government put forth a mammoth $11 billion public investment program envisioning 50 percent foreign financing to support export-led growth. The program was endorsed by the World Bank on the basis of favorable commodity price projections. Operating within the complicated political environment of a newly formed democracy marked by extreme inequalities and a rapidly declining international economy, the neoliberal project exacerbated these tensions and was never fully launched. Though Belaunde had succeeded in assembling Peru's most sophisticated economic team to date, most of these technocrats had sat out the military experiment abroad and quickly found that the apparently simple political-economic truths of the 1960s no longer held.

The public foreign debt had increased nine-fold since 1968 and service payments consumed 50 percent of export earnings by 1980. Increasing capital flight indicated that private investors would not be easily won back, and rapid price hikes on government-controlled goods, currency devaluations, and compensatory wage increases carried out under the aegis of orthodox stabilization introduced Peru to the inertial hyperinflation that has plagued the Southern Cone for years. The privatization drive was again stalled by the lack of a specific program to sell off the public firms, and by the fact that civilians close to the government held well-paid jobs in those firms. As the international economic shocks of the early 1980s began to register their full toll on the Peruvian economy, the lesson of IMF-sponsored stabilization in this more severe crisis context became clear: even market approaches demand a basic level of capacity, coordination, and will power within the state to be carried out effectively. In the absence of favorable world markets and easy availability of foreign credit to boost the neoliberal project along, the policy process was shattered by 1983. Enormous rifts emerged among Congress, the executive, and the major financial institutions, with each going its own way and making policy according to its own narrow interests until the end of Belaunde's term in 1985.

Political Realignment and the National-Industrial Project

The poor timing of a traditional export-led policy in the midst of increasingly volatile world commodity prices, and the bad luck of natural disasters that further undermined Peru's primary export base, converged in late 1983 to produce economic results among the worst in the region. GDP fell by 12 percent, led by a 17 percent decline in manufacturing industry. By mid-1984, one fifth of the country's industrial workers had been fired, and at least 60 percent of the total labor force had become underemployed. The public external debt had jumped 21 percent since the Belaunde government began; servicing it took an ever larger share of shrinking foreign exchange revenues. Without a social policy to soften the harsh impact of the recession or any internally coherent means of legitimating the need for more economic sacrifices, the government broke with the IMF in 1984, and Peru slipped into an *ad hoc* moratorium on its debt payments.

At this delicate point in its democratic transition, Peru's democracy was only surface deep. The Belaunde administration showed no inclination to reform state institutions suffused with biases toward the rich and powerful, and the fallout from nearly a decade of repressive austerity measures together with the government's "dirty war" tactics against a mounting guerrilla insurgency led to increasing violence. The nationwide municipal elections in late 1983 gave Peru's newly enfranchised poor a chance to register their discontent with the existing state of affairs. Not unexpectedly, the center-left opposition gained ground on the AP/PPC coalition. The APRA captured 33 percent of the vote, and the IU another 29 percent, with the latter electing its leader, Alfonso Barrantes, mayor of Lima on a Marxist ticket. The results confirmed Belaunde's lame duck status, brought on by a combination of the President's own ineptitude and the imposition of a five-year non-renewable term for the executive. The elections also highlighted two unfolding political trends related to the democratization process and shaped by the crisis.

The first concerns the greater concentration of state power in the executive, promoted by the new constitutional reforms and bolstered by the traditional propensity of social groups and interest associations to seek influence with the executive through direct personal ties independent of political parties and legislative lobbying. In the absence of a stable institutional backup to counteract these pressures, the present arrangements almost guarantee self-destruction as the executive becomes rapidly overwhelmed by such demands. Constitutional powers to legislate a program have yet to translate into the autonomy to carry one out, and the executive's ultimate inability to orchestrate policy and exert control over other political and economic actors remains a serious challenge to the formulation of medium- and longer-term solutions to the crisis. The second reality brought home by the 1983 elections was the final demise of the classic primary export-led model as a viable development option for Peru, and the dissolution of the traditional alliance among the landed oligarchy, state elites, and foreign capital that had held it together.

The vote confirmed that there was no turning back the clock or eradicating the various legacies of the military experiment, as Belaunde's neoliberal project had intended. On the one hand, the labor, industrial, and agricultural reforms of the Velasco period had changed ownership patterns and paved new organizational inroads for popular participation, leaving Peru's poor and oppressed in a stronger position to assert themselves. Domestic capitalists had also succeeded in revamping their operations, forming more modern groups based in the financial system and exercising a considerable degree of market power in such sectors as agro-processing, export manufacturing, and services.[6] On the other hand, the political and economic debacle of the early 1980s had given those opposition parties that had made a strong showing in the 1978 constituent assembly elections, and then floundered during the 1980 presidential campaign, a chance to regroup. The electoral emergence of the APRA and the more leftist IU as credible political machines, able to incorporate the diverse interests of this new constellation of social forces into winning party platforms, marked another major turning point in Peruvian politics.

The electoral rise of the IU as the country's second-largest political force, especially striking in view of Peru's basically conservative past, can be explained by a decade of grassroots outreach, the cultivation of organized labor as a core constituency, and the eventual ability of all six parties in the coalition to compromise on the moderate leftist Barrantes as an acceptable leader and candidate. The

APRA's ability to win a victory in a legally contested race was even more remarkable, given the party's unsuccessful attempts to do so since its inception in 1924. Although it is not possible to recount here the story of the APRA's electoral breakthrough to assume its historic role as the country's governing party, the death of legendary APRA founder and party boss Víctor Raúl Haya de la Torre and the party's negotiated resolution of old enmities with the military in the late 1980s are important parts of an explanation. Haya's death loosened the Aprista old guard's tight vertical grip on the party, and made way for a new generation of leaders embodied in the election of Alan García as APRA general secretary in 1982. By opening up the party to intellectual crosscurrents more appropriate to the 1980s and reaching out to non-aligned voters across classes and income groups, García's generation had done much to clean up the APRA's traditional image as provincial, sectarian, and violent.[7]

The political realignment of 1983 kicked off the presidential campaign, and even though elections would not be held until 1985, García quickly moved to the front of the race. There were few substantive differences between the APRA and IU campaign platforms. Both revived the theme of constructing a multi-class national alliance and advocated civilian solutions to the guerrilla-military conflict raging in the Andean emergency zone. Both geared their positions to Peru's large, young electorate. Each party's platform centered on the declaration of a partial debt moratorium to provide breathing space for redistributional policies and for a reactivation strategy linking industrial and agricultural production according to a more integrated and regionally-decentralized plan. The main differences were the IU's status as a recently formed coalition of parties lacking the internal discipline of a single party, and its more extreme position favoring full nationalization of the financial sector and key areas of raw material production where the grip of foreign capital remained strong. García, taking advantage of the organizational strength of his party, was able to combine personality and image with a program that courted the private sector.

The APRA recognized that economic reactivation in the wake of the debt crisis would require greater cooperation with domestic business and financial groups and sought a social pact with private industry along these lines. In contrast to the IU's controversial stance on nationalization, the APRA proposed to rationalize the state sector through privatization and administrative reform. García won the confidence of the newly formed association of private business institutions (CONFIEP) in 1984 by appealing to those quarters of domestic capital hurt by the neoliberal policies of the early 1980s and shaken by the rising guerrilla threat. Perhaps more important, the APRA forged personal ties and solicited campaign support from Peru's prominent post-oligarchic economic groups. These groups proved to be quite flexible and nonpartisan in their political outlook.[8] The rise of a more sophisticated and charismatic leader personified by García, a more modern domestic capitalist class, and some measured successes during the late 1970s in promoting nontraditional exports, provided the vision for a locally-financed national industrial project meant to generate employment and decrease Peru's dependence on foreign imports and financing.

García's Policies, 1985-1987:
From Emergency Plan to Heterodox Reactivation

By the time García assumed office in July 1985, the APRA had been working on its development plan for two years. While the finer policy points for promoting economic reactivation had yet to be defined, the party did have an emergency plan for the first hundred days of government. Combined with 50 percent of the popular vote and a majority in both houses of Congress, these circumstances enabled García to act quickly. Controlling domestic inflation and currency speculation and alleviating the pressure that excessive imports and foreign debt payments had placed on the current account were immediate priorities in order to counter the economic recession. The APRA's earlier calls for a unilateral debt moratorium were substantiated by the fact that service payments on the debt now surpassed 100 percent of the country's export earnings, and Peruvian debt had already been written down to less than half its value on the secondary market in New York. These deep discounts implied that an imminent return to voluntary lending was unlikely. The country's recent catastrophic experiences with IMF stabilization programs had prompted two former Peruvian Central Bank presidents with fairly conservative biases to advise García that he had little choice but to temporarily go it alone without the banks and the IMF.

García's inaugural announcement of the "10 percent solution," limiting service payments on Peru's medium- and long-term public debt to no more than 10 percent of annual export earnings, differed from Belaunde's *ad hoc* moratorium in two ways. First, the debt issue was explicitly used as a political rallying point. By making debt nonpayment a prerequisite for economic reactivation, García won a wide consensus for his unilateral stance and was therefore able to turn the problem around and make it work for him. Second, with its focus on selectively honoring those obligations necessary to maintain trade and development financing, and on seeking alternative methods of debt repayment, the 10 percent solution represented Peru's first attempt at a coherent debt strategy since the problem originated in the mid-1970s. Stated policy through 1987 was to keep up on payments to the major multilateral development agencies and on food imports and regional trade agreements. The García administration also vowed to service punctually any debt contracted after July 1985 and to promote debt-equity swaps and counter-trade deals to repay previously-contracted loans. One important defense mechanism was for the country to continue servicing its short-term working capital debt to the banks, and the Peruvian private sector remained current on its commercial interest payments as well.[9]

On the domestic side, the emergency plan, borrowed from the heterodox stabilization policies that were simultaneously in effect in Argentina, presented an alternative to the IMF's prescription of tight monetary approaches to halt inflation. Instead, inflation was to be fought through direct price administration and the control of imports and foreign exchange. Peru's venture away from conventional orthodox wisdom was a long time coming and obviously a response to past policy failures. The attraction to this more ambitious and sophisticated mix of policies can be explained, ironically, by the very limited and weak technical expertise within the ranks of the APRA. As García brought in consultants from the EEC, the ILO, and academia, neostructuralist policy influences from other countries in the region quickly took hold. The first phase of heterodox shock froze prices on all goods and services. The exchange rate was also frozen, as were dollar accounts. The frozen exchange rate was combined with wage hikes and lower interest rates to encourage a transfer of income from financial and speculative activities to the productive sector.

The partial debt moratorium, combined with import controls and arms cuts, did provide foreign exchange to spur economic reactivation. Reserves were also built up by the Central Bank's highly unorthodox decision to purchase dollars from regional banks flush with the proceeds of Peru's illicit $500-800 million annual cocaine trade. By early 1986, the economic program began to move forward in a series of quarterly packages aimed at taking advantage of the high level of idle capacity present in the economy. The National Planning Institute, which had not played a prominent role in the policy process since the Velasco government, was designated as the lead development agency, and from there the economic team produced an impressive medium-term plan reflecting an eclectic approach to Peru's economic problems.[10] The development plan was based primarily on the Kaleckian model, which recognized the importance of balancing the expansion of productive capacity with the expansion of mass consumption, and saw the need to capture and reinvest the economic surplus in order to sustain a consumer-led economic recovery. The plan also expressed broader neostructuralist concerns over import substitution, export promotion, and the integration of the popular sectors via redistributive reforms.

The reactivation strategy deepened throughout 1986 with periodic wage hikes, emergency work programs, and generous subsidies for Peru's depressed agricultural sector. García had begun urging business executives to invest, and offered tax refunds and credit incentives for companies that created new jobs. By year's end, a complex economic superstructure had evolved that combined import controls with multiple exchange and interest rates. The bulk of the tax breaks and subsidies were channeled into manufacturing and agro-industry. The short-term success of the program was tremendous: real wages increased by 30 percent in the countryside and 25 percent in the cities, while GDP rose by 8.5 percent. The maintenance of selective controls over key prices brought inflation down from a yearly rate of 250 percent to 63 percent. Finally, industry grew an astounding 15 to 20 percent, and private investment was up nearly 25 percent over 1985. The boom gave APRA a

Concertación = negotiation

clean sweep in the November 1986 municipal elections, and García held his ground as perhaps the most popular president in Peruvian history.

These immediate gains aside, some predictable longer-range challenges had surfaced. First was the difficulty of moving out of the price freeze without precipitating a new inflationary spiral, a dilemma that has plagued all of the region's recent attempts at heterodox stabilization. Second, the promised negotiations with the major economic groups and representatives of organized labor over the new development policy did not take off with the same alacrity as did the reactivation. It was not until early 1987 that the government formed the National Investment Board as the first formal step toward negotiation, or *concertación*. Third, because of the prolonged freeze on government-controlled prices and a continued world depression in oil and mineral prices, tax collections dipped to their lowest point in a decade. García's supply-side tax cuts for the business sector also failed to generate the expected new revenues, as many firms evaded taxes by fleeing into the informal economy. The projected income from the sale of 30 to 40 public firms was blocked by the lack of interested buyers and by the government's reluctance to take on the complex problem of privatization, for which there were few fast solutions. The partial debt moratorium failed to help as much as expected, as it had been necessary to pay out close to 30 percent of export earnings during this first year—rather than the announced 10 percent—to maintain the necessary trade and development inflows.

The success of the heterodox reactivation came to hinge on moving into its longer-term goal of stimulating new private-sector investment before foreign reserves were depleted. García met with representatives from the country's top twelve business groups (the so-called twelve apostles), and steps were finally taken to implement the national industrial project. Priority investments were defined as those that are decentralized, save foreign exchange, and promote employment and intra-industry links. A special Employment and Investment Fund was created to offer bonds that could be exchanged for a share in an approved project, whereupon the government would contribute 50 percent to the rate of return, and a new foreign trade institute was set up to seek markets and promote in-kind debt payment schemes based on the expected returns from nontraditional export projects. With all the generous tax and credit incentives, the APRA government succeeded in taking the *concertación* process up to the letter of intent stage, but because the negotiations with the private sector had been fraught with delays and inconsistent messages related to the party's lack of administrative skill, most of the $400 million in new projects failed to move forward as planned.

Potential investors had been discouraged by some of the government's less appealing measures, such as a mandatory bond-purchasing scheme for the most profitable firms of 1986. There was also a confidence gap generated by the guerrilla insurgency, which was targeting local industrial plants for expensive physical damage. Peruvian entrepreneurs, though increasingly modern in their outlook, were still not accustomed to investing without the backing of foreign capital, and there were the usual suspicions about the ability of an inefficient state sector to execute the highly interventionist heterodox program successfully. Policy debates taking place within the government at the time did not help relieve these anxieties, as there was open confusion over the problem of reconciling popular demands with the attempted industrialist pact, given the state's rapidly diminishing resources. By initially promising tripartite participation in the negotiations and then pushing ahead with the business-government side of the investment deals behind closed doors, García had already alienated labor leaders aligned with the IU and distrustful of the APRA's legislative maneuvers to weaken the rights of organized workers. As the demands of labor and business began bearing down on the executive, the ongoing policy debate within the government erupted into a major dispute between state agencies.

Much of the tension centered on the specifics of moving into a viable longer-term development strategy. The more fiscally-conservative Central Bank and Finance Ministry pointed to the deficit and the imperative for slowed state spending accompanied by a tax overhaul. At the same time, the expansionist economic team operating out of the INP favored a deepening of consumer-led growth and more aggressive promotion of the export projects being discussed with the private sector. In April 1987 the President announced a major economic package that was meant to strike a compromise among the various factions. The fiscalists won some tax and exchange rate adjustments, while the expansionists won more wage hikes for labor and lower interest rates for the private sector. In order to preserve foreign exchange and fend off IU accusations that the APRA had sold out on its debt policy, García vowed strictly to uphold the 10 percent ceiling. Although intended to ameliorate conflict and win more time for the program to work, the economic package was the first clear sign that the heterodox policy was in serious trouble and that García had begun to lose control. This was confirmed just a month later when organized labor staged its first successful national strike since 1984.[11]

It was within the context of an increasingly difficult foreign exchange situation, the unraveling of economic strategy, and more vociferous opposition from the left, that García announced his intention to nationalize all private banks, finance, and insurance companies in mid-1987. The immediate explanation centered on the need to democratize credit and make more working capital available for Peru's small and medium entrepreneurs. The decision is probably best interpreted in the light of the government's frustration over the continuing levels of capital flight and the slow pace at which the process of *concertación* was achieving its ambitious private investment goals. Up to that point the APRA had expressed little concern for small capitalists, assigning them a marginal role in the national industrial alliance. As a result of the nationalization, García co-opted a major position of the IU and thus further consolidated his largely unorganized grassroots political support base. Yet at the same time he alienated the powerful economic groups with whom he had been cultivating a working relationship since the early 1980s.

Anti-Populist Backlash and Other Political Implications

With the collapse of public finances in late 1987 and the growing alienation of those groups within the state and business community whose cooperation would have been essential for any realistic attempt at economic restructuring, another Peruvian experiment had come to an end. Because the nationalization caught the IU and even some of the APRA off guard, the ensuing congressional debate centered mainly on the highly charged ideological aspects of the measure. The outcome was the passing of a vague nationalization law that left the government and the private sector to battle out many of the poorly-defined initiatives in the courts. The divisive issue brought the dormant AP/PPC coalition back to life, giving rise to a conservative opposition Democratic Front that championed private property rights and succeeded in keeping the conflict alive. Although the issues and actors were quite different, the standoff was similar to the pattern of the previous administration, whereby government policy broke down halfway through the presidential term and the executive became extremely isolated. The pattern is obviously rooted in the complexities of constructing a constitutional democracy in the midst of an ongoing economic crisis. Yet it was also reinforced under García by a combination of political miscalculations and the interaction of the chosen economic policy with unresolved structural limitations of the state.

As for García's domestic political strategy, a quick injection of populist wage policies and a brief reversal in the terms of trade between industry and agriculture, followed by a retraction, led to an urgent search for other ways of maintaining alliances with organized labor and the popular sector. Rash actions to solve one problem created problems elsewhere, the ramifications of the bank nationalization law being the strongest case in point. The erratic handling of *concertación*, and the President's insistence on negotiating directly and in private with the major representatives of economic power instead of utilizing institutional channels within the state and the CONFIEP, left both sides vulnerable and with little recourse when personalistic ties began to sour. The complete exclusion of organized labor from the negotiations made that alliance all the more difficult to maintain. This inability of base groups to find effective political representation once they had played a key part in supporting candidates and parties in democratic transitions has been a paradox common to all democratizing countries in the region.[12] In the Peruvian case, even the interests of the influential economic elites who had promoted García were left behind, as the APRA oscillated between a populist stance and its modernization pact, and pursued neither course very efficiently. On the external front one is left to wonder if greater economic breathing space could have been gained from a more consistent political approach. The U.S. government, taking the guerrilla insurgency seriously and sensitive to Peru's first democratic presidential succession in 75 years, was treading softly with García. The government's Inter-Agency Review Committee did order the banks to downgrade Peru's debt in November 1985, but the country's honoring of its short-term debt and the banks' low level of exposure helped delay other commonly feared sanctions such as the freezing of the country's foreign assets and the interruption of trade finance. The APRA also held Peru's commercial and multilateral creditors at bay by posing the moratorium as temporary and declaring its intentions to form a new foreign debt committee that would negotiate directly with the country's creditors. The space afforded by international actors and the high growth rates of 1986 and 1987 had the perverse effect of permanently postponing these negotiations from the Peruvian side. As a result, the IMF declared Peru an "ineligible" borrower in August 1986, and approximately $900 million in multilateral loan disbursements to Peru were subsequently frozen.

In view of Peru's very precarious financial position of 1988, the lesson of the partial debt moratorium is twofold. First, even small, highly underdeveloped countries with formidable internal security threats will not be let entirely off the hook, particularly when little effort is made toward a dialogue with the international financial community. Paying out 10 to 30 percent of annual export earnings to service the debt did not prevent the usual trade and aid sanctions, although it did help to slow the pace with which they were applied. Second, the fiscal crisis resulting from this one-shot financing based on debt nonpayment and import and exchange controls confirmed the APRA's original economic policy position during the electoral campaign: In the absence of sufficient quantities of external financing, sustainable growth policies will require a substantial increase in domestic resources through taxes and private savings. The double bind, of course, was that rigid limitations from the external sector quickly transformed what had been envisioned as a long-term policy for garnering domestic resources into a short-term crisis management program, and not a particularly well-managed one at that. Heterodox policy as nothing more than a short-run inflation management strategy had the disastrous effect of holding down those key prices, including interest and exchange rates, necessary to build a strong private-sector economy.[13] Having lost its momentum as a long-run force for restructuring the economy, heterodoxy only intensified the inverse relationship between a more interventionist model and the capacity of the Peruvian state to intervene.

At the level of the state, the most glaring limit to García's program was the continued lack of any one development institution to take the lead in formulating and carrying out public policy. The battles within the Central Bank and Finance Ministry effectively paralyzed the main pool of technocrats, and the INP did not have the capacity to operate alone. The political stalemate in the public enterprise sector also created a bottleneck in the government's modernization drive, as these firms now control half of Peru's modern sector capital stock, yet remain in managerial limbo for want of a definition of their scope and objectives. Despite García's intention to reform Peru's corrupt public administration, the filtering of the APRA party into the state bureaucracy brought out the worst traits in both. Having taken over with a 60-year backlog of pent-up political ambitions within the party, the spoils of office augmented the APRA's clientelistic tendencies and enhanced intra-party conflicts that had been temporarily assuaged by the prospects of finally winning office. The older and more sectarian party bosses, not entirely at ease with

García's fast pace and independent leadership style, have frequently challenged state policy decisions on these grounds alone. The APRA's younger generation has undermined party cohesion and the overall policy-making process by going to battle early over the crucial question of who will succeed García. Important both in symbolic and real terms was the rivalry between the President and APRA Premier and Finance Minister Luis Alva Castro, which resulted in Alva's resignation and further disruption of the policy process.

Conclusion

As Peru moves into another inflation-recession cycle and the discussion turns from economic reactivation to ways of distributing the adjustment burden more equitably, it is difficult to avoid a rather bleak assessment of the APRA's first few years in office. The present wavering between a rapprochement with the international economic community and a deepening of the autarkic route that began with the partial debt moratorium is reminiscent of the policy paralysis that set in during Belaunde's last two years. The decisions this time around are further complicated by the strengthening of the guerrilla insurgency, and the APRA's inability to rein in the military's autonomy without reviving historic animosities between the two. Relations with business, labor, and the popular classes are at best tenuous, and it is safe to say at this point that Peruvian democracy has become bogged down by the pressures and demands of those groups that helped bring it about. The political and social contingencies point to an even greater need for an economic program that addresses these demands, yet at a time when the state's capacity and financial resources for such an effort are at their lowest. This situation makes Peru a top candidate for debt relief and a massive infusion of development aid and, if nothing else, the outgoing administration would do well to open this possibility.

Apart from these immediate observations, if we look at the García administration from a long-run perspective and as another of Peru's modernizing spurts, this period offers some instructive insights. First, this phase clarifies the extent to which democratization, beyond the formal trappings of elections and constitutional reforms, also demands a gradual building up of state institutions and technical capabilities over time. Second, it upsets the wishful notion shared by many underdeveloped democratizing societies that this political process can be ushered in free of conflict. A more likely scenario is that many of the solutions will be hammered out as a result of the domestic conflicts that have plagued civilian governments in the Peru during the 1980s.

The outcome of this first attempt at forging a more viable development pact between the state and Peru's economic and social groups was not very successful, and all sides remain without an affirmative project. Given the limitations on the executive and the state capacity problems discussed throughout this chapter, it is tempting to see the demise of García's program as almost structurally determined by the political economy and the chaotic nature of the Peruvian state. Yet the

APRA's modernization effort also brought these various institutional drawbacks more clearly into focus and helped raise important policy questions about how to proceed, even if many of the answers are still a long way off.

Notes

Background research for this chapter was supported by the John D. and Catherine T. MacArthur Fellowship in Conflict, Peace, and Security, and by a grant from the Institute for the Study of World Politics. The author would like to thank Barbara Durr, Manuel Pastor, Jr., Carla Anne Robbins, Alex Secada, and Rosemary Thorp for their helpful comments, as well as the editors, for their patience and encouragement through various drafts of this chapter.

1. This alternative periodization for analyzing Peruvian development patterns is suggested by James M. Malloy, "Peru's Troubled Return to Democratic Government," *Universities Field Staff Report*, no. 15, 1982.

2. José Matos Mar, *Desborde popular y crisis del estado* (Lima: Instituto de Estudios Peruanos, 1984), chapter 4.

3. Dietrich Rueschemeyer and Peter B. Evans, "The State and Economic Transformation: Toward an Analysis of the Conditions Underlying Effective Intervention," in *Bringing the State Back In*, ed. Peter B. Evans, Dietrich Rueschemeyer, and Theda Skocpol (Cambridge: Cambridge University Press, 1985), provide a helpful framework for pinpointing those kinds of state-building precedents that enhance the effectiveness of interventionist development models.

4. Statistical trends cited throughout this chapter are based on data gathered from the Central Reserve Bank of Peru, the Ministry of Economy and Finance, and the National Planning Institute.

5. Carlos Eduardo Paredes and Alberto Pasco-Font, *The Behavior of the Public Sector in Peru, 1970-85: A Macroeconomic Approach* (Washington, DC: World Bank, 1987), 54.

6. Peru's more modern economic groups are profiled by Michael Reid, *Peru: Paths to Poverty* (London: Latin American Bureau, 1985), 86-88.

7. The political consolidation of the IU and the APRA's rejuvenation as a party are dealt with in *The Andean Report*, Lima, September 1984, and by Cynthia Sanborn, "*El futuro diferente?* The Legacy of the 1970s for Peruvian Populism in the 1980s" (Paper presented at the Latin American Studies Association Meetings, XIV Congress, New Orleans, 1988).

8. The emergent alliance and attempted political pact between the APRA and Peru's domestic capitalist class are the major themes of Francisco Durand, "Los empresarios y alianzas políticas: el caso del Perú bajo Alan García" (Paper presented at the Latin American Studies Association Meetings, XIV Congress, New Orleans, 1988).

9. The most comprehensive account of García's unilateral moratorium and of Peru's overall debt policy is provided by Drago Kisic, *De la corresponsibilidad a la moratoria: el caso de la deuda peruana 1970-1986* (Lima: Fundación Friedrich Ebert and Centro Peruano de Estudios Internacionales, 1987).

10. A synthesis of the theoretical underpinnings and accompanying development strategies set forth in the INP plan can be found in Daniel Carbonetto et al., *Un modelo ecónomico heterodoxo: el caso peruano* (Lima: Instituto Nacional de Planificación, 1987), See also Rosemary Thorp, "The APRA Alternative in Peru: Preliminary Evaluation of García's Economic Policies," *The Peru Report* 1, no. 6 (1987).

11. The May and June 1987 issues of *The Peru Report* provide a useful chronology of

the unraveling of heterodox policy and the weakening of García's political support base.

12. This paradox, and the manner in which it has been played out during Peru's democratic transition, is explored at length by Sanborn, *"El futuro diferente?"*

13. Thorp, "The APRA Alternative in Peru," more fully explains the potentially disastrous effects of Peruvian heterodoxy when only applied as a short-term inflation management strategy.

Suggestions for Further Reading

Cotler, Julio. "Military Interventions and 'Transfer of Power to Civilians' in Peru." In *Transitions from Authoritarian Rule: Latin America*, ed. Guillermo O'Donnell, Philippe C. Schmitter, and Laurence Whitehead. Baltimore: Johns Hopkins University Press, 1986.

FitzGerald, E. V. K. *The Political Economy of Peru 1956-1978: Economic Development and the Restructuring of Capital*. Cambridge: Cambridge University Press, 1979.

Kisic, Drago. *De la corresponsabilidad a la moratoria: el caso de la deuda peruana 1970-1986*. Lima: Fundación Friedrich Ebert and Centro Peruano de Estudios Internacionales, 1987.

McClintock, Cynthia, and Abraham F. Lowenthal, eds. *The Peruvian Experiment Reconsidered*. Princeton: Princeton University Press, 1983.

Saulniers, Alfred H. *Public Enterprises in Peru: Public Sector Growth and Reform*. Boulder CO: Westview Press, 1988.

Thorp, Rosemary, and Geoffrey Bertram. *Peru 1890-1977: Growth and Policy in an Open Economy*. New York: Columbia University Press, 1978.

11

Political Economy of Democratic Transition: Chile in the 1980s

Barbara Stallings

Chile has one of the longest histories of democracy in Latin America. Indeed, its democratic tradition was perhaps the thing of which Chileans were most proud, thinking it set them apart from their neighbors who were often plagued by political instability and periods of military rule. In this context, the 1973 coup represented a sharp break with the past. Even more incongruous is the fact that only Chile, among the major Latin American nations, remains a military stronghold 15 years later after Brazil, Argentina, Peru and others have returned to democratic rule.

While Chile had a political system that was more similar to the Western European countries than to its Latin American neighbors, its economy was quite typical of Latin America. Dependence on a single export product, foreign control of important parts of the economy, an inefficient and heavily-protected industrial sector, sharp inequalities, and stop-go cycles linked to frequent balance-of-payments crises were some of the major characteristics as of 1970. The Allende policies in 1970-73 were an attempt to deal with these problems via a stronger role for the state. The military who overthrew Allende took the opposite tack and moved sharply toward laissez-faire.

By the late 1970s, the laissez-faire model was producing impressive results in terms of growth, although inequality was increasing and external disequilibria were building up. The authoritarian political system, which made the economic model possible, was maintained through a combination of repression and acquiescence, since many in the middle and upper classes had agreed to trade political freedoms for a higher standard of living. In 1982, however, the economy crashed, and Chileans found themselves with the worst possible combination—severe economic problems *and* oppressive political dictatorship. Not surprisingly, calls began ringing out for a change of regime. By late 1983, it looked as if Chile would soon join the list of Latin American countries returning to democracy, but this did not happen, and the military regained their control of the political situation as well as the economy.

Why did a transition not occur in Chile during the difficult years of 1982-84? This question becomes especially intriguing from the vantage point of 1988. In contrast to the early 1980s, the Chilean economy is currently functioning as well as any in Latin America, yet surveys suggest that the military may be voted out of power in the upcoming plebiscite. Understanding this paradox requires both economic and political analysis. On the one hand, the very economic success achieved by the military government had as its corollary the poverty of a substantial portion of the population that did not share in the benefits. This provided a base of people who were determined opponents of the government. On the other hand, political factors are also relevant. The scheduling of a plebiscite in 1988 on whether to continue the military government for another eight years brought a return to "normal" political activity. It also provided enough of an incentive for the opposition finally to forge a tactical alliance and present a joint social-economic program.

This chapter will explore these issues. The first section provides a political-economic background. The next two parts focus on the economic crisis of the early 1980s and the protests demanding a return to democracy. The chapter then turns to the post-1985 recovery and the plebiscite. Finally, the concluding section reflects on the Chilean experience within the broader subject of transitions to democracy.

Political-Economic Background

In the early 1950s, Chile faced a series of choices.[1] The economic strategy of import-substitution industrialization that had provided the dynamic for growth since the 1930s seemed to have exhausted itself. In a closely-related fashion, the middle-class political coalition that had governed over that period had lost its hold on the electorate. There was no agreed-upon solution to these dilemmas. On the contrary, there were at least three alternatives, whose proponents fought among themselves and which were tried in turn over the period from 1958 to 1973.

The first alternative was the government of Jorge Alessandri (1958-64), which was based on a coalition of right-wing political parties and followed what were considered at the time to be orthodox economic policies. That is, the private sector was given extensive privileges and allowed to dominate the economy. Foreign investment was invited in as a welcome partner, and wages and consumption were constrained in favor of investment. Nevertheless, the state maintained an important role in regulating the economy and assisting the private sector.

The lack of conspicuous success of the Alessandri government, and fear of a leftist victory, led in 1964 to a coalition of right and center parties that produced an electoral majority for Eduardo Frei and the Christian Democrats. As was typical of "reformist" governments in Latin America in that era, the Frei administration (1964-70) wanted to modernize the economy. The state increased its role in the economy, yet still relied on the private sector for the bulk of production and investment. Foreign capital was sought but forced to operate within government guidelines. "Communitarian" organizational structures were set up to permit greater distributive efforts without inhibiting growth and investment. Certain structural reforms were also seen as necessary prerequisites for such a strategy to work. In particular, an agrarian reform was carried out to increase the market for industrial products, and state participation in the crucial copper industry was instituted to provide greater leverage for dealing with external problems.

While they achieved some economic success, the Christian Democrats and their allies lost strength as disagreements arose over the speed and nature of economic and social reforms. By the end of the 1960s, the three alternative coalitions were again in contention, but the weight of public opinion had shifted toward the left. The Popular Unity alliance, oriented around the Socialist and Communist parties and supporting the candidacy of Salvador Allende, won the 1970 election by a narrow plurality. Its victory led to a government (1970-73) committed to prepare the way for a transition to socialism. Agrarian reform and control of foreign capital were stepped up. The state also increased its domestic strength through takeovers of certain strategic firms, increased regulation of others, and higher public expenditure on both consumption and investment. Not surprisingly, the responses of international capital and the U.S. government were extremely unfavorable. Domestic opposition to the government also grew, as new groups were organized and polarization sharply increased. By the 1973 civilian opposition enlisted the support of the military, which overthrew Allende in a bloody coup.

The political mobilization of the country ended abruptly with the coup.[2] Although the armed opposition expected by the military did not materialize, they nevertheless went ahead with an internal war of unprecedented dimension and duration. Thousands of Popular Unity leaders and supporters were killed, put in concentration camps, exiled, or fired from their jobs. The Congress was closed, political parties disbanded, labor organizations made illegal, and even business groups discouraged. Elections at all levels were forbidden.

The coup was originally carried out as a combined operation by the four branches of the armed forces (army, navy, air force, and militarized police), but army chief Augusto Pinochet rapidly became the dominant leader of the ruling Military Junta. Although many of its civilian supporters had expected the military government to be of short duration, followed by new elections within a period of months, the military themselves had a longer-term project in mind: to depoliticize the country, eliminate the power of labor and the left, and put a new economic model into place. Thus, the increasingly leftward orientation of the preceding decades ended, and a shift to the right began.

After the coup, there was an initial period of indecision about economic policy, while an *ad hoc* "shock treatment" was applied in an attempt to lower inflation by cutting domestic demand. The GDP fell by 6 percent in 1973 and another 13 percent in 1975, but inflation stayed well above 300 percent per year. It was not until 1976 that a coherent line emerged from the group of economists who came to be known as the "Chicago Boys." That group, based in the Catholic University in Santiago but with close ties to the University of Chicago through a U.S.-financed exchange program, had been preparing an alternative economic project since the late 1960s. Although their extreme free-market ideas were revolutionary within the Chilean tradition of a strong state and protected economy, after 1976 they were applied in almost textbook fashion under the leadership of Finance Minister Sergio de Castro.

Government expenditure was cut so dramatically that the large fiscal deficit was eliminated. Many state firms were returned to their previous owners or sold at bargain-basement prices. Tariffs were cut from an average of 100 percent to a uniform 10 percent, and the capital market was deregulated. Perhaps most controversially, the exchange rate was pegged to the dollar in mid-1979. This encouraged foreign borrowing by the private sector and resulted in a vast foreign debt.

By the late 1970s, these policies began to produce GDP growth rates that were very high by Chilean standards. The so-called miracle years of 1977-81 saw growth average around 8 percent per year, while inflation fell to about 35 percent per year. Nevertheless, it was not until 1981 that per capita GDP exceeded the previous peak achieved in 1971, and real wages never returned to their 1971 high. Unemployment also remained high throughout the "miracle" period.

Even leaving social questions aside, there were major problems with the type of growth that was occurring. The most obvious issue was the current account deficit that reached some 15 percent of GDP in 1981. This gap was filled by a huge volume of foreign loans, most of which was spent on consumer imports and/or speculation. Productive activities were becoming unattractive, and industry in particular was in decline. By 1981, many firms were in bankruptcy, and the financial system was increasingly insolvent. The end of foreign lending the next year brought the "miracle" to an abrupt halt.[3]

The Economic Crisis and Government Response

The crisis in Chile was part of the world-wide economic problems that emerged in the early 1980s. As recession hit the advanced industrial countries and interest rates rose, these trends were passed on to Latin America through balance-of-payments problems. At the same time, foreign loans that had stimulated growth in the 1970s were cut off as a result of the Mexican debt crisis. Despite being part of this international pattern, however, Chile's crisis had some unique characteristics that need to be pointed out. Table 11.1 presents a set of economic indicators for the country during this period.

Characteristics of the Crisis

Inflation more than doubled between 1981 and 1982, from 9.5 to 20.7 percent, while the fiscal balance went from a surplus to a deficit equivalent to 2.3 percent of GDP. Neither of these figures was especially high, either by historical or cross-national standards, but the plunge in growth and the rise in unemployment were extraordinary. Chile's GDP fell by 14 percent in 1982, and open unemployment jumped to 22 percent of the labor force. Likewise, a balance-of-payments crisis manifested itself in a large loss of reserves, even though the trade balance moved

Table 11.1
Chilean Economic Performance Indicators, 1980-87

	1980	1981	1982	1983	1984	1985	1986	1987
GDP Growth Rate (%)	7.8	5.5	-14.1	-0.7	6.3	2.3	5.7	5.5
Inflation[a] (%)	31.2	9.5	20.7	23.1	23.0	26.4	17.4	22.9
Balance of Payments[b] ($ million)	-1971	-4733	-2304	-1117	-2060	-1329	-1137	-808
Fiscal Deficit[c] (% of GDP)	3.1	1.7	-2.3	-3.8	-4.0	-6.3	-2.8	-0.1
Unemployment (% of Labor Force)	11.8	11.1	22.1	22.2	19.2	16.2	13.1	12.4
Real Wages[d] (%)	9.0	8.9	-0.2	-10.7	0.1	-3.8	1.7	-0.3

[a]Consumer prices, end of year
[b]Current account
[c]Central government
[d]Average change in non-agricultural wages
Sources: Banco Central de Chile, *Indicadores Económicos y Sociales*, 1960-85 and *Boletín Mensual*; U.N. Economic Commission for Latin America, *Preliminary Overview of the Latin American Economy, 1987.*

into a small surplus. The problem was a rise in the debt-service ratio, together with a sudden fall in capital inflow and an increase in capital flight. In addition, there was a domestic financial crisis of enormous proportions, involving the largest banks in the country as well as industrial firms.

An extensive debate has taken place in Chile about the relative importance of domestic versus international factors as causes of the crisis.[4] External shocks did hit Chile especially hard, through a fall in the terms of trade and a rise in interest rates, but government policy decisions were at least as important. The balance-of-payments problems, for instance, were not only attributable to international prices and interest rates. The dramatic reduction of tariffs, the elimination of capital controls, and the fixed exchange rate were also key causal factors. In an even more obvious way, the domestic financial crisis came about because the Central Bank both withdrew from its normal regulatory functions and encouraged massive foreign borrowing by the private sector. These initial policies, undertaken in the 1976-81 period, were extended once the crisis hit since the government refused to intervene.

From the point of view of the economic team in Chile, any governmental response to the crisis would have been at least as traumatic as the crisis itself because of their near-total commitment to market mechanisms, including an "automatic adjustment" to macroeconomic disequilibria. Thus government intervention was seen as tantamount to admitting that the model had failed. These proclivities on the part of the economists, who had enjoyed an extraordinary amount of autonomy during the "miracle" years, finally ran up against the political limits of the system by early 1982. Allowing the crisis to run its course would have threatened the government's very survival; rebellion could have been expected from business and the military itself as well as opposition groups.

To prevent such a scenario, Pinochet and his political advisors began to take a more active role in economic policy making.[5] Over the next few years, they frequently changed finance ministers and allowed or even encouraged policies that deviated substantially from the laissez-faire model of the Chicago Boys. The period can be divided into several phases.

April-December 1982

With the dismissal of Sergio de Castro from the Finance Ministry in April 1982, a number of policies began to be called into question. The most important concerned the exchange rate and possible devaluation of the currency that had been pegged at 39 pesos per dollar since mid-1979. The resulting overvaluation was impeding exports and making it extremely difficult for local industry to compete with imports. On the positive side, however, the fixed exchange rate had been instrumental in bringing down inflation to the single-digit level for the first time in decades, and was keeping debt payments manageable for those who had borrowed abroad. Consequently, a devaluation was controversial for practical as well as theoretical reasons. Those who wanted to maintain the fixed exchange system argued that a preferable way to deal with the macroeconomic disequilibria was to lower nominal wages. The latter would require a conflictive process of cutting wages and eliminating the indexation system established through the 1979 labor reform, whereby wages were automatically increased in line with inflation.

The alternative positions were presented to Pinochet, who felt that the size of wage drop needed to reequilibrate the economy was politically impossible. Thus the economic team, at that time led by Sergio de la Cuadra, another Catholic University economist who had replaced his colleague Sergio de Castro, was ordered to devalue the peso in June 1982. At the same time, the basis for wage indexation was altered and later eliminated altogether. The devaluation quickly slashed imports, leading to a small trade surplus in 1982 and a much larger one in 1983.

January 1983

An even more dramatic departure from previous policy occurred at the beginning of 1983 when the government assumed control of two major banks in order to stem the financial crisis. The financial crisis had been exacerbated by the devaluation since many local businesses had obtained dollar loans, and more pesos would be required to repay the same amount of dollar debt. Many became insolvent and thus unable to service their loans from Chilean banks, which were already in trouble because of speculative activities. The two banks in greatest difficulty were the Banco de Chile and the Banco de Santiago, leaders of the two largest conglomerates in the country.[6]

Three options were considered for dealing with the banks: they could be provided with resources to refinance debtors and remain solvent themselves; they could be allowed to go bankrupt; or they could be taken over by the state. Again the question was referred to Pinochet and his advisors, and the decision was made to intervene the banks, i.e. to take them over on a temporary basis.

For lack of reliable information, interpretations abound as to why a right-wing government would take over the business groups that were its strongest supporters. One possibility is that the conglomerates were getting too powerful, and the military did not want so much competition. Another is that the government needed a scapegoat to deflect blame for the economic problems. A third is that the conglomerates were behaving so badly, in their penchant for speculation and short-term profitmaking, that they were seriously undermining the government's economic project. Whatever the reason(s), the process of intervention threatened to create yet more problems, since some of the losers in the transaction were foreign banks that had lent money to several smaller banks scheduled for liquidation. Through various types of leverage, the foreign banks eventually forced the government to take responsibility for the debt of the private financial sector. Ironically, the Finance Minister who presided over the intervention, Rolf Luders, had been one of the key figures in the Banco de Chile and himself ended up in jail for alleged illegal activities while a banker.

February 1983-April 1984

It thus fell to Carlos Cáceres, the fourth Finance Minister in less than a year, to deal with the aftermath of the intervention and other problems facing the economy. During this period, the banks were put back on their feet through state initiatives involving enormous expenditures. These expenditures were compensated by otherwise tight demand-management policies that caused wages to fall dramatically and production to remain in a depressed condition.

The decision to intervene the banks left the government in a truly anomalous position. Firm proponents of a small state, they found themselves with more control over the economy than even Allende had had. Pundits referred to the process as "the Chicago road to socialism." Although the long-run issue was how to return the firms to the private sector, the immediate problem was how to rescue the ailing private sector. The means chosen represented huge subsidies to the banks and the largest corporations, including the purchase of bad loans by the Central Bank, a preferential exchange rate for holders of dollar debt, the option to turn dollar debt into pesos, and ultimately a government guarantee for a substantial part of the privately-contracted foreign debt. It is estimated that these policies cost the government some $7 billion between 1982 and 1985, equivalent to a staggering 44 percent of GDP in the latter year.[7] Smaller debtors had to make do with much less, and their problems are still pending.

International financial problems were also high on Cáceres' agenda. His predecessor, Rolf Luders, had negotiated a two-year standby agreement with the International Monetary Fund (IMF) as the typical first step toward a renegotiation of the foreign debt, but the intervention of the banks and the rescue measures made the program inoperable even before it began. The government therefore decided to follow very tight policies to curb the current account deficit, the public sector deficit, and inflation and to return to the originally-agreed economic targets. The agreement made it possible to proceed with a renegotiation of foreign loans due for repayment in 1983-84. Terms were similar to those obtained elsewhere in Latin America, except that the government reluctantly agreed to guarantee the debt of the private financial sector and assumed responsibility for the debt of bankrupt financial institutions.[8]

The Political Protests: A Demand for Democracy

Although Cáceres' policies would eventually provide a basis for reequilibrating the economy, the costs were extraordinarily high. The IMF agreement, and the government's own preferences, meant that austerity measures continued. GDP fell again in 1983, although by less than 1 percent. Real wages fell by 11 percent, however, while median family income in Greater Santiago plunged by 28 percent.[9] Given the previous year's crash in GDP, and indications that policy was not about to change, the situation became politically explosive.

Several types of protest resulted. As early as 1981, a movement was initiated by small businesses, especially farmers in the south, to demand a change in economic policy to alleviate the growing bankruptcies. These groups had helped overthrow the Allende government, but had not been favored by the military government's policies. After first limiting themselves to individual public statements about their problems, by 1982 the small businesspeople moved to broader organizational cohesion and more militant tactics. Large public meetings, demonstrations, and attempts to forcibly prevent banks from taking possession of bankrupt firms all became part of their growing mobilization.[10]

The larger firms were more cautious in their approach, since they had close ties with the government and had benefited from many of its policies. By mid-1982, however, the severity of the crisis led to new leadership in the umbrella organization, the Confederation of Production and Commerce (CPC). Its new president surprised observers during his inaugural address by saying: "Either we unite and work together or we will all go under together." In July 1983, the CPC presented a document to the government that called for lowering the interest rate on all debts to 5 percent; transformation of dollar debts into pesos; increased government expenditure, including a deficit up to 4 percent of GDP; labor-intensive public investment projects; and greater flexibility in dealing with the IMF.

The third type of protest was openly political in nature.[11] In May 1983, the copper workers' union called for a national "day of protest" that saw participation by various sectors of workers, students, shantytown dwellers, and the population in general. Despite government repression, the protest days became monthly events. Activities included partial labor strikes, school absenteeism, commercial boycotts, demonstrations in downtown streets, and barricades in the shantytowns. Sponsorship spread to the political parties and party alliances, and the demand for a return to democracy became the central issue.

On August 10, 1983, after three monthly "days of protest," Pinochet announced a cabinet shuffle that featured the appointment of Sergio Onofre Jarpa as Minister of Interior. Jarpa was a veteran politician from the right-wing National Party that favored a controlled return to democracy. It is unclear whether Jarpa's appointment was part of a long-term Pinochet plan or if events were simply shaped as they went along. In either case, the appointment enabled the government to gain the upper hand by exacerbating divisions within the opposition between the center-right parties and organizations and those of the left. The former agreed to enter into a "dialogue" with Jarpa, while the latter refused.

This division was but one more instance of the bitter, long-standing feuds that have wracked the opposition since the 1973 coup. The divisions were not new. They had their origins much earlier in the century, but were especially aggravated in the Allende years. During the Pinochet government, they were manifested through two different approaches: one strategy called for a return to democracy through negotiation; the other emphasized mobilization of the population. At the extreme end of this spectrum was the Communist Party, which had reversed its historic position in Chile and had come to advocate armed struggle as the only way to remove Pinochet. The role of the Communists within the opposition was, in itself, a major source of conflict.

In addition to fomenting and reinforcing divisions within the opposition ranks, the government also used two other tactics to deal with the protests. One was repression. Repression was especially prevalent in the shantytowns, although arrests and violent dispersion of demonstrations occurred in other areas as well. During some of the days of protest, massive military force was deployed. After the October 1984 event, a state of siege was declared, marking the virtual end of the protest movement.

The other tactic was economic co-optation, especially directed toward the crucial business constituency. Two types of economic incentives were offered. One was specifically-targeted favors, aimed to buy off opponents. Examples included exclusion of protesters from minimum employment program benefits, and special privileges for truckers to keep them from joining the protest movement.[12] In addition, more general economic policy was altered to placate business allies. Thus, in April 1984, Jarpa finally convinced Pinochet to replace Cáceres in the Finance Ministry. His successor was Luis Escobar Cerda, a minister during the Alessandri government.

The usual interpretation is that Escobar's ten months in office represented an important break with the "Chicago-style" policies. To some extent that was true. He definitely favored reflation and greater protectionism and, with Jarpa's support, introduced policies to bring them about. Nevertheless, two factors should be kept in mind. On the one hand, many of the policies often attributed to Escobar were actually instituted earlier. For example, the special price and credit policies for agriculture, the subsidies for the housing industry, and the tariff increase from 10 to 20 percent all preceded the change in finance ministers. On the other hand, Escobar saw himself obliged to carry out certain measures that were inconsistent with his own policy preferences. For instance, monetary policy became quite contractionary in the latter part of 1984, and his elevation of tariffs to an even higher 35 percent was scheduled for rollback.

These conflicting trends were manifestations of the divergent views within the government over how to deal with the crisis. In general, the orthodox positions prevailed, but small incursions were made by officials connected with business. These incursions introduced some flexibility into the system and improved performance. The change in agricultural policy, for instance, substantially increased output in that sector. Likewise, the increase in tariffs and credit rescued certain industries. At the same time, however, the austerity policies prevented the resurgence of inflation and, together with the devaluation, brought the balance of payments under control. The economy began to revive, and the worst of the crisis was over.

A New Version of Laissez-Faire Economics

The combination of economic recovery, repression and serious divisions within the opposition ranks meant that Pinochet was able to survive the crisis, unlike his counterparts elsewhere in the region. The political protests petered out, and the business groups were placated by the favors they received. Putting these factors together, Pinochet and his advisors concluded that they could risk a return toward the pre-crisis economic model—which they still believed was the best for the country, even if particular aspects had gone awry previously—and in February both Jarpa and Escobar were dismissed. Escobar's replacement was Hernán Büchi, an engineer who had served in various posts under the military: secretary general of the Economics Ministry, director of the planning agency, and superintendent of banks. The holder of an M.A. from Columbia University, Büchi is a strange figure in a military government. He is a long-haired jogger who eats health food and is rumored to have been on the fringes of the Revolutionary Left Movement (MIR) during the Allende years. Nevertheless, he is widely respected as a technocrat and has the full confidence of Pinochet.

Büchi's appointment resolved many problems facing the government. His policies combined the earlier laissez-faire model with the more interventionist approach of Escobar. The almost universal shorthand is that Büchi is a more "pragmatic" and "flexible" version of the Chicago Boys. As one observer with close government connections put it: "Büchi favors the business organizations' line but is friends with the Catholic University group. As a consequence, he has been able to unite the two factions in the government." Perhaps the most accurate way of expressing the synthesis is a long-term model resting on a small state and open economy, but a short-term model that is mildly interventionist. In other words, the former has not changed much from the pre-crisis period, but the latter looks quite different.

The style of the economic team has changed as well. While de Castro refused even to receive Chilean business leaders and appeared to hold them in complete disdain, Büchi listens to them and tries to obtain their backing for government policies. The combination seems to have regained the support of most of the business class as well as the international actors who will be discussed later. Furthermore, it has united the government itself, eliminating the tensions and divisions of the 1982-84 period.

The macroeconomic model in place since February 1985 has been aimed at a moderate rate of growth and low inflation through promotion of investment and exports and containment of public and private consumption.[13] (Indicators of economic trends can be seen by referring back to Table 11.1.) Within this panorama, a tight fiscal policy has played a key role. The main emphasis has been on cutting social expenditure, since public investment has been increased while taxes have been lowered. Public-sector firms have also raised their prices, thus creating surpluses that have been transferred to the central government coffers. Through this combination, the fiscal deficit was lowered to only 2.8 percent of GDP in 1986 and was virtually eliminated in 1987.

Another basic component of the short-term model has been the limit on private consumption in general and wages in particular. The automatic inflation adjustment of wages, which was eliminated in 1982, has not been restored. Private-sector wages have been left to be determined by firm-level agreements, while public-sector wages have been kept down as part of the campaign to cut government expenditure. As a result, real wages fell by 2.2 percent between 1982 and 1987. The minimum wage has stayed even further behind inflation as have wages in the government minimum employment programs.

Trade policy has centered on two main instruments—the exchange rate and tariffs. The peso has been gradually lowered (through a "crawling peg"), combined with occasional larger devaluations, in order to maintain an expensive dollar. This is considered to be the most important incentive for exports and import substitution. When Büchi became Finance Minister, tariffs were 35 percent. They were soon returned to a flat 20 percent rate (and later 15 percent), although the use of surcharges has been continued in special cases. Other incentives for non-traditional exports also exist.

Prices for most goods remain market-determined with the main exception being in agriculture. The special treatment provided to agriculture after the protests in

1982-83 has been continued. This includes subsidized prices and special credit facilities; the new exchange rate policy has also helped agriculture. The other sector with special help has been construction, which benefits from the subsidies offered to homebuyers. Through this plan, people can obtain different types of subsidized credit, depending their income level.

This more interventionist set of macroeconomic policies has been linked to a medium-term "structural adjustment" strategy. On the one hand, this strategy has stressed an increase in investment and a reorientation of production toward exports. On the other hand, both as a complement to these objectives and as an aim in itself, there has been an increasing emphasis on strengthening the private sector. The policies to deal with the insolvency of banks and non-financial enterprises have already been discussed. Beyond the question of debts, there remained the issue of property rights, both with respect to the banks themselves and the firms they had controlled. In 1984, while Büchi was still superintendent of banks, a plan evolved to sell the two banks that had been intervened to the public through the process known as "people's capitalism."[14] Stock in firms was sold to individual investors, making it possible for the banks to get the additional capital they needed and the state to get out of its undesired position of control.

The success of the bank sales encouraged the main structural change that has occurred since 1985—a significant increase in privatization. Following the coup in 1973, firms that had been under temporary government control were returned to their owners, but a large number remained in public hands because of military veto over their sale.[15] By 1985, the economic and especially the political conjunctures were different. Privatization via people's capitalism had two major political advantages for the government. On the one hand, it would increase the number of small property owners, who might then be expected to become government supporters. On the other hand, the shrinking of the public sector would limit the room for maneuver of a successor government, whenever one might take over. The economic benefits of privatization were much more dubious. Little money would be obtained, and a major source of revenue would be lost. According to the latest figures, 14 non-financial firms have been completely privatized, and 14 more will be all or partially sold. The 28 firms include the main providers of steel, communications, transportation, electricity, paper, and chemicals.[16]

The other important initiative in terms of reducing the size of the state has been the lowering of taxes. In the last five years, reforms have cut taxes by approximately $1 billion on an annual basis, compared to what they would otherwise have been, which is about 20 percent of total government income (excluding public enterprises). These sets of reforms have included: (1) an income tax cut for corporations and high-income groups; (2) cuts in various indirect taxes including tariffs, gasoline, and dividends; and (3) a cut in the value-added tax from 20 to 16 percent. Unlike the U.S. tax cuts of the 1980s, these are not projected to lead to government deficits, but are already being compensated by higher tax collection and expenditure cuts. The alternative would have been to use some or all of the surplus to increase

social services, which have been substantially reduced during the military government, but this alternative was rejected in favor of reducing the size of the state.[17]

These domestic changes were not unrelated to Chile's international economic
problems, although the exact nature of the link is debated. The government claims
its policies represent its own ideas, while the opposition points to the IMF, World
Bank, and private banks as the source of many of the policies. What is undeniable
is that Chile's large foreign debt makes the balance of payments a major constraint
on economic policy, now that private bank loans have virtually dried up. Nearly half
of export revenues have gone for debt service since the crisis began. The government's
basic stance in favor of private enterprise and an open economy means that the debt
must be serviced, but government negotiators have nevertheless sought the best deal
possible. Under Büchi, relations with both the international agencies and the private
banks have been extremely cordial. Since 1985, the government has signed an
Extended Fund Facility (EFF) with the International Monetary Fund and three
Structural Adjustment Loans (SALs) with the World Bank. In addition, three sets
of negotiations have been completed with private bank creditors. These negotiations have brought in some $3 billion, which has been crucial in enabling the
government to meet its debt-servicing obligations.

At the same time, Chile has eliminated $4 billion from its foreign debt through
the controversial debt-equity swaps. This program enables foreign corporations, or
Chilean citizens who hold foreign currency, to purchase Chilean debt at a discount
and then exchange it for the full face-value equivalent of local currency to make
direct investments. The resulting profits cannot be remitted for four years and then
only in a phased manner. Critics charge that these mechanisms provide a cheap
means of making investments that would occur in any case and lead to increased
denationalization of assets. Often debt-equity swaps have been used to purchase
companies being sold by the government.[18]

All of these international financial negotiations, of course, have been affected by
Chile's relations with the United States.[19] The most appropriate words to describe
these relations are inconsistent or even contradictory. The basic problem is concern
over Chile's human rights record set against strong approval of its economic policy.
The contradiction came into play most sharply in terms of the second World Bank
loan, which the U.S. government considered voting against. Ultimately, it abstained
and the loan was approved with a 51 percent majority. The ambivalent position of
the United States has enabled Chile to continue its authoritarian policies and still
deal adequately with its potentially debilitating foreign exchange situation.

The Plebiscite: Another Opportunity for Redemocratization

Even though the government had managed to resolve many of its economic
problems and to co-opt business to a certain extent, there still remained an
unfinished political agenda. The emphasis on legality that pervades Chilean society,
including the military, made it advisable—perhaps even necessary—to establish a

legal basis for Pinochet's rule. This was done through the constitution, approved in a controversial referendum in 1980. Among the provisions of that constitution was the requirement for a plebiscite in 1988. The members of the Military Junta were to nominate a candidate who had to be approved or rejected by popular vote. If the government candidate were to win, he would serve another eight-year term. If he were defeated, open elections would be held. As it turns out, the plebiscite that was set up to increase support for Pinochet may end up removing him from office.

As the time for the plebiscite approached, it became the source of increased division within the opposition over whether to participate or to hold out for free elections. In early 1988, the Christian Democrats and the moderate left agreed to take part, and other groups agreed at least to back a voter registration drive. Shortly thereafter, the "Campaign for the No" was set up to coordinate activities related to the plebiscite; this was a broad coalition that eventually came to include 16 parties. In mid-June, the Communists decided to join the "No" campaign although they were not formally affiliated with the coalition.

The organizational alliance finally made possible a degree of programmatic unity, after 15 years of divisiveness, and in May the 21-point "Social-Economic Program of the Campaign for the No" was published. A very moderate document, it promised greater political participation for all and an improved standard of living for the poorest sectors of the population, while still "maintaining the indispensible fiscal, monetary and external equilibrium." The additional revenues to fulfill the promises were to come from higher taxes on upper-income groups, redistribution of public expenditure, and renegotiation of the foreign debt.

Government supporters immediately attacked the proposals as not affordable, even if desirable in principle. A group of ex-ministers of the Pinochet government issued a statement declaring the measures "contrary to the factors required for economic growth." A few days later, however, the value-added tax was lowered, raising questions about what could be afforded. As in 1983-84, the government has attempted to use economic measures to gain support. Some special one-time social expenditures were authorized, taking advantage of the high price of copper and other favorable international trends, and it is expected that the individual consumer and home-mortgage debts will be alleviated. At the rhetorical level, government supporters argue that the orderly economy and economic growth achieved since 1985 cannot survive a "No" vote, despite the opposition's claims to the contrary.

Although opinion polls are divided, and a large "undecided" group appears in all of them, the opposition is convinced that it can win the plebiscite. Lack of access to television is a major problem in getting across the opposition message, but increasing numbers of political debate programs are being aired. Once the government announces its candidate and a date for the plebiscite, and the campaign officially begins, the two sides will have 15 minutes of free television time each day. Furthermore, since the state of emergency has been lifted, the opposition will be able to hold public meetings with prior authorization.

Beyond the uncertainty over the outcome of the plebiscite, there is of course uncertainty over the succeeding events. Few expect that Pinochet will willingly give up power, and fraud and violence are considered possible. The opposition will not easily admit defeat either, but they have fewer means at their disposal. Regardless of which side wins, however, the political-economic trajectory of the next few years is the most uncertain aspect of all.

Conclusion: The Economics and Politics of Democratic Transition

Reflecting on the Chilean experience during the 1980s provides some interesting insights about transitions to democracy.[20] There have been two moments since the military coup when democracy has been on the agenda in Chile: 1983-84 and 1987-88. The differences in the circumstances of the two periods—and the possibility of different outcomes—provide the opportunity to examine the role of both economic and political variables in the transition process.

Economic factors have been central in both 1983-84 and 1987-88, although the way in which they have operated is somewhat different in the two periods. In 1983, Chile was in the throes of the most serious economic crisis of the postwar period. GDP had fallen 15 percent in two years, wages had fallen 11 percent, open unemployment was above 22 percent, and the balance of payments was out of control. Bankruptcies were exacting a heavy toll on large as well as small businesses. In that context, there was a direct relationship between economics and politics: the economic crisis was clearly the major cause of the political protests that began that year, bringing together a diverse group of parties, organizations, and individuals to demand a return to democracy.

By 1988, Chile had recovered from the crisis and achieved a level of economic stability and growth that is the envy of most other Latin American countries. GDP growth has averaged 5 percent per year over the last half decade, and inflation is expected to fall to around 15 percent in 1988. The external accounts have been brought under control, and bankruptcies have tapered off. There is, however, another side to this picture. The term "boom" is often used to refer to the Chilean economy in the late 1980s, but the boom conditions are not shared by the entire population. The government's own data (see Table 11.1) show that wages have stagnated since the crisis began, and unemployment remains very high. Debts that became unmanageable during the crisis still hold many individual consumers in bondage. For this group of people, opposition to the government is a continuation of the direct relationship between economics and politics.

In both periods, therefore, economic hardship has stimulated demand for political change. Nevertheless, the interest in democracy in 1988 is not limited to those who have failed to share in the new prosperity. Many who are doing well are also supporting the demand for change. For the latter group, it would seem that the very success of the economy has made it possible to seek change. Opposition to the government is less likely to bring about the loss of a job. Economic uncertainty and strategies to cope with poverty occupy less of people's time. The idea of a simple link between economic problems and a return to democracy seems less defensible in 1988, and the nature of the relationship needs to be reconceptualized in a more complex way.

Beyond rethinking the economic link, however, we also need to look at political variables that have changed from the 1983-84 period to the present. The single most important political change is the increased unity of the opposition. For 15 years, divisions between left and center parties rendered ineffectual the attempts to end the military dictatorship. The divisions, left over from the bitter disputes during the Allende years, pitted Christian Democrats against the Marxist left, the various factions of the Socialist Party against one another, and all against the Communists. Indeed, the 1983-84 protests came to naught in part because of conflicts within the opposition over whether to engage in negotiations with the government after Jarpa's appointment.

In early 1988, however, a tactical alliance was finally worked out, and most oppositon forces came together in the "Campaign for the No." Not only was an organizational alliance achieved, but a common social-economic program was negotiated as well. The role of the Communists remains divisive, but Christian Democrats are working together with the bulk of the left in an attempt to defeat the government in the plebiscite. Whether the new-found unity will survive the plebiscite—whatever the outcome—is uncertain, but in the meantime it is making a difference in that the opposition can present itself as a viable alternative to the military government.

Other political factors have also changed. The different form of political combat in the two periods means that different actors have been important, and different power resources relevant. In the protest period, there were two separate, although related, arenas of conflict. On the one hand, there were mass protests in the streets and occasional strikes in the workplace. The aim was to mobilize as many participants as possible in a situation where the costs they faced were potentially very high. Workers could and did lose their jobs, and people were injured or arrested in demonstrations. The goal of the opposition was to convince the military that they could not control the country and that their only alternative was to withdraw.

On the other hand, there were business protests, which were more important to the government than mass demonstrations. For a right-wing government following a laissez-faire economic strategy, the private sector is a crucial part of a support coalition. Its support is important for practical reasons as well as ideological ones. Without private-sector investment, a laissez-faire economy cannot function. Behind-the-scenes business negotiations with the government were thus a vital aspect part of the 1983-84 process. The problem for those seeking a return to democracy was that the business groups were pacified by change in economic policy rather than holding out for change in political regime.

During the plebiscite period, by contrast, there is only a single arena of conflict, the ballot box. (Of course, no one knows for sure what will happen after the plebiscite, regardless of the outcome, but the initial arena is clear.) Although money is always useful in an election, businesspeople do not have the overriding importance they had earlier. Their votes count the same as anyone else's, and at least in urban areas there is little chance of coercing subordinates to vote in a particular way. The cost of voting is less than the cost of protesting, both in terms of time involved and potential sanctions. Therefore, many more Chileans will be participants in the voting process.

The types of power at the government's disposal also differ somewhat in the two situations. General economic policy, as well as more targeted favors, have of course been useful in both periods. It was basically through changes in economic policy that the business protests were defused in 1983-84. Farmers received subsidized prices, for example, while they and urban entrepreneurs also obtained higher tariffs, more credit, and some relief on debt problems. In 1987-88, the government has lowered taxes, with the 20 percent cut in the value-added tax widely interpreted as an election ploy. Other one-time social expenditures are being made, and further debt relief may well be offered. The economic incentives in 1988 are more widespread than the earlier ones, in line with the need to attract a much larger group of people to vote "Yes" in the plebiscite.

The main difference in tactics available to the government concerns repression. Large-scale repression and military deployment were very effective in the 1983-84 context, but would be counter-productive in 1988. Indeed, public pressure from the opposition, the Catholic Church, and foreign governments has convinced the government that it must move in the opposite direction, and lift the state of emergency so as to allow the opposition more freedom of action. To a significant extent, then, the government has to rely on the same method as the opposition — ideological persuasion.

The bottom line in terms of these various differences is that the odds have shifted in favor of the opposition in 1988 in comparison to 1983-84. Although fewer people are motivated by economic concerns, the weaker economic stimulus has been more than compensated by the favorable changes in political context. The opposition is a more unified, credible alternative force. The costs of supporting the opposition in a way that will help displace the government are lower. Businesspeople, who are dubious supporters of democracy at best, have a less dominant role. And the government itself has lost the use of some important power resources that were previously at its disposal, particularly repression.

None of this, of course, guarantees that the "No" will win or produce a return to democracy. The government may be able to persuade Chileans to vote "Yes," or it may spend enough to buy their votes. Alternatively, it may refuse to step down even if it loses the plebiscite, opting instead for a return to open repression. Nevertheless, the circumstances of 1988—ironically initiated by the government itself—offer the best possibility yet that Chile will return to its historic place among Latin American democracies.

Notes

The author would like to thank Charles Gillespie, Robert Kaufman, Carlos Portales, and Peter Winn for comments on earlier drafts of this chapter. The chapter is part of a larger project on "The Politics of Economic Stabilization and Structural Change in Developing Nations," financed by the Ford and Rockefeller Foundations.

1. For a comparison of Chilean development strategies in the period 1958-73, see Barbara Stallings, *Class Conflict and Economic Development in Chile, 1958-73* (Stanford: Stanford University Press, 1978).

2. The background to the coup is described in Arturo Valenzuela, *The Breakdown of Democratic Regimes: Chile* (Baltimore: Johns Hopkins University Press, 1978).

3. For several perspectives on Chile since the coup, see Alejandro Foxley, *Latin American Experiments in Neoconservative Economics* (Berkeley: University of California Press, 1983); Sebastian Edwards and Alejandra Cox Edwards, *Monetarism and Liberalization: The Chilean Experiment* (Cambridge, MA: Ballinger, 1987); and Samuel Valenzuela and Arturo Valenzuela, eds., *Military Rule in Chile: Dictatorship and Oppositions* (Baltimore: Johns Hopkins University Press, 1986).

4. A summary of this discussion can be found in Laurence Whitehead, "The Adjustment Process in Chile: A Comparative Perspective," in *Latin American Debt and the Adjustment Crisis*, ed. Rosemary Thorp and Laurence Whitehead (Pittsburgh: University of Pittsburgh Press, 1987).

5. For discussion of Pinochet's relations with his advisors, see Arturo Fontaine Aldunate, *Los economistas y el Presidente Pinochet* (Santiago: Zig-Zag, 1988).

6. On the conglomerates in general, see Andrés Sanfuentes, "Los grupos económicos: control y política," *Colección Estudios CIEPLAN* 15 (1984).

7. Sergio Infante, *Los claroscuros de la normalización bancaria*, Documento de Trabajo (Santiago: PET, 1986).

8. The first debt restructurings are discussed in Ricardo Ffrench-Davis and José de Gregorio, "La renegociación de la deuda externa de Chile en 1985: antecedentes y comentarios," *Colección Estudios CIEPLAN* 17 (1985).

9. Banco Central de Chile, *Indicadores económicos y sociales, 1960-85*.

10. The most extensive analysis of the relationship between the government and the business sector under the military is found in Guillermo Campero, *Los gremios empresariales en el período 1970-83* (Santiago: Estudios ILET, 1984).

11. For detailed information on the protests in the period 1983-84, see Gonzalo de la Maza and Mario Garcés, *La explosión de las mayorías* (Santiago: ECO, 1985). For an interpretation, see Manuel Antonio Garretón, "Protests and Politics in Chile," in *Power and Popular Protest: Latin American Social Movements*, ed. Susan Eckstein (Berkeley: University of California Press, 1988).

12. Carlos Huneeus, "La política de la apertura y sus implicancias para la inauguración de la democracia en Chile," *Revista de Ciencia Política* 7, no. 1 (1985).

13. The most useful overall discussion of the "new" economic model in Chile is Jorge Leiva, "Reformulación y rescate del modelo económico," *Coyuntura Económica* 13 (1985). See also articles on more specific aspects in *Colección Estudios CIEPLAN* and *Coyuntura Económica*.

14. On "people's capitalism" in Chile, see Enrique Errázuriz and Jacqueline Weinstein, *Capitalismo popular y privatización de las empresas*, Documento de Trabajo 15 (Santiago:

PET, 1986).

15. For data on the trends in public-sector ownership between 1965 and 1981, see Cristián Larroulet, "El estado empresario en Chile," *Estudios Públicos* 14 (1984). Larroulet is now the main advisor to Finance Minister Büchi.

16. Mario Marcel, "Privatización de las empresas públicas en Chile, 1985-87" (Santiago: CIEPLAN, forthcoming).

17. For a discussion of the tax cuts, see Mario Marcel and Manuel Marfán, "La cuestión tributaria," *Revista de CIEPLAN* 13 (July 1988).

18. A critical analysis of debt-equity swaps is Ricardo Ffrench-Davis, "Conversión de pagarés de la deuda externa en Chile," *Colección Estudios CIEPLAN* 22 (1987). Data through June 1988 are from *El Mercurio,* July 26, 1988.

19. On U.S.-Chile relations, see Heraldo Muñoz and Carlos Portales, *Una amistad esquiva: las relaciones de Estados Unidos y Chile* (Santiago: Pehuén, 1987).

20. To put the Chilean experience in comparative perspective, see the articles in Guillermo O'Donnell et al., eds., *Transitions from Authoritarian Rule,* 4 vols. (Baltimore: Johns Hopkins Univeristy Press, 1986). A useful review of the O'Donnell work and some of the rest of the redemocratization literature is Charles Gillespie, "From Authoritarian Crises to Democratic Transitions," *Latin American Research Review* 22, no. 3 (1987).

Suggestions for Further Reading

Edwards, Sebastian, and Alejandra Cox Edwards. *Monetarism and Liberalization: The Chilean Experiment.* Cambridge, MA: Ballinger, 1987.

Foxley, Alejandro. *Latin American Experiments in Neoconservative Economics.* Berkeley: University of California Press, 1983.

Garretón, Manuel Antonio. "Protests and Politics in Chile." In *Power and Popular Protest: Latin American Social Movements,* ed. Susan Eckstein. Berkeley: University of California Press, 1988.

Muñoz, Heraldo and Carlos Portales. *Una amistad esquiva: las relaciones de Estados Unidos y Chile.* Santiago: Pehuén, 1987.

Stallings, Barbara. *Class Conflict and Economic Development in Chile, 1958-73.* Stanford: Stanford University Press, 1978.

Valenzuela, Arturo. *The Breakdown of Democratic Regimes: Chile.* Baltimore: Johns Hopkins University Press, 1978.

Valenzuela, Samuel and Arturo Valenzuela, eds. *Military Rule in Chile: Dictatorship and Oppositions.* Baltimore: Johns Hopkins University Press, 1986.

Whitehead, Laurence. "The Adjustment Process in Chile: A Comparative Perspective." In *Latin American Debt and the Adjustment Crisis,* ed. Rosemary Thorp and Laurence Whitehead. Pittsburgh: University of Pittsburgh Press, 1987.

PART IV

Conclusion

12

Debt and Democracy in the 1980s: The Latin American Experience

Robert Kaufman and Barbara Stallings

The debate over whether there are systematic differences in the way democratic and authoritarian regimes deal with distributive conflicts and economic policy choices has raged for several decades.[1] In the 1960s and 1970s, as democracies in the region were shaken by political immobilism and severe stagflation crises, much of the conventional wisdom held that it was especially difficult for governments to manage economies in the context of competitive elections, populist politics, and interest group pluralism. Subsequent comparative studies, however, have suggested that for much of the post-war period the macroeconomic performance of authoritarian regimes has not been any better. Indeed, during the 1970s and early 1980s, the historical record has been cluttered with vivid examples of political stalemate and monumental blunders committed by authoritarian rulers: economic and foreign policy adventurism in Argentina, growing fiscal deficits and misman-aged oil wealth in Mexico and highly erratic monetary and exchange rate policies in Brazil.

The debt crisis of the 1980s offers an opportunity to explore the "regime issue" in a very different type of political and economic setting from those of earlier decades. From the late 1960s to the early 1980s, the abundance of funds on international financial markets provided a crucial resource for all regimes in dealing with politically dangerous distributive conflicts. In contrast, the cut-off of interna-tional credit after 1982 has forced extraordinarily severe adjustments on all of the countries in the region—the worst of the postwar era. In their relations with creditor countries, governments of Latin America have had to confront the question of how to deal with massive net outflows of financial resources, estimated at 5 percent of GDP. At home, the issues of stabilization and economic adjustment have exacer-bated distributive conflicts. It is a crisis that has contributed to the collapse of most authoritarian regimes, posed threats to the stability of constitutional governments, and stimulated wide debate almost everywhere about what kinds of recovery strategies should be adopted and who should pay the costs. What do distinctions between democracy and authoritarianism tell us about the way governments have dealt with the economic challenges of the 1980s? And, conversely, what are the effects of such challenges on contemporary efforts at redemocratization? The chapters in this volume have all focused on important aspects of these questions, exploring changes in the power relations among key actors or the responses of governments in specific countries. Here, we will attempt to build on these contributions in order to explore the two-way connection between debt and democracy. The first part of this chapter sets the stage for this analysis by discussing the need for economic adjustment and some of the political determinants of government policies. The second examines the evidence about whether and how type of regime influenced economic policy choice. The third section looks at the influence of regime type on economic outcomes. The fourth part turns the debt/democracy issues around, and explores the way debt-related economic problems have affected the consolidation of democratic systems. In the concluding pages, we point to some areas of further research.

Determinants of Policy Choice in the 1980s

Debate over the origins of the economic crisis of the 1980s has generally turned on the relative weight of international and domestic factors. For our purposes, it is not necessary to enter this debate. Both were important, and both pushed in the same direction.

Following Mexico's dramatic declaration of bankruptcy in August 1982, international factors—rising interest rates, declining commodity prices, and a sudden freeze on new commercial lending—contributed to the spread of the crisis to the region as a whole. Since that time, profound asymmetries in the bargaining relations between debtors and creditors have forced the former to bear the heaviest burdens of adjustment. Creditor governments, private banks, and official lenders have been able, as Roett has discussed, to coordinate their bargaining strategies and deal with debtors on a case-by-case basis. As a consequence, a number of crucial issues have been left off the North/South bargaining agenda, including creditor countries' trade, fiscal and interest rate polices. And while a number of countries have experimented with full or partial moratoria, none has been able to negotiate the type of debt-reduction formulas recommended in this volume by Dornbusch.

At the same time, as Dornbusch has also suggested, domestic policies pursued by most Latin American governments in the 1970s and early 1980s left them highly vulnerable to such problems. The maintenance of overvalued exchange rates was particularly damaging, since it discouraged exports, strengthened speculative pressures against local currencies, and facilitated massive capital flight. These governmental choices, in turn, were made against the backdrop of long-standing difficulties associated with the fiscal drain of state enterprises, limited tax capacities, and weak export sectors.

In the context of such problems, it seems clear that politically controversial domestic policy adjustments will be necessary, if not sufficient, components of any economic recovery. This does not imply wholesale acceptance of the kinds of orthodox austerity packages and economic liberalization measures conventionally associated with the International Monetary Fund (IMF). Indeed, such packages may well be counterproductive in terms of their effects on long-term prospects for growth. Nevertheless, policies must be found to control domestic inflation and to reduce current account and fiscal deficits. A crucial ingredient is lowering expenditure on debt service, but more conventional approaches—raising taxes and/or lowering domestic expenditures—will probably be necessary as well. Longer-term recovery will involve significant efforts to promote more internationally-competitive economies with more dynamic and diversified export sectors.

It is possible that such policy changes can be managed in ways that involve relatively equitable sharing of domestic costs. Even so, it is certain that some groups will suffer more than others. Several chapters, including those by Jeffry Frieden, Sylvia Maxfield, and Ian Roxborough, have dealt at length with this issue. As Roxborough has shown, the costs until now have been particularly high for organized labor. Within the business sector, smaller firms and those with fixed assets seem most vulnerable. At the other end of the spectrum, if they are to avoid further capital flight and expand exports, most governments are likely to find themselves under considerable pressure to offer tax incentives and other inducements to larger, export-oriented firms and those who hold liquid assets abroad. If governments are to change the current allocation of costs, alternative policies must be devised and new political coalitions formed to support them.

What factors can be expected to condition responses to economic crises? We will argue that political regime type has been an important determinant of policy choice in the 1980s, even if it was not necessarily crucial in the more affluent 1960s and 1970s. Nevertheless, regimes were not the only relevant factor, and before looking at the nature of their impact, we need to examine four sets of variables suggested in the general literature.[2]

First, the orientations and resources of the people who staff the policy-making apparatus obviously make a difference in the choice of policy. This is not simply a question of orthodox "will"—the favorite word of many IMF analysts. The variable refers to the degree of consensus among top policy-makers, the backing they receive from the head of state, and perhaps most important, their capacity to mobilize and coordinate the activities of the state apparatus as a whole. All of the countries of Latin America have had trouble on this score (as have many more advanced industrial societies). Even so, we might reasonably expect the capacity to plan and coordinate complex recovery policies to be greater in the more advanced Latin American countries like Brazil, Mexico, or Colombia than in Bolivia or Haiti.

Second, economic policies also reflect the interests and ideological orientations of a government's support coalition. Since such coalitions are usually fragile and internally divided, this relationship is likely to be complex. A left-wing government, for example, may be impelled by circumstances to adapt an austerity program even if this risks alienating its supporters. Conversely, right-wing coalitions of military nationalists and domestic businesses may well oppose both IMF-type policies *and* populist appeals. Despite these reservations, however, support coalitions do influence choices of recovery strategies. Governments that include significant popular-sector components within their support coalitions are less likely to accept orthodox recovery programs than governments of the right or center-right. Exactly what their alternatives will consist of, and whether they will be economically and politically viable, remains to be seen.

Third, if the economic program of an outgoing government proved extremely unpopular—and especially if it was widely regarded as having been a failure in terms of outcomes—this fact will place important constraints on the ability of a new government to follow similar policies. This factor is particularly important when the outgoing administration or regime has polarized the political system into relatively well-defined coalitions of supporters and opponents. When the opposition takes power in such situations, we can expect substantial shifts away from the policy orientations (whether orthodox or heterodox) of the preceding government.

Fourth, choices regarding economic adjustment are also conditioned by the need to regain confidence of external creditors and the leverage available through financing from other sources. Some authors have suggested that substantial increases in resources—from export windfalls or external loans—have typically induced governments to abandon IMF agreements. Conversely, as it became increasingly evident that "good behavior" would not generate additional funding, a number of governments in the mid-1980s began to seek relief through full or partial moratoria. These included governments as diverse as Peru, Bolivia, Ecuador, Costa Rica, and Brazil.

Each of these sets of variables can be presumed to have an influence on policy that is partially independent of the procedural rules of the game associated with authoritarianism and democracy. Indeed, since the distinction between democracy and authoritarianism refers primarily to the rules governing the political *process*, and not to the actors involved in that process, we cannot expect it to tell us much about policy choices without reference to other clusters of variables sketched above. Authoritarian regimes attempting to appeal to labor and popular-sector support— as was the case, for example, under Velasco in Peru (1968-75)—may behave in ways that are parallel to democratic governments appealing to similar constituencies. The same may also be true of elected and non-elected governments of the center-right. In societies where the state apparatus is weak and fragmented, differences in regime type may also have limited effect on policy since none can be successfully implemented.

Despite these considerations, it is wrong to conclude that the presence or absence of democratic rules and institutions governing political competition is irrelevant to economic policy choice and outcomes. Never more than partial components of any political system, the operation of democratic institutions will depend on the autonomy and technical capacity of the state bureaucracy, on historic patterns of antagonism and cooperation among the principal civil and military groups, and on the economic and strategic location of the country in the international context. Yet within these contexts, competitive democratic institutions may have a substantial impact on the calculus of policy-making elites and their capacity to implement decisions. The analytic challenge is not to discard the "democracy variable," but to refine it by distinguishing more clearly between *types* of democratic regimes and by situating them more explicitly with reference to the other variables discussed above.[3]

To unravel these relationships fully is a major task of theory-building and well beyond the scope of this chapter. Nevertheless, in many of the major countries of the region, the experiences of the 1980s have provided some important pieces of evidence that might contribute to such an endeavor. In the following section, we will look more specifically at the policy experiences of different types of political regimes, drawing primarily, although not exclusively, on the country studies included in this volume. We will then offer some propositions about the ways regime characteristics affected policy choices and outcomes and the ways they did not.

Political Regimes and Economic Policy Choice

For the purposes of our analysis, we divide political regimes into three types: authoritarian regimes, established democracies, and transitional democracies. Authoritarian regimes are those that do not permit competitive elections and restrict the space allowed to either oppositional or interest group activity. Among the countries discussed in this volume, this applies most clearly to Chile's military-backed regime, in power since 1973. Mexico is also considered authoritarian, despite a number of democratic features, since presidents have been imposed from above and have governed without extensive institutionalized checks on their authority.

Established democracies are systems in which executive authority has long been limited by institutionalized processes of electoral competition and bargaining among independent and relatively evenly-balanced political parties. Costa Rica, with a forty-year history of constitutional government, clearly falls into this category. Other countries that are also considered to be established democracies are Colombia and Venezuela. In Venezuela, after a brief transitional period of coalition among the major parties, the political system has been characterized by vigorous competition between two major "catch-all" parties, Democratic Action and Copei, which have alternated in office since the early 1960s. In Colombia, the National Front pact of 1958-1974 placed more severe limitations on the competition between the Liberals and Conservatives. Nevertheless, the power-sharing agreement did not preclude substantial electoral competition among factions within the major parties, and in any event it was formally terminated in 1974.

Transitional democracies, finally, are systems that have recently moved toward competitive electoral systems after prolonged experience with authoritarian rule. Of the countries covered in this volume, this would include Brazil since 1985 and Peru since 1980. To broaden the comparisons, we will also refer to the Alfonsín government in Argentina, in power since 1983, and to Uruguay's Sanguinetti administration, inaugurated in 1985.

This is not, it should be noted, either a comprehensive survey of all experiences nor a particularly representative sample. The cases included for consideration are generally among the larger and/or more modern economies of the region, with Brazil and Mexico often classified among the NICs (newly industrializing countries) of the world economy. Omitted entirely are very interesting experiences of the less-developed countries, such as Bolivia, Paraguay, and most of Central America. A full exploration of the debt-democracy issue would eventually have to take such cases into account. Nevertheless, by narrowing the range of economies under consideration, we have a firmer (though still precarious) ground of comparison for assessing political effects.

In terms of policy responses to the 1980s debt crisis, we distinguish broadly between "orthodox" and "heterodox" approaches. Although the specific content of orthodoxy has changed over the last decade, it continues to be characterized by market-oriented approaches that stress fiscal and monetary restraint, reduction in the size of the state sector, liberalization of the domestic economy, and collaboration with creditors. "Heterodox" approaches do not reject all elements of this package, but they generally advocate a more active state investment and regulatory role, are more willing to risk confrontation with creditors, and attach a higher priority to issues of distribution and employment. As we shall see below, authoritarian regimes have generally followed the most orthodox policies, while transitional democracies have been most inclined toward heterodoxy. Established democracies tend to fall in between.

Authoritarian Regimes

Throughout the 1980s, despite its inability to bring its fiscal deficit under control, the de la Madrid government pursued some of the most consistently orthodox policies in the region. In an effort to reduce inflation and current account deficits, it relied heavily on restrictive credit and wage policies. Trade flows were liberalized and exports diversified substantially by the end of the de la Madrid period. Although there were some tense moments, the government maintained collaborative ties with both the IMF and private creditors.

Of the other governments in the region, only Pinochet's Chile consistently matched this record for such a prolonged period. After experiencing the worst economic crisis in the region in 1982, the regime did temporarily move away from the strict laissez-faire approach of earlier years, in an attempt to fend off pressures from domestically-oriented industrialists and opposition groups mobilizing in the streets. By 1985, however, the opposition was under control, and the regime had returned to a slightly-modified version of its market-oriented strategy. This strategy included tight monetary and fiscal policies, restriction of consumption, and increased privatization of state firms. The extensive trade liberalization continued despite its negative effects on domestic industry. Relations with the IMF and the World Bank remained close, and many bankers saw Chile as the most successful Latin American economy.

To understand such performance, of course, we need to consider more than simply the authoritarian structures of these societies. The driving forces behind orthodoxy in both cases were highly cohesive technocratic elites with strong neo-classical convictions. Mexico, in addition, faced considerable pressure from con-servative financial-industrial groups to liberalize capital and trade flows and maintain good relations with creditors. Although authoritarian concentrations of executive power could not entirely shield either Pinochet or de la Madrid from the need to offer concessions to power contenders seeking cushions from the disloca-tions of market adjustments, they were nevertheless able to implement highly unpopular programs. The capacity to do so rested heavily on executives that could operate with limited institutional restraints and on extensive bureaucratic or coercive control of popular-sector protest.

Not surprisingly, the more thoroughly exclusionary Pinochet regime went much further in this regard, relying on a combination of overt coercion and more subtle divide-and-conquer tactics to keep the center and left opposition off balance. De la Madrid, in contrast, operated under greater constraints. In part, this was due to the coalitional base of the regime, which (despite the shift to the right after 1982) was still far broader than in Chile and continued to include the official labor sector. In part, the constraints on Mexican orthodoxy were also due to the greater intermixture of democratic elements within the structure of the regime. Unlike Pinochet, for example, the de la Madrid government could not, without seriously undermining its own legitimacy, simply repress unions that blocked attempts to rationalize or reduce public enterprises. Perhaps more significant, although electoral outcomes were foreordained, their importance in the legitimation process provided a powerful inhibition against clamping down hard on the fiscal brakes. Thus, fiscal problems increased prior to the presidential elections of 1970, 1976, and 1982, and in the six months preceding the gubernatorial elections of 1985.

Established Democracies

Costa Rica followed a somewhat more mixed policy course. Although the government took some important steps to promote exports and rationalize state enterprises, there was little movement toward either a reduction in the size of the public sector or the liberalization of trade. And, unlike Mexico or Chile, authorities eventually felt compelled to declare a temporary moratorium on interest payments in 1986. Nevertheless, as Joan Nelson has discussed in detail, the newly-elected government of Alberto Monge was able to impose fiscal and monetary restrictions with speed and effectiveness in order to deal with the extraordinarily severe stabilization crisis of 1980-1982.

Nelson attributes the early success of Costa Rica's crisis management to several political factors that might be generalized to other established democracies. The Monge administration (1982-86) was able to learn from mistakes of its predecessors, in this case the failure of the Carazo government to respond more quickly to skyrocketing trade deficits of the late 1970s. Acceptance of painful short-term measures was facilitated by public perception that there were no viable alternatives, by broad patterns of trust and consultation between Monge and key union and business groups, and by governmental efforts to provide various forms of aid for low-income groups that were most vulnerable to the stabilization shocks.

Were similar patterns evident in other countries that we have placed in the "established democracy" category? In Colombia, even after the formal termination of the National Front agreement in 1974, the heads of the major parties have shared in a broad consensus on a conservative approach to macroeconomic policy.[4] During the 1980s, despite drug trafficking and guerrilla challenges, this enabled the government to follow a moderately orthodox, and relatively successful, economic course. After a two-year policy of modest reflation that was accompanied by rising inflation and falling reserves, the Betancur government adopted a stabilization program in mid-1984. The budget deficit was reduced both by raising taxes and cutting government expenditures, including investment and wages in the public sector. To deal with the trade deficit, the rate of devaluation was sharply increased. These steps were taken without a formal agreement with the IMF, given Betancur's antipathy toward the Fund, but an informal monitoring arrangement was devised in order to get new money from banks. Even this relatively mild program aroused opposition, especially from labor, but it was dealt with in a conciliatory fashion: by a differentiated wage adjustment favoring the poor and by appointment of a union official as minister of labor. The successor Barco government has changed policy very little.

As in Colombia and Costa Rica, the two dominant parties in Venezuela have also generally agreed on the parameters of political and economic life.[5] During most of the twentieth century, Venezuela's economy has been dominated by oil, and when Jaime Lusinchi took over the presidency in 1984, he found an economy that had been in the doldrums since the oil-field boom of the 1970s ended. In confronting Venezuela's economic problems, he steered a cautious course, trying to placate both business and labor. Until oil prices plummeted in 1986, he generally followed austere fiscal and monetary policies; at that point domestic demand was increased to counterbalance the fall in oil revenue. The other significant characteristic of Lusinchi's policy was its international dimension. During his term in office, Venezuela refused to deal with the IMF, yet it was the only country in the region to keep interest payments up to date without new loans, and even to repay principal as it fell due.

We can summarize the differences and similarities among authoritarian regimes and established democracies in the following broad-brush manner: (1) Although both types of regime encountered problems in fiscal management, they were able, in crisis conditions, to impose relatively tough credit restrictions and devaluations.

Within the established democracies, successful stabilization policies were facilitated by the capacity of governments to appeal to centrist tendencies within public opinion, to the economic moderation of the major parties, and to comparatively broad patterns of trust and cooperation in the relations between the government and major interest groups. (2) Nevertheless, established democracies did not go as far as the authoritarian regimes in reorganizing economic structures. Only in Chile and Mexico was there significant trade liberalization or privatization. (3) All of the governments in both categories attempted to avoid confrontations with creditors. Colombia and Venezuela refused to make traditional agreements with the IMF, however, and Costa Rica was impelled to suspend interest payments to private commercial banks. Chile and Mexico, by contrast, maintained close relations with both the banks and the IMF.

Transitional Democracies

In the 1980s, the transitional democratic governments in Brazil and Peru followed the most heterodox policy course of the countries discussed in this volume. In Brazil, President Sarney, although personally linked to the old order, was nevertheless under strong pressure to respond quickly to the expansionary aspirations of populist and leftist groups in the PMDB and the unions that had long been in opposition to the outgoing military government. Consequently, his administration adopted measures that stimulated consumption, relying on administrative controls rather than fiscal and monetary demand-management to contain inflation. The government also clashed bitterly with the local business class, broke off relations with the IMF, and took unilateral action in 1987 to reduce interest payments on the foreign debt.

After the return to democracy in Peru, two phases can be identified.In 1980 reactions against the leftward movement of the military years led to the election of a civilian government, headed by Fernando Belaunde, that espoused orthodox policies including trade liberalization, sale of public enterprises, and austerity measures. Indeed, Belaunde's economic policies are often portrayed as a milder version of Pinochet's. Rhetoric aside, however, the government headed in populist directions not that different from Sarney's. No state firms were sold; trade liberalization was swiftly abandoned, as domestic opposition arose; interest rates were raised, but never reached positive levels; and the budget deficit mushroomed with large spending increases. By the end of Belaunde's term, the disarray of the economy had led to abandonment of the IMF program and an informal moratorium on debt payments.

The abject failure of the Belaunde policies, together with the orthodox rhetoric, opened the way for an explicitly heterodox experiment under Alan García and the APRA. Elected in 1985, García based his economic program on demand stimulation, especially wage increases, and on administrative control of prices. Limits were placed on foreign debt payments, and relations were formally severed with the IMF.

Although he initially tried to negotiate with local business leaders, the President alienated them through nationalization of the banking system.

Despite some differences on detail, there are underlying similarities that made it difficult for all three governments to steer a more orthodox policy course. First, each transitional democracy had to deal with an authoritarian legacy that had both reflected and deepened political polarization and bitter distributive struggles. The transition to democracy expanded the arena in which such struggles could legitimately occur and increased opportunities for popular-sector groups to resist orthodox policies. Second, unlike more established democracies, economic policy choices were not moderated by long-standing patterns of consultation between executive and legislature, competing parties, or major interest groups. Executives had wide discretionary authority. As was true in authoritarian regimes, this expanded the scope for the types of blunders that characterized the Cruzado Plan in Brazil or the bank nationalization in Peru. Political logic also led executives to try to build support by populist appeals directed over the heads of legislative, party, and interest group leaders.

Brief reference to experiences in two other transitional democracies—Argentina and Uruguay—can be used to round out and partially modify these comparative generalizations. On the whole, the experience of the Alfonsín government in Argentina ran parallel to that of Brazil.[6] The heterodoxy of the Austral Plan reflected the strong resurgence of distributive politics within both the Radical and Peronist movements, substantial executive discretion, and strong political pressures to resist the orthodox fiscal and monetary policies being urged by the IMF and private creditors. At the same time, Alfonsín's room for maneuver was seriously limited by the financial disarray and trade problems inherited from the military government. By 1985, these constraints had led the administration to combine its heterodox approach to price controls with demand-management policies that were more acceptable to the IMF and creditors.

Uruguay, finally, represents something of a deviant case among transitional democracies.[7] Since coming to power in 1985, after a negotiated end to 12 years of authoritarian rule, the Sanguinetti administration has behaved with surprising caution in responding to distributive demands. Government spending has been cut in real terms, and wage increases have been kept under control. Agreements have been worked out with the IMF and creditor banks. Reserves have consequently increased although the balance of payments has been buffeted by international factors. Moderate growth has resulted after a number of bad years. A full discussion of the reasons behind this performance is beyond the scope of this chapter. Yet striking political-institutional parallels with Costa Rica, Colombia, and Venezuela suggest that Uruguayan authorities have been able to draw on some of the resources available to the more established democracies, especially a party system that discourages sharp polarization among ideological or economic interests.

Table 12.1 summarizes the preceding discussion, considering policy choice with respect to macroeconomic stabilization, trade liberalization, and relations with

Table 12.1
Economic Policies by Type of Regime in Latin America, 1980s

Country	Administration Dates	Political Regime Type	Stabilization Type	Trade Liberalization	Relations with IMF and Banks
Chile	Pinochet 1982-	Authoritarian	Orthodox	Substantial	Collaborative
Mexico	de la Madrid 1982-	Authoritarian	Orthodox	Substantial	Collaborative
Costa Rica	Monge 1982-86 Arias 1986-	Established Democracy	Moderate Orthodox	Limited	Collaborative with IMF, but suspended interest payments
Venezuela	Lusinchi 1984-	Established Democracy	Moderate Orthodox	Limited	Broke with IMF, but collaborative with banks
Colombia	Betancur 1982-86 Barco 1986-	Established Democracy	Moderate Orthodox	Limited	Broke with IMF, but collaborative with banks
Brazil	Sarney 1985-	Transitional Democracy	Heterodox	None	Broke with IMF, moratorium
Peru	Belaunde 1980-85/ García 1985-	Transitional Democracy	Moderate Orthodox/ Heterodox	None/ None	Broke with IMF, moratorium/ Broke with IMF, moratorium
Argentina	Alfonsín 1983-	Transitional Democracy	Moderate Heterodox	None	Collaborative
Uruguay	Sanguinetti 1985-	Transitional Democracy	Moderate Orthodox	Limited	Collaborative

external creditors. There are some notable regularities. Each of the authoritarian regimes followed relatively orthodox policies in all three categories, the only countries to have done so. Five of the seven transitional or established democracies either avoided collaboration with the IMF and/or unilaterally reduced interest payments. Established democracies chose moderately orthodox stabilization programs, whereas most of the transitional democracies experimented with more heterodox approaches. None carried through with fundamental structural changes such as trade liberalization. Although such findings are hardly conclusive, they do strongly suggest that regime type in the 1980s has had a systematic impact on policy choice.

Political Regimes and Economic Outcomes

The preceding section suggested the existence of a high correlation between political regime type and *economic policy choice* during the crisis period of the 1980s. Is there also a connection with *economic performance?* Since performance is influenced by a variety of factors outside the scope of domestic politics—such as international conditions, size of the economy, and natural resources—the distinctions among political regimes may not be as strong as they were with respect to policy choices. Nevertheless, just as the effect of regime on policy may be stronger in the crisis period of the 1980s than in earlier decades, so also might be the effect on performance.

The data presented in Table 12.2 allow us to comment on several categories of economic outcomes: domestic stabilization (inflation, fiscal deficits, and wages), economic growth, and external accounts. Countries are grouped according to the three regime types—authoritarian, established democracies, and transitional democracies—to facilitate comparisons within and across categories.

Economic Stabilization: Inflation, Fiscal Deficits, and Wages

Transitional democracies, as might be expected from their reluctance to impose orthodox stabilization plans, tended to have substantial difficulty with both inflation and budget deficits. Three of the four countries in this category were well above the average on both measures.[8] Notwithstanding relatively low budget deficits, Uruguay also had fairly high rates of inflation. Conversely, established democracies had lower than average figures on these variables, as did the right-wing authoritarian government in Chile—findings that appear in line with our preceding discussion of policy choices. The main deviant case was Mexico, which despite its orthodox policy orientation, did as poorly on both budget deficits and inflation as did the transitional democracies. Part of the explanation may lie in the democratic features that are mixed into the regime's authoritarian structure. Although labor and opposition groups do not have a direct influence on policy, the regime was under strong pressure to provide them with some material rewards in order to sustain its legitimacy.

Real wages also show some predictable results and some surprises. With respect to this variable, both authoritarian regimes—Mexico as well as Chile—experienced a sharp contraction of real wages during the 1980s. Conversely, in Costa Rica and Colombia, the two established democracies for which data were available, fiscal moderation was successfully combined with fairly large real wage increases. Among transitional democracies, there were still higher increases: Brazil in 1985-86, Peru in 1986-87, Argentina in 1983-84, and Uruguay in 1985-87. The durability of real wage increases, however, was linked closely to inflationary trends. That is, a government's intention to raise real wages will be cancelled out if inflation increases even faster than nominal wages. This would appear to be the case for Brazil in 1987 and Argentina in 1985-87; it is also happening in Peru in 1988. It probably explains part of the real wage trend in Mexico as well. An alternative explanation is that the transitional governments may have decided to cut back after permitting increases that were themselves seen as contributing to inflation.

Rates of Growth

An integral part of earlier debates on the economic effects of political regimes was the proposition that authoritarian regimes would experience higher rates of growth because of their capacity to provide security for private investment. This hypothesis does not receive much support from the data in Table 12.2. With the exception of the disastrous performance in 1982, Chile has indeed had higher-than-average growth, but Mexico has had a very poor record since the crisis began in 1982. The highest growth rates have actually been found in the transitional democracies—especially Brazil in 1985-86 and Peru in 1986-87. Among the established democracies, Costa Rica and Colombia have done reasonably well, but Venezuela—despite its oil resources—had a very poor growth record in the 1980s.

The evidence suggests that the hypothesis is mis-specified. High growth rates can result either from demand stimulation and the use of idle capacity or from investment over the long term. It seems clear that the Brazilian and Peruvian spurts were of the former type and associated with attempts at regime, or government, legitimation. Both Brazil (under the military) and Mexico in the 1970s were examples of investment-stimulated growth, in both cases based on the international loans that are now causing a large part of the economic difficulties in the region. Interestingly enough, the authoritarian regime in Chile—even in the 1970s—did not manage to generate a large amount of investment in productive activities. Most of the Chilean loans, like those of Argentina during the same period, were directed toward speculation and import of consumer goods.

Balance of Payments

Finally, we consider the way political regimes affect external accounts pressures. Since authoritarian regimes presumably have greater capacity than democracies to contain domestic demand and generate trade surpluses, it is conceivable that they

Table 12.2
Economic Outcomes by Selected Countries in the Latin American Region, 1982-1987

Country	1982	1983	1984	1985	1986	1987[a]	Average 1982-87
GDP GROWTH RATES							
Chile	-13.1	-0.5	6.0	2.4	5.4	5.5	1.0
Mexico	-0.6	-4.2	3.6	2.6	-4.0	1.0	-0.3
Costa Rica	-7.3	2.7	7.9	0.9	4.4	3.0	1.9
Venezuela	-1.3	-5.6	-1.0	-0.6	5.5	1.5	-0.3
Colombia	1.0	1.9	3.8	3.1	5.1	5.5	3.4
Brazil	0.9	-2.4	5.7	8.3	8.2	3.0	4.0
Peru	0.3	-11.8	4.7	2.5	8.0	7.0	1.8
Argentina	-5.3	2.4	2.3	-4.7	6.0	2.0	0.5
Uruguay	-10.1	-6.1	-1.2	-0.2	6.6	5.5	-0.9
Avg. of 9 countries[b]	-3.9	-2.6	3.5	1.6	5.0	3.8	1.2
INFLATION RATES[c]							
Chile	20.7	23.6	23.0	26.4	17.4	22.9	22.3
Mexico	98.8	80.8	59.2	63.7	105.7	143.6	92.0
Costa Rica	81.7	10.7	17.3	11.1	15.4	13.6	25.0
Venezuela	7.3	7.0	18.3	5.7	12.3	36.1	14.5
Colombia	24.1	16.5	18.3	22.3	21.0	24.7	21.2
Brazil	97.9	179.2	203.3	228.0	58.4	337.9	184.1
Peru	72.9	125.1	111.5	158.3	62.9	104.8	105.9
Argentina	209.7	433.7	688.0	385.4	81.9	178.3	329.5
Uruguay	20.5	51.5	66.1	83.0	76.4	59.9	59.6
Avg. of 9 countries[b]	70.4	103.1	133.9	109.3	50.2	102.4	94.9
REAL WAGE INCREASES[d]							
Chile	-0.2	-10.7	0.1	-3.8	1.7	-0.3	-2.2
Mexico	0.9	-22.7	-6.6	1.6	-4.9	n.a.	-6.3
Costa Rica	-19.8	10.9	7.8	8.9	6.1	n.a.	2.8
Venezuela	n.a.	n.a.	n.a.	n.a.	n.a.	n.a.	n.a.
Colombia	3.7	5.0	7.3	-3.0	4.9	1.4	3.2
Brazil	7.3	-9.8	-1.9	15.1	17.1	-7.7	3.4
Peru	2.3	-16.7	-15.5	-15.0	26.7	6.7	-1.9
Argentina	-10.4	25.5	26.4	-15.2	1.6	-8.4	3.3
Uruguay	-0.3	-20.7	-9.2	14.1	6.7	4.2	-0.9
Avg. of 9 countries[b]	-2.1	-4.9	-1.1	0.3	7.5	-0.7	-0.2

Country	1982	1983	1984	1985	1986	1987[a]	Average 1982-87
		BALANCE OF PAYMENTS (% OF EXPORTS)[e]					
Chile	-62.2	-27.9	-56.4	-35.3	-27.1	-18.8	-38.0
Mexico	-28.4	23.8	17.5	1.7	-9.0	19.0	4.1
Costa Rica	-30.5	-32.9	-16.0	-36.6	-19.4	-15.3	-25.1
Venezuela	-26.0	30.4	33.9	21.9	-18.6	-1.7	6.7
Colombia	-93.2	-92.6	-68.0	-38.0	8.3	-7.3	-48.5
Brazil	-80.9	-31.0	0.2	-1.1	-18.0	-5.8	-22.8
Peru	-48.6	-28.8	-7.9	-2.4	-45.8	-52.9	-31.1
Argentina	-31.3	-31.2	-29.5	-11.4	-41.2	-60.9	-34.3
Uruguay	-18.6	-5.2	-13.0	-14.1	6.4	-17.4	-10.3
Avg. of 9 countries[b]	-46.6	-21.7	-15.5	-12.8	-18.3	-17.9	-22.1
		GOVERNMENT BUDGET DEFICITS (% OF GDP)[f]					
Chile	-2.6	-3.6	-2.9	-1.9	-0.5	2.5	-1.5
Mexico	-12.4	-8.1	-7.5	-7.7	-13.0	-14.0	-10.5
Costa Rica	-3.3	-3.6	-3.0	-2.0	-3.3	-2.1	-2.9
Venezuela	-4.9	-0.6	2.8	2.0	-0.4	-0.7	-0.3
Colombia	-4.1	-3.5	-4.2	-2.6	-1.6	-0.9	-2.8
Brazil	-2.7	-4.6	-5.8	-11.8	n.a.	n.a.	-6.2
Peru	-3.9	-7.2	-4.1	-2.0	-3.6	-5.7	-4.4
Argentina	-3.7	-14.1	-7.2	-4.5	-3.1	-8.0	-6.8
Uruguay	-8.7	-3.7	-5.0	-1.9	-1.4	-1.3	-3.7
Avg. of 9 countries[b]	-5.1	-5.4	-4.1	-3.6	-3.4	-3.8	-4.3

[a]Preliminary data
[b]Unweighted average
[c]Inflation rate=increase in consumer price index (December-December)
[d]Real wage increases=Average wages for countries; Brazil is average for Rio de Janeiro and São Paulo
[e]Balance of payments=current account deficit or surplus
[f]Government budget deficits=central government only
Sources: U.N. Economic Commission for Latin America, *Preliminary Overview of the Latin American Economy*, 1987 (for GDP, inflation, and wages); Inter-American Development Bank, Economic and Social Progress in Latin America, various years (for balance of payments and budget deficits).

are in a better position to reduce the size of their balance-of-payments deficits. But performance with respect to the balance of payments is also the variable most heavily influenced by external factors. Chile provides an interesting example. Although, as hypothesized, the government has been successful at producing a merchandise surplus, the outflow to keep up with debt payments since lending ceased in 1982 has led to a large deficit on the overall current account.

More generally, Table 12.2 suggests little relationship between regime type and the *average size* of the current account deficit (measured here as a percentage of export revenues). Among the two authoritarian regimes, Chile had the second-highest average deficit, while Mexico had a surplus. The former was attributable largely to the size of the foreign debt, while the latter was due to oil exports. Indeed, the pattern of Mexico's current account balance, like that of Venezuela, has been dominated by the "oil effect;" the sudden deficits in 1986 were mainly the result of the drop in international oil prices. Leaving Venezuela aside, the average deficits for established and transitional democracies did not vary substantially. The highest was actually for Colombia, due to very large trade deficits in 1982-83. Among the other democracies, average deficits of 20-30 percent of export revenues were the norm, with Uruguay well below that range.

A slightly stronger relationship between regime type and balance of payments is found if we focus on trends rather than averages for the six-year period. Deficits have fallen sharply in Chile since 1984, while they have increased in Argentina and Peru since the Alfonsín and García governments took office. In Brazil and Uruguay, however, deficits have not increased following the accession to the presidency of Sarney and Sanguinetti. In general, while efforts at promotion of exports and restraint of imports are important factors in determining the magnitude of current account deficits, price trends for particular export products and the size of external debt payments must also be taken into account.

A look at the evidence on economic outcomes during the 1980s, then, suggests that regime type has a discernable, if partial, impact on performance. This impact may be more important during a crisis period than a boom. Although economic success is far from guaranteed under conditions of affluence—the problems associated with "bonanza development" or the "Dutch disease" have been discussed at length in the literature[9]—such conditions tend to create outcomes that are relatively similar across countries. The differences become more pronounced when resources dry up. It is then that the political regime variable may be particularly useful in predicting both policy intentions and certain types of economic outcomes.

The Effects of Debt on Democracy: Can Democracies Survive?

Most political scientists assume, sometimes tacitly, that there is a connection between the legitimacy of a political regime and its effectiveness in meeting the material demands of its citizens.[10] To be sure, this may not be a tight or immediate relationship; not even fragile governments are likely to be overthrown at the first sign of an economic downturn. Nevertheless, there is a strong assumption that regimes that cannot "deliver the goods" for prolonged periods of time are likely to experience dangerous erosion of support and intensified challenges to their right to rule.

This seems especially plausible in Latin America where commitments to democratic regimes have often been much more tentative and conditional than in many advanced industrial democracies.[11] In view of the generally grim economic conditions that have prevailed throughout the region during the 1980s, the prospects for the survival of contemporary democratic regimes would not appear to be particularly good. In his chapter in this volume, Roett paints a possible scenario for the upcoming elections in various countries. Given their disillusionment with new democratic governments that have failed to improve the standard of living of their citizens, voters will turn to populist leaders who promise a "real" change. The resulting governments may so radicalize the policy process that polarization will inevitably result, with the armed forces then becoming a serious threat in the 1990s.

Upon further consideration, however, there may turn out to be more separation between the economic and political spheres than is generally believed. The role that economic crisis played in the collapse of democratic regimes in the 1960s and 1970s has been strongly contested.[12] And, after almost a decade of region-wide recession during the 1980s, there have so far been no military overthrows of elected civilian governments. Paul Drake notes this fact in his contribution to this volume. All seven of the governments he classifies as "democratic" survived the economic shocks of the current decade.[13] Only three of thirteen cases in his "dictatorship" category survived. This does not mean, of course, that we should underestimate the seriousness of the social and political problems caused by the debt crisis, but there is a need for caution in drawing out the implications for political regimes.

Drake provides a useful starting point for speculation on this subject. Although a sudden cutoff of external financing is likely to shake any regime, he suggests that democracies may actually have more resources than dictatorships for surviving such shocks. Democracies are not as dependent as many Latin American dictatorships have been on delivering material benefits to their supporters. Non-material political values, civil liberties and opportunities for public contestation are also included among their claims to legitimacy. Furthermore, democracies offer opponents of incumbent governments the chance to obtain power in the future by peaceful means.

We can expand on such insights by considering in more detail the experiences of the transitional and established democracies we have discussed above. Among the latter, general support for the system appears to have remained high, at least in the case of Costa Rica. As already indicated, the low degree of ideological or class polarization between the major parties also seems to have been an important factor in cushioning the system from the social and political turmoil associated with economic shocks. In these societies, elections and changes of administration have not produced highly disruptive discontinuities in underlying political alignments or policy orientations. At the same time, as Nelson has suggested, democratic competition within such societies has sometimes offered opportunities to try out constructive new approaches for dealing with the crisis itself.

This said, it is important to emphasize that these types of party systems have by no means offered a sure guarantee against political destabilization.[14] In recent years, the stability of Colombia's constitutional regime has been seriously threatened by drug trafficking and by the resurgence of guerrilla war that has long plagued the country. Since the Colombian economy has performed fairly well during the 1980s, however, it is difficult to attribute these problems directly to the debt crisis itself.

Transitional democracies, on the whole, appear to be in more precarious situations. With the possible exception of Uruguay, civilian governments have come to power in more polarized circumstances than in the established democracies. They must deal with a stronger political left and/or more powerful and independent union movements. In Peru and Brazil, as well as in Argentina during the first year of the Alfonsín administration, this encouraged expansionary policies that eventually deepened the economic crisis itself. These policies, in turn, have increased polarization since they are generally opposed by conservative business groups and the military establishment.

Yet it would be a mistake to assume that past cycles of military intervention are necessarily destined to repeat themselves. Opposition to the authoritarian regimes of the 1960s and 1970s was growing before the debt shocks of the 1980s, even among groups that had initially supported their rise to power. The public sense of failure and disillusionment may have been most pronounced in Argentina, where one of the most murderous regimes in the region's history marched the country directly toward economic and military disaster. But the Brazilian and Peruvian military regimes were widely regarded as failures as well—unresponsive to popular interests, riddled with corruption, and paralyzed by policy ineptitude. Such perceptions provide an important cushion for new democracies. Despite their current difficulties, most sectors of society continue to see the alternatives as worse.

Furthermore, the experience of authoritarian rule itself has moderated the beliefs and behavior of political actors. The changes in political orientation seem most pronounced among leftist and popular-sector groups in Brazil, Argentina, and Uruguay, which suffered through a long period of exclusionary military rule. Expectations about social transformations are much lower than they were in the late 1960s. The leaders of these movements place a higher, less conditional value on the political freedoms offered by "bourgeois democracy." The same appears to be true of most of the opposition groups in Chile, with the exception of the Communist Party.

The revaluation of democratic institutions does not appear to have gone as far in Peru, where the left was not the main target of the preceding authoritarian regime. Even so, it is noteworthy that guerrilla terrorism did not prevent the successful transfer of power from one elected government to another in 1985, and the main leftist parties have taken a strong stand against the guerrilla movement. The longer such processes continue, the more likely it is that political attitudes will change in ways that support democratic consolidation. Opposition groups have more incentive to wait their turn for power. Experiences in power offer opportunities to learn from mistakes.

The pivotal actors in efforts to consolidate transitional democracies, however, will not be the left or the popular sector, but the military establishment and its conservative allies among politicians and businesspeople. A major question is whether such groups will allow the process of democratic learning and consolidation to play itself out. On the positive side, it is clear that the calculus of these groups, as well as those of the center and the left, has been affected by the previous difficulties of authoritarian regimes. As Maxfield discusses, even the ostensibly pro-business regimes in Brazil and the Southern Cone blocked access to political power by important industrial groups and conservative politicians. More important, the authoritarian experience placed serious strains on the internal unity of the military establishments themselves and damaged their prestige and support among other social sectors. Consequently, there seems to be little inclination to repeat the military "revolutions" of earlier decades. In contrast to the 1960s and 1970s, the military find it in their own interest to allow civilian leaders to wrestle with economic crisis.

The greater danger to democracy in the next decade is not military overthrow, but military subversion. This threat seems especially high in societies like Peru and Colombia, which have been plagued by incessant guerrilla warfare. In such situations, "national security" doctrines provide an important spur for the incremental expansion of military power into economic and political issues more appropriately left to elected civilian authority. Military subversion also poses a severe threat to democracy in Brazil, where the military possesses a powerful intelligence apparatus and extensive legal prerogatives.[15] Even without the pretext of guerrilla threat, these resources have allowed the military to play a major role in the bargaining over the new constitution. And as Sarney has become increasingly isolated from party and interest group leaders, he has turned more and more to the military as a source of support.

If such tendencies are not effectively countered, elected civilian governments may be left to rule in name only—the facades for far more unaccountable forms of decision-making authority. The Uruguayan coup of 1973 provides a possible prototype. Avoiding such outcomes, however, will not depend exclusively on the state's capacity to reduce the profound deprivation and frustration that has gone along with economic austerity. Independent of the economic situation, it also depends on the capacity of contending party and interest group leaders, acting in their own long-term interests, to build a framework of mutual accommodation among themselves and to close ranks against both terrorist violence and military encroachments.

Concluding Comments and Future Directions

The main purpose of this chapter, and the book as a whole, has been to explore the two-way relationship between economic crisis and political change. In particular, we have been interested in the debt-related problems of the 1980s and the process of democratization. Are new democratic regimes, compared to authoritarian governments or established democracies, particularly inclined toward certain types of economic policies? Are they more or less likely to succeed in implementing them? Do they thus affect political outcomes? Turning things around, what effect does the economic crisis have on the redemocratization process? To what extent is it true that the debt crisis facilitated the transition to democracy but will also prevent its consolidation?

Despite some strong evidence to the contrary, based on the 1960s and 1970s, we have found that the political regime variable has been important in the crisis-ridden 1980s. Furthermore, it has been important both for understanding policy choice and for explaining certain types of economic outcomes. In part, our differing conclusions may be related to the fact that we have distinguished not only between authoritarianism and democracy, but also between types of democratic regime. We also suspect that the difference between our findings and those of earlier studies arise because regime type weighs more heavily in conditions of crisis, when there are sharply contrasting views about how to allocate costs.

When turning to the effect of crisis on democracy itself, we are less convinced of the importance of the relationship. While we do agree that economics is a very powerful force in influencing the political process, other factors are also important. The very effect of living through authoritarian periods has made political actors more willing to seek the compromises necessary for democracy to function. In addition, the dissatisfaction with military rule—both on the part of civilians and the armed forces themselves—should help to prevent its return in the near future. Of course, as Roett discusses in his chapter, large-scale economic assistance from the United States, Europe and Japan would substantially improve the long-term prospects for democracy in Latin America.

Although we have been able to clarify some relationships in the book, there are many topics that require further research. We need, for example, more refined specifications of democratic processes and institutions and their links to economic policy making. Numerous studies of European democracies have suggested that societal corporatist institutions have facilitated the negotiation of the costs of adjustment among labor and business peak associations. More recently, it has been argued that the effects of wealth, localism, and zero-sum distributional struggles can be reduced by large electoral districts, list-system proportional representation (which encourages party centralization), and parliamentary systems. Some of this must clearly be taken into account in considering past and potential effects of democracy.

To be sure, it is doubtful that European institutional formulas will provide magic cures for adjustment problems in Latin America. For example, societal corporatist approaches, which rely heavily on peak association bargaining, would be particularly difficult to engineer in contexts where the union movement itself is so deeply divided. In this volume, Roxborough has provided a vivid account of the difficulties of reaching social pact agreements in Argentina and Brazil. Nevertheless, experiences in Costa Rica, Colombia, Venezuela, and Uruguay suggest that the alternatives do not necessarily have to be destructive partisan conflicts or adversarial relations among government, business and labor. The implications for economic policy making suggest the need for a closer look at such issues as the way electoral districts are organized, at systems of voting and territorial representation, and at patterns of party financing and candidate selection.

Eul-Soo Pang's reference to the debate over parliamentarism in Brazil also raises some interesting questions about policy effects of alternative patterns of executive/ legislative relations. It is true that in transitional democracies, bitter debates over these issues can themselves become impediments to constructive policy making, as Pang suggests was the case in Brazil. And it must be added that presidential systems in the established democracies have had some success in dealing with independent legislatures. Nevertheless, it remains an open question as to whether (and under what conditions) carefully-designed parliamentary systems might eventually reduce the typical pattern of tension between executive and legislative elites, and encourage more extensive patterns of consultation and compromise.

On the relationship running from economics to politics, there are also some important questions to be asked. One chapter we had originally hoped to have in the book, for example, concerned the views of the mass public on the nature of the economic crisis, the relative ability of democratic governments to deal with it, and the value placed on democracy per se. In other words, it is not only the opinions of the elite that are relevant . In most of the coups that brought military governments to power in the 1960s and 1970s, substantial sectors of the respective societies were active participants. It is important to know how the public views political and economic questions, how this opinion varies by class and region, and how citizens want to participate in the future.

Finally, we cannot conclude the book without stressing the necessity of broadening the framework in which we have been operating. We have focused exclusively on political democracy and ignored the issues of *economic* and *social* democracy. It was attempts to attain democracy in this broader sense that was partially responsible for the demise of political democracy itself in the 1960s and early 1970s. Most Latin Americans have not given up the hope that all can be combined. Can political democracy be a way to attain greater equality in the region, both equality of a material sort and greater participation in decisions beyond the voting booth? Clearly this question constitutes a project in and of itself, but it is arguably the most basic issue on the agenda for the future.

Notes

1. Relevant literature on the impact of political regimes includes Thomas E. Skidmore, "The Politics of Economic Stabilization in Post War Latin America," in *Authoritarianism and Corporatism in Latin America*, ed. James M. Malloy (Pittsburgh: University of Pittsburgh Press, 1977); Carlos Díaz-Alejandro, "Southern Cone Stabilization Plans," in *Economic Stabilization in Developing Countries*, ed. William Cline and Sidney Weintraub (Washington, DC: The Brookings Institution, 1981); Karen Remmer, "The Politics of Economic Stabilization: IMF Standby Programs in Latin America, 1954-84" *Comparative Politics* (October 1986); Jonathan Hartlyn and Samuel A. Morley, "Political Regimes and Economic Performances in Latin America," in *Latin American Political Economy: Finan-*

cial Crisis and Political Change, ed. Jonathan Hartlyn and Samuel A. Morley (Boulder, CO: Westview Press, 1986); Stephan Haggard, "The Politics of Adjustment: Lessons from the IMF's Extended Fund Facility," and Robert R. Kaufman, "Democratic and Authoritarian Responses to the Debt Issue: Argentina, Brazil, Mexico," both in *The Politics of International Debt*, ed. Miles Kahler (Ithaca: Cornell University Press, 1986); Youssef Cohen, "The Impact of Bureaucratic-Authoritarian Rule on Economic Growth," *Comparative Political Studies* 18, no. 1 (1985).

2. For an attempt to synthesize some of the broader strands found in the literature, see Stephan Haggard and Robert Kaufman, "The Politics of Stabilization and Structural Adjustment," in *Developing Country Debt*, ed. Jeffrey Sachs (Chicago: University of Chicago Press, forthcoming 1989) and the concluding chapter in Joan Nelson, ed., *The Politics of Economic Adjustment in Developing Nations* (forthcoming).

3. In this chapter, we concentrate on distinguishing between two types of democracies—established and transitional. In further work, it would also be necessary to look at different types of authoritarian regimes as well. A start on this type of analysis can be found in Stephan Haggard's analysis of strong and weak authoritarian governments. See Haggard, "Politics of Adjustment."

4. For further information on the Colombian political and economic systems, see Albert Berry et al., *The Politics of Compromise: Coalition Government in Colombia* (New Brunswick: Transaction Books, 1980); Bruce Bagley, "Colombia: National Front and Economic Development," in *Politics, Policies, and Economic Development in Latin America*, ed. Robert Wesson (Stanford: Hoover Institution, 1984); and Eduardo Lora and José Antonio Ocampo, *Stabilization and Adjustment Policies and Programs: Country Study-Colombia* (Helsinki: WIDER, 1987).

5. On the basis for the current Venezuelan political system, see Terry Karl, "Petroleum and Political Pacts: The Transition to Democracy in Venezuela," in *Transitions from Authoritarian Rule: Latin America*, ed. Guillermo O'Donnell et al. (Baltimore: Johns Hopkins University Press, 1986). For an economic and political analysis of the more recent period, see Michael Coppedge, "Debt, Democracy and Acción Democrática" (Ph.D. dissertation, Yale University, 1988).

6. Sources on the Argentine political economy include Gary Wynia, *Argentina in the Post-War Era* (Albuquerque: University of New Mexico Press, 1978); Guillermo O'Donnell, "Estado y alianzas en la Argentina, 1966-76," *Desarrollo Económico* 16, no. 64 (1977); and Luigi Manzetti and Marco Dell'Aquila, "Economic Stabilization in Argentina: The Austral Plan," *Journal of Latin American Studies* 20 (1988).

7. Uruguay's recent transition to democracy is discussed in Charles Gillespie, "Uruguay's Transition from Collegial Military-Technocratic Rule," in *Transitions from Authoritarian Rule: Latin America*, ed. Guillermo O'Donnell et al. (Baltimore: Johns Hopkins University Press, 1986). See also Luis Macadar, *Uruguay 1974-80: ¿un nuevo ensayo de reajuste económico?* (Montevideo: Banda Oriental, 1982) and Martin Weinstein, *Uruguay: Democracy at the Crossroads* (Boulder, CO: Westview Press, 1988).

8. Since both authoritarian and democratic regimes in Argentina and Brazil have experienced high rates of inflation, it might be argued that these cross-national comparisons exaggerate the inflationary impact of transitional democracies. Nevertheless, in these two countries—as well as in Peru—inflation rates shot up significantly *after* the shift away from authoritarianism. Conversely, during the course of the Pinochet regime in Chile, historically

high rates of inflation were substantially reduced.

9. Recent discussion by economists of problems caused by sudden inflows of foreign exchange goes under the rubric of the "Dutch disease." For a review of this literature, see Max Corden, "The Economic Effects of a Booming Sector," *International Social Sciences Journal* 35, no. 3 (1983). For a political science analysis of similar problems, referred to as "bonanza development," see David Becker, *The New Bourgeoisie and the Limits of Dependency: Mining, Class, and Power in "Revolutionary" Peru* (Princeton: Princeton University Press, 1983).

10. A classic discussion of the relationship between legitimacy and effectiveness is found in Seymour Martin Lipset, *Political Man: The Social Bases of Politics* (Garden City, New York: Anchor Books, 1959), 64-80.

11. See Charles W. Anderson, *Politics and Economic Change in Latin America* (Princeton: D. Van Nostrand Co., 1967) and Douglas A. Chalmers, "The Politicized State in Latin America," in *Authoritarianism and Corporatism in Latin America*, ed. James M. Malloy (Pittsburgh: University of Pittsburgh Press, 1977).

12. David Collier, ed., *The New Authoritarianism in Latin America* (Princeton: Princeton University Press, 1979); Juan J. Linz, "Crisis, Breakdown, and Reequilibration," and Arturo Valenzuela, "Chile," both in *The Breakdown of Democratic Regimes*, ed. Juan J. Linz and Alfred Stepan (Baltimore: Johns Hopkins University Press, 1978).

13. It should be noted that Drake includes Mexico in his list of democracies. Our differing classification reflects the long-standing controversy on the nature of the Mexican political system.

14. In 1973, for example, a very similar type of party system was overthrown by a coup in Uruguay.

15. Alfred Stepan, *Rethinking Military Politics* (Princeton: Princeton University Press, 1987).

About the Contributors

Rudiger Dornbusch is Ford International Professor of Economics at the Massachusetts Institute of Technology. He is the author of many books and articles on the international debt crisis of which the most recent is *Dollars, Debts, and Deficits*. He has also written several leading textbooks and has been a consultant to various Latin American governments.

Paul Drake is Institute of the Americas Professor and Director of the Center for Iberian and Latin American Studies at the University of California, San Diego. He is the author of *The Money Doctor in the Andes, Socialism and Populism in Chile, 1932-52*, and the co-editor of *Elections and Democratization in Latin America, 1980-85*.

Jeffry Frieden is Assistant Professor of Political Science at UCLA. He has published *Banking on the World: The Politics of American International Finance*. He has also written various articles on international political economy.

Robert Kaufman is Professor of Political Science at Rutgers University. He is the author of *The Politics of Debt in Argentina, Brazil, and Mexico: Economic Stabilization in the 1980s* and many articles on Latin American politics.

Sylvia Maxfield is Assistant Professor of Political Science and Management at Yale University. She is co-editor of *Government and the Private Sector in Contemporary Mexico* and author of several articles on Latin America and international political economy.

Joan Nelson is a Visiting Fellow of the Overseas Development Council. She is the author of several books and many articles on politics in the Third World and editor of a forthcoming volume on *The Politics of Economic Adjustment in Developing Nations*.

Eul-Soo Pang is Professor of Global Systems and Culture and Director of the Latin American Center at the Colorado School of Mines. He is author of three books of which the most recent is *In Pursuit of Honor and Power: Noblemen of the Southern Cross in 19th Century Brazil*. He is a frequent contributor to *Current History*.

Riordan Roett is Sarita and Don Johnston Professor and Director of the Latin American Studies Program at the Johns Hopkins School of Advanced International Studies, Washington, D.C. He is the editor and coauthor of *Mexico and the United States: Managing the Relationship* (Westview Press).

Ian Roxborough is Lecturer in Political Sociology at the London School of Economics. He is the author of *Unions and Politics in Mexico, Chile: State and Revolution, Theories of Underdevelopment*, and several articles on the labor movement in Latin America.

Barbara Stallings is Professor of Political Science at the University of Wisconsin-Madison. She recently published *Banker to the Third World: U.S. Portfolio Investment in Latin America, 1900–1986*, and she is also the author of *Class Conflict and Economic Development in Chile, 1958–73* and various articles on international political economy.

Carol Wise is a Fellow of the Kellogg Institute at the University of Notre Dame and a Ph.D candidate in Political Science at Columbia University. She has published several articles on the political economy of Peru.

Index